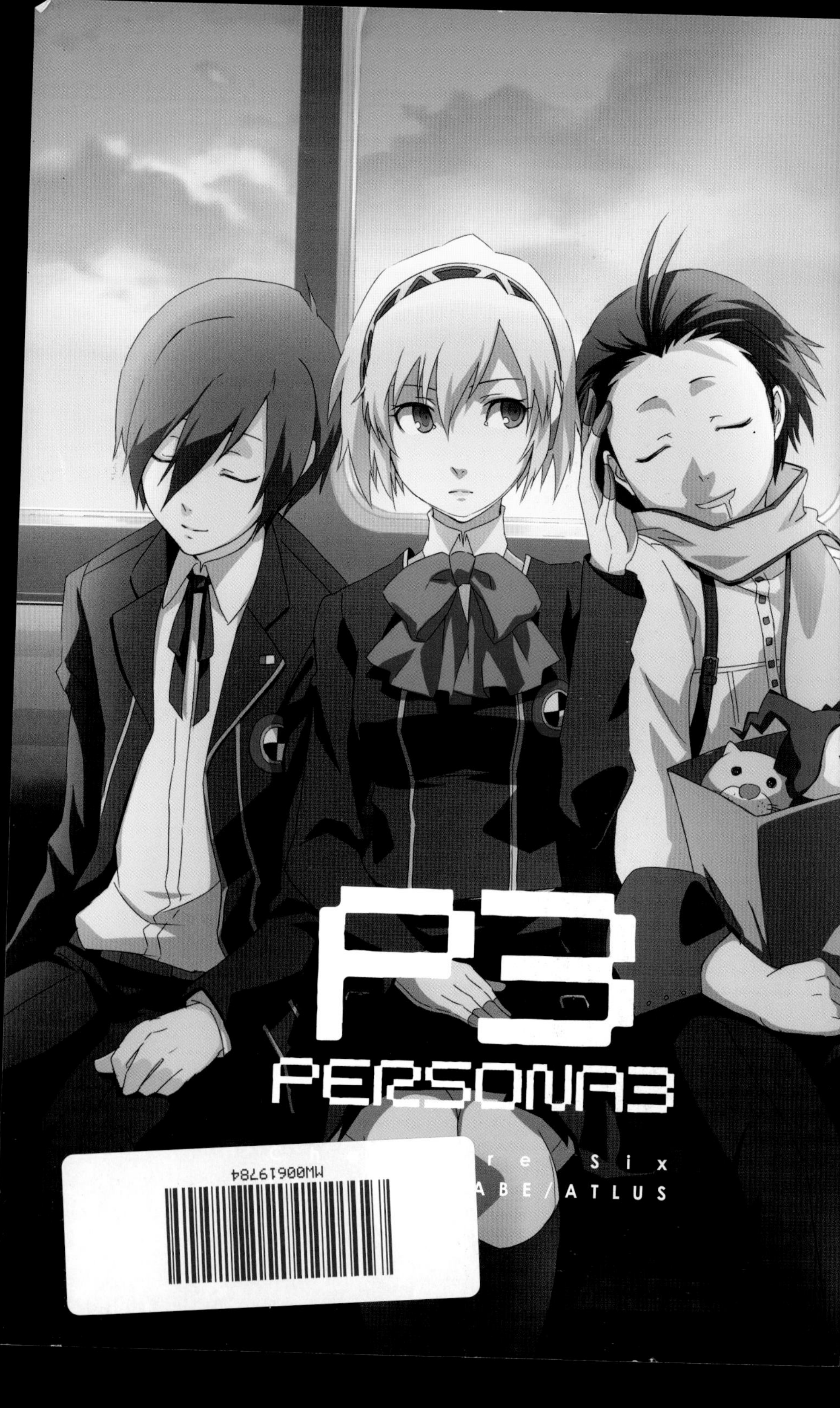
P3
PERSONA3
re Six
ABE/ATLUS

001 illust
002 this page
003 #23 start
004
005
006
007
008
009
010
011
012
013
014
015
016
017
018
019
020
021
022
023
024
025
026
027
028
029
030
031
032
033
034
035 #23 end
036 bridge
037 #24 start
038
039
040
041
042
043
044
045
046
047 #24 end
048 s.now
049 #25 start
050
051
052
053
054
055
056
057
058
059
060
061
062
063
064
065
066
067
068
069
070
071
072
073
074
075
076
077
078
079 #25 end
080 bridge

081 #26 start
082
083
084
085
086
087
088
089
090
091
092
093
094
095
096
097
098
099
100
101
102
103
104
105 #26 end
106 illust
107 #27 start
108
109
110
111
112
113
114
115
116
117
118
119
120
121
122
123
124
125
126
127
128
129 #27 end
130 illust
131 #28 start
132
133
134
135
136
137
138
139
140
141
142
143
144
145 #28 end
146 staff list
147 #29 end
148
149
150
151
152
153
154
155
156
157
158
159 #29 end
160 s.now
161 -
162 imprint

story

The end is inevitable and equalizes all, but within the finite realm of life exists limitless possibilities.

In November of 2009, "his" story was still seeking its ending, though none could know which path he would choose or for what reason.

With their school trip at an end, the S.E.E.S. members returned to the abnormalities of their normal lives. As events progressed, tragedy would befall them once again.

Meanwhile, the tale of Junpei and his enigmatic lady friend continued to be shaped by a strong will and powerful wish.

Junpei's Persona evolved into Trismegistus, but he was clearly letting himself fall deeper into the embrace of negative energies whenever he utilized his new Persona's powers.

Following the battle, everyone reflected on Chidori's existence in their own way. When her sketchbook was recovered from her hospital room, Junpei finally saw what Chidori's eyes had seen.

A brief respite brings with it thoughts of things and memories lost. Once fate resumed its course, it would confirm a dire suspicion.

LastPiece **PERIOD**
Mémoire de la Mort
23
003
S.E.E.S. Battle report
2009 11 03 tue V.S.
Hangedman

Perspective04 **RECURSION**
Interlude
24
037

Perspective05 **CONFLICT 2**
triste bataille
25
049

Perspective06 **REBIRTH**
La vie de deux personnes
26
081

Perspective07 **NEGATIVE TRAIN**
Chaîne de la douleur
27
107

Perspective08 **STARRY-EYED**
Les paysages qu'elle contemplait
28
131

Perspective09 **ANOTHER ECHO**
Détestable pressentiment
29
147

2009 12~2012 02
151/162p 93.2%
monochrome B6

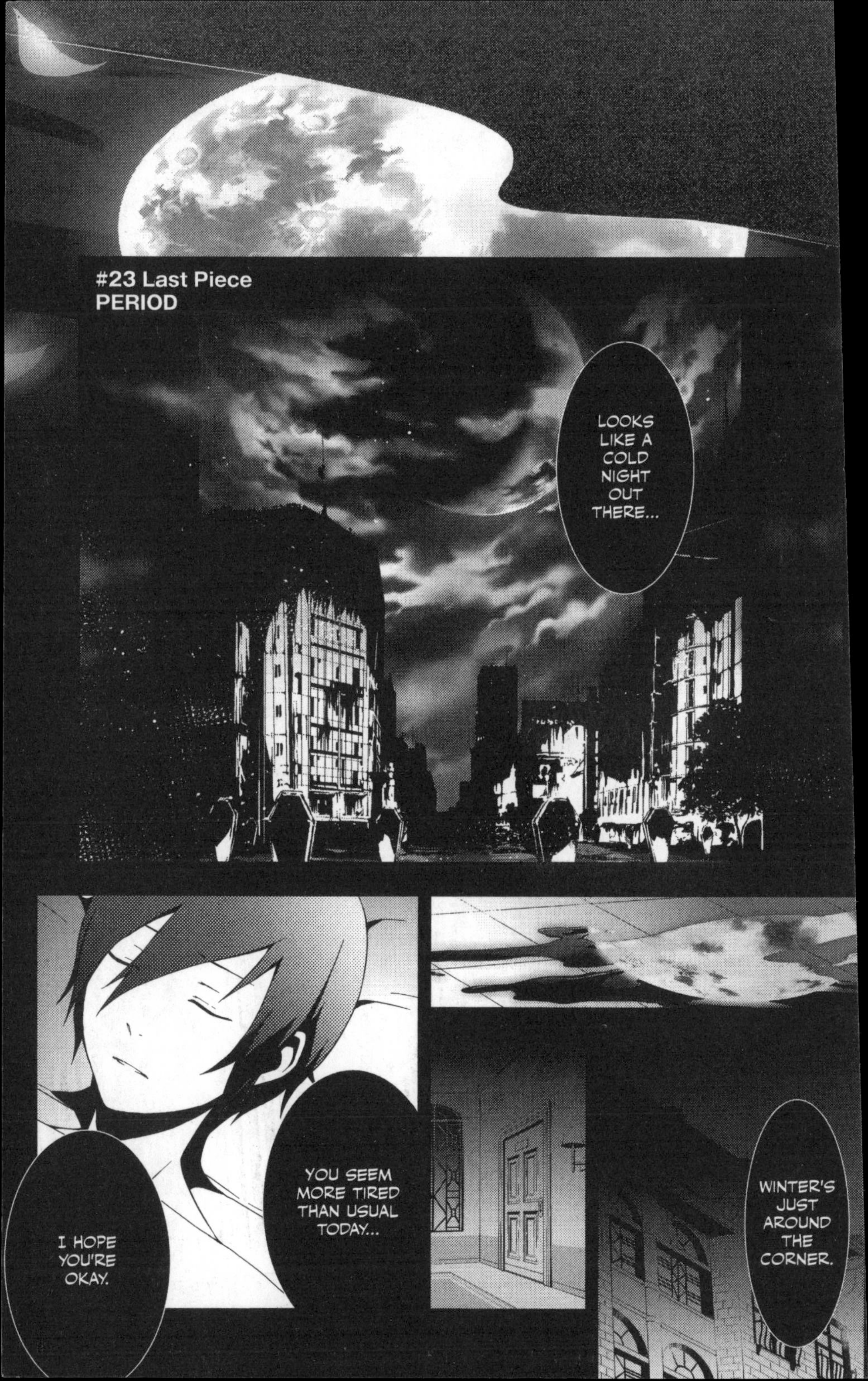
#23 Last Piece
PERIOD
LOOKS LIKE A COLD NIGHT OUT THERE...
WINTER'S JUST AROUND THE CORNER.
YOU SEEM MORE TIRED THAN USUAL TODAY...
I HOPE YOU'RE OKAY.

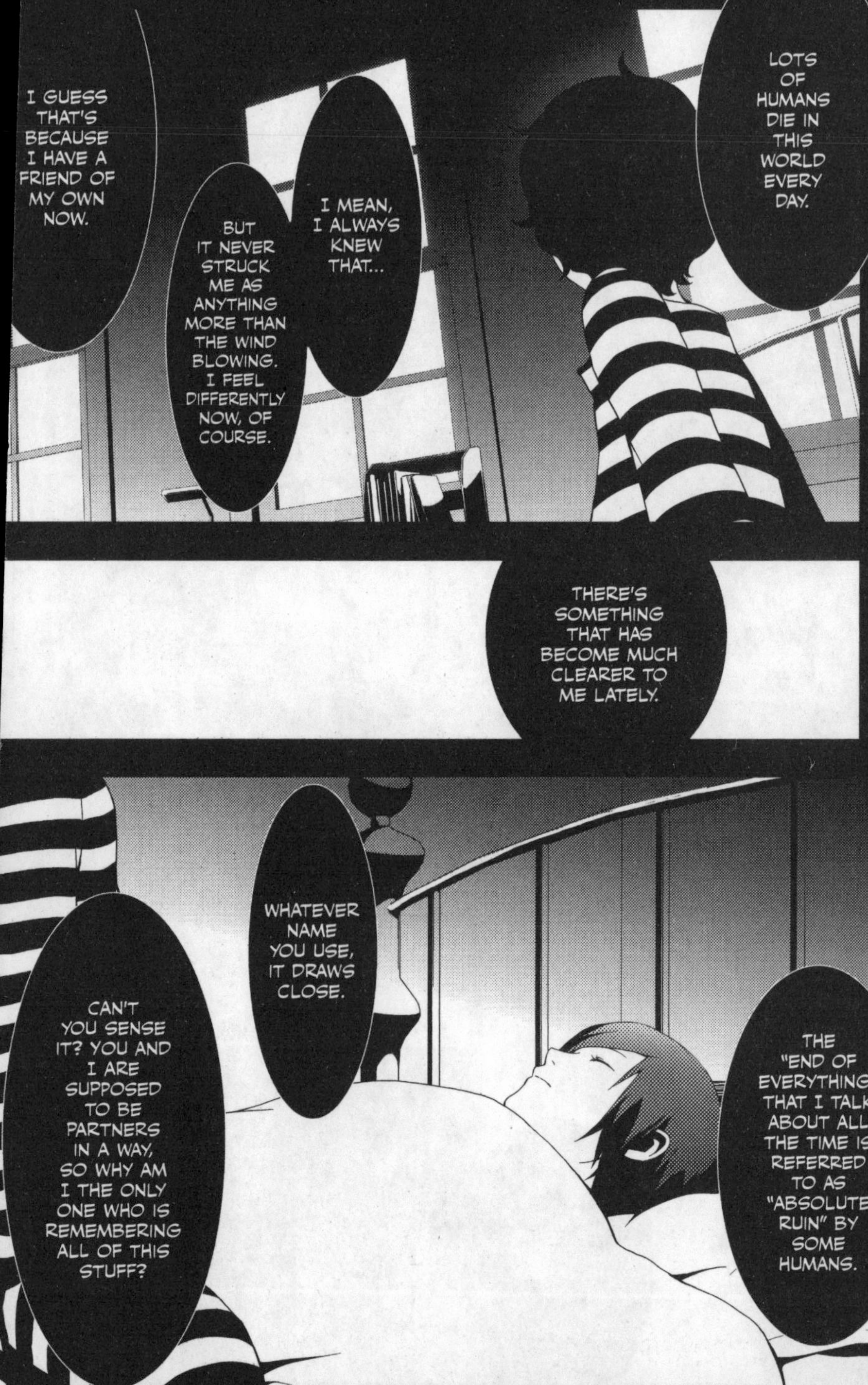
LOTS OF HUMANS DIE IN THIS WORLD EVERY DAY.
I MEAN, I ALWAYS KNEW THAT...
BUT IT NEVER STRUCK ME AS ANYTHING MORE THAN THE WIND BLOWING. I FEEL DIFFERENTLY NOW, OF COURSE.
I GUESS THAT'S BECAUSE I HAVE A FRIEND OF MY OWN NOW.
THERE'S SOMETHING THAT HAS BECOME MUCH CLEARER TO ME LATELY.
THE "END OF EVERYTHING" THAT I TALK ABOUT ALL THE TIME IS REFERRED TO AS "ABSOLUTE RUIN" BY SOME HUMANS.
WHATEVER NAME YOU USE, IT DRAWS CLOSE.
CAN'T YOU SENSE IT? YOU AND I ARE SUPPOSED TO BE PARTNERS IN A WAY, SO WHY AM I THE ONLY ONE WHO IS REMEMBERING ALL OF THIS STUFF?

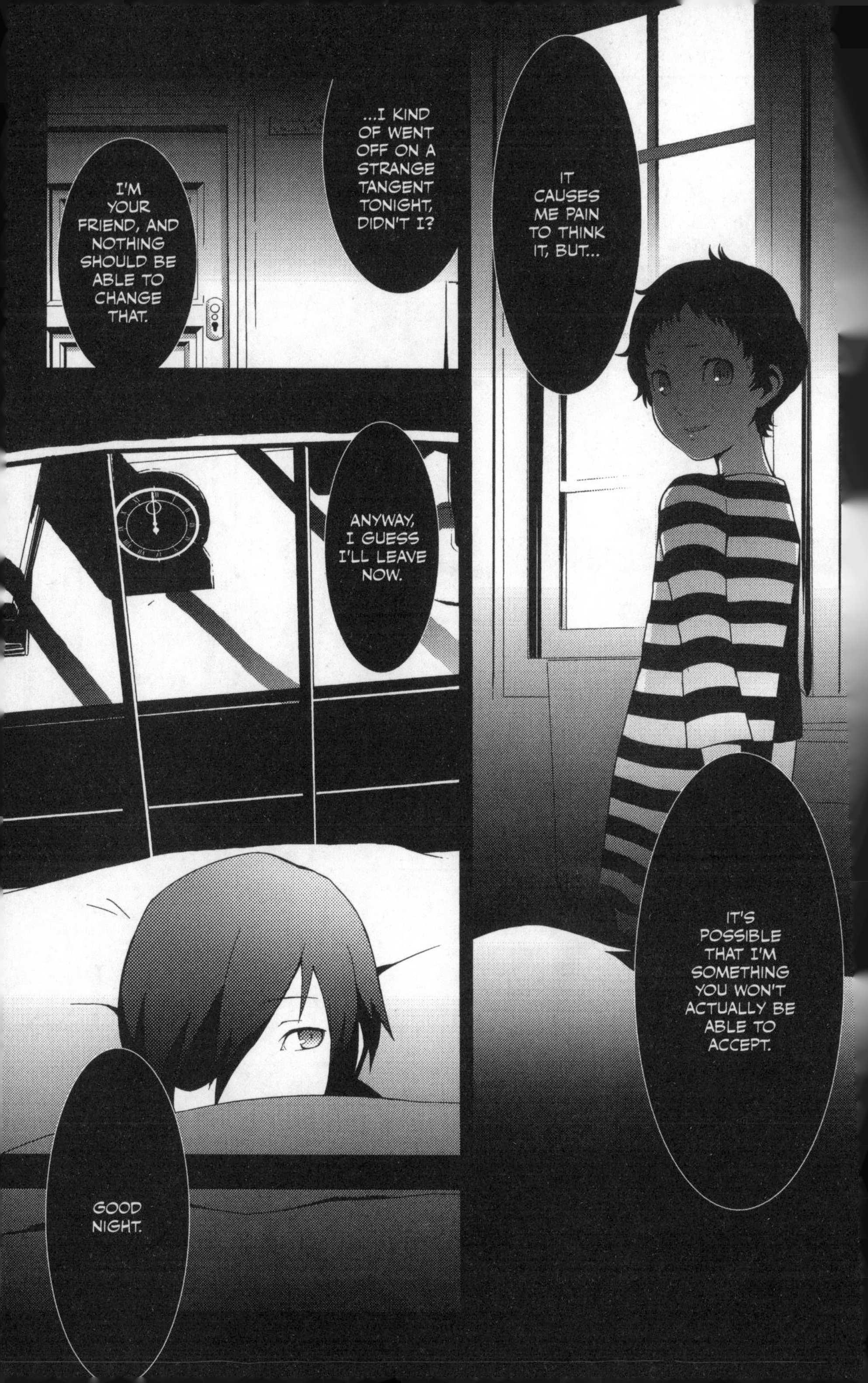
IT CAUSES ME PAIN TO THINK IT, BUT...
IT'S POSSIBLE THAT I'M SOMETHING YOU WON'T ACTUALLY BE ABLE TO ACCEPT.
...I KIND OF WENT OFF ON A STRANGE TANGENT TONIGHT, DIDN'T I?
I'M YOUR FRIEND, AND NOTHING SHOULD BE ABLE TO CHANGE THAT.
ANYWAY, I GUESS I'LL LEAVE NOW.
GOOD NIGHT.

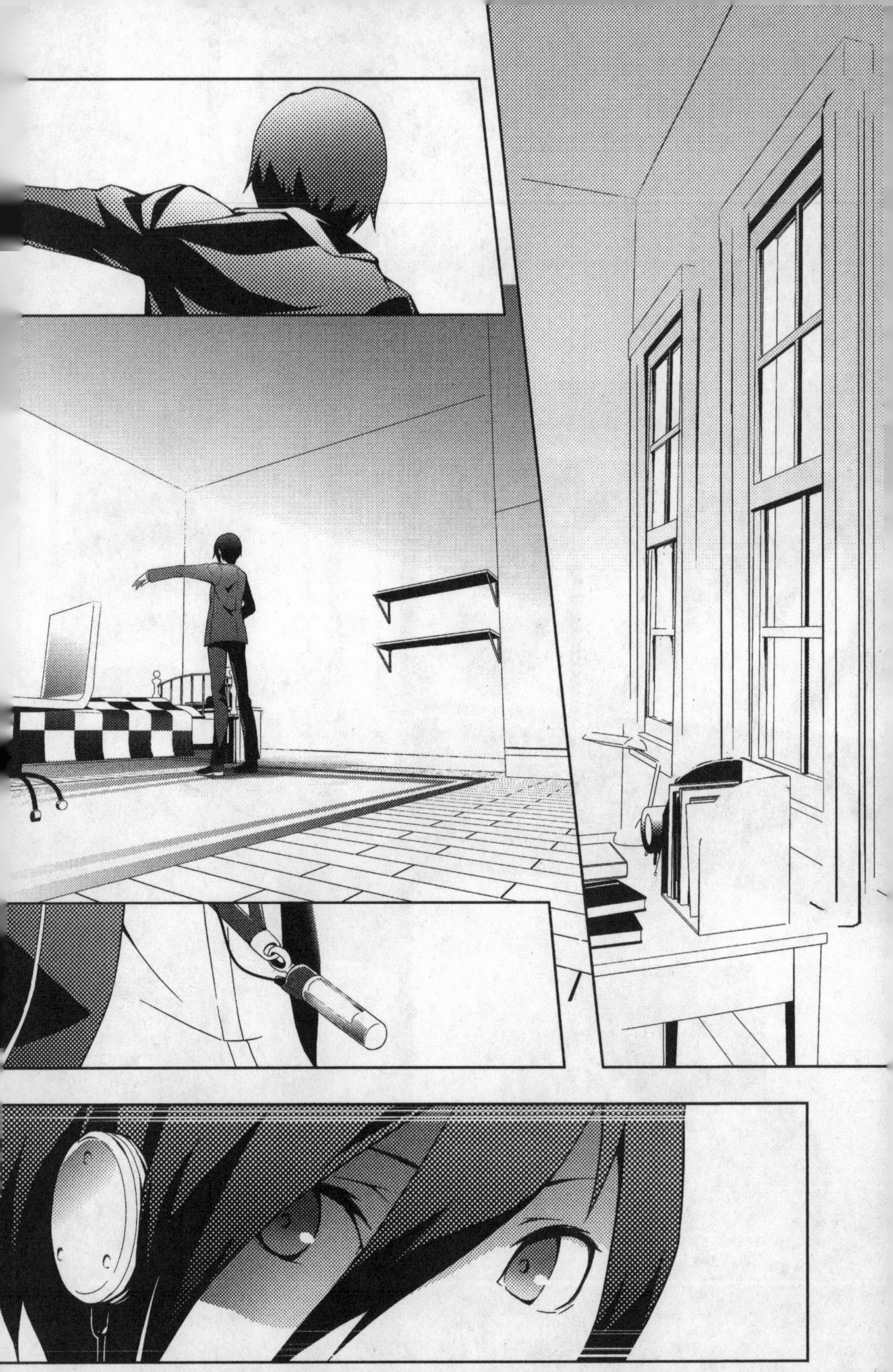

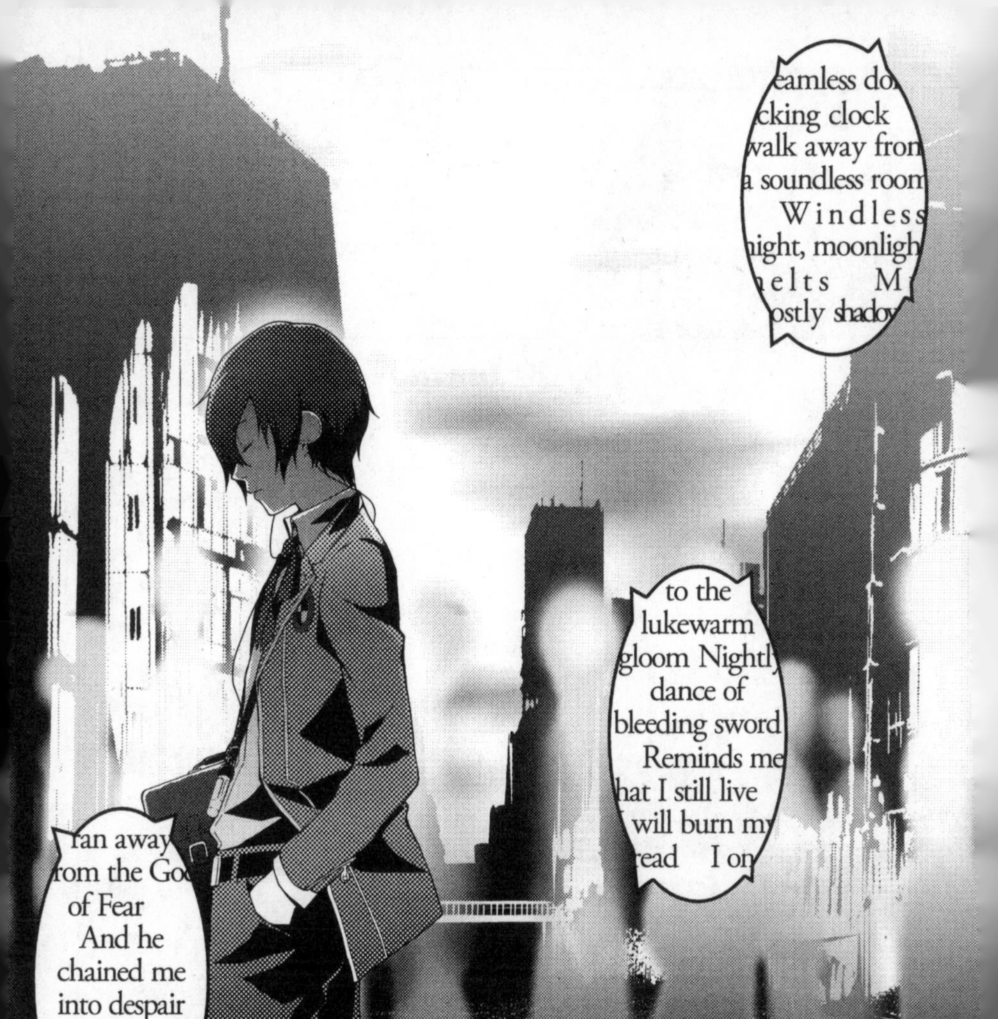
eamless do cking clock walk away fron a soundless room Windless night, moonligh elts M ostly shadov
to the lukewarm gloom Nightl dance of bleeding sword Reminds me hat I still live will burn my read I on
ran away rom the Go of Fear And he chained me into despair Burn my dread I will break the

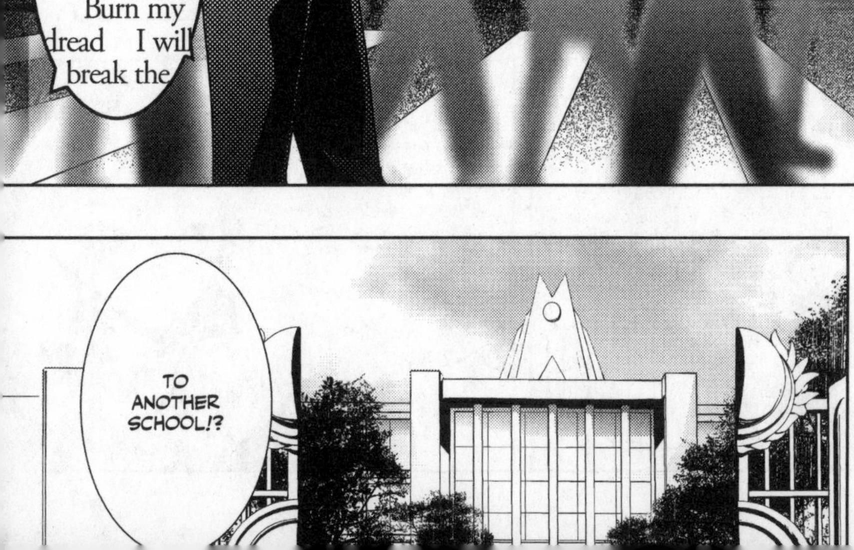
TO ANOTHER SCHOOL!?

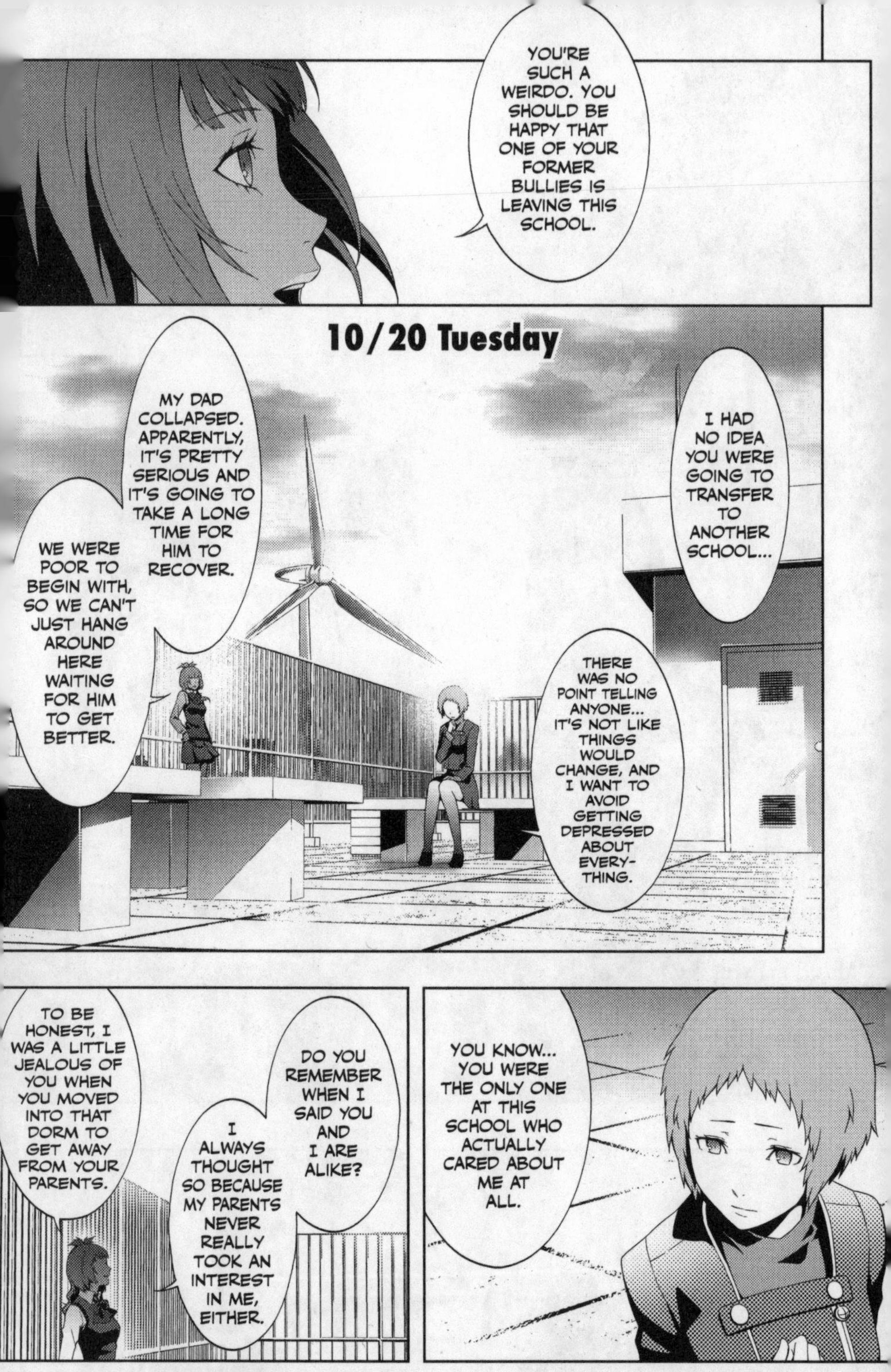
YOU'RE SUCH A WEIRDO. YOU SHOULD BE HAPPY THAT ONE OF YOUR FORMER BULLIES IS LEAVING THIS SCHOOL.
10/20 Tuesday
I HAD NO IDEA YOU WERE GOING TO TRANSFER TO ANOTHER SCHOOL...
THERE WAS NO POINT TELLING ANYONE... IT'S NOT LIKE THINGS WOULD CHANGE, AND I WANT TO AVOID GETTING DEPRESSED ABOUT EVERY-THING.
MY DAD COLLAPSED. APPARENTLY, IT'S PRETTY SERIOUS AND IT'S GOING TO TAKE A LONG TIME FOR HIM TO RECOVER.
WE WERE POOR TO BEGIN WITH, SO WE CAN'T JUST HANG AROUND HERE WAITING FOR HIM TO GET BETTER.
YOU KNOW... YOU WERE THE ONLY ONE AT THIS SCHOOL WHO ACTUALLY CARED ABOUT ME AT ALL.
DO YOU REMEMBER WHEN I SAID YOU AND I ARE ALIKE?
I ALWAYS THOUGHT SO BECAUSE MY PARENTS NEVER REALLY TOOK AN INTEREST IN ME, EITHER.
TO BE HONEST, I WAS A LITTLE JEALOUS OF YOU WHEN YOU MOVED INTO THAT DORM TO GET AWAY FROM YOUR PARENTS.

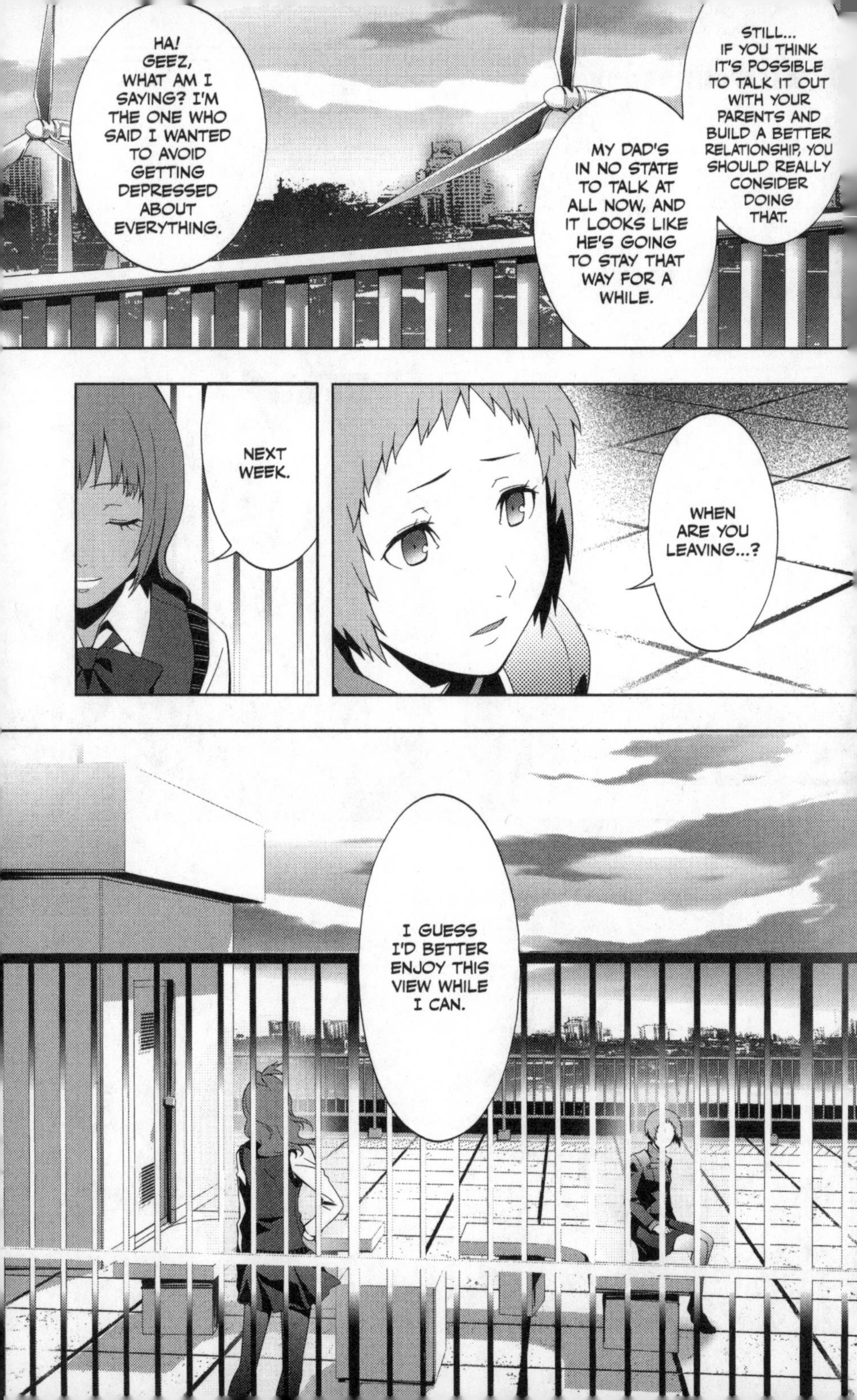
STILL... IF YOU THINK IT'S POSSIBLE TO TALK IT OUT WITH YOUR PARENTS AND BUILD A BETTER RELATIONSHIP, YOU SHOULD REALLY CONSIDER DOING THAT.
MY DAD'S IN NO STATE TO TALK AT ALL NOW, AND IT LOOKS LIKE HE'S GOING TO STAY THAT WAY FOR A WHILE.
HA! GEEZ, WHAT AM I SAYING? I'M THE ONE WHO SAID I WANTED TO AVOID GETTING DEPRESSED ABOUT EVERYTHING.
WHEN ARE YOU LEAVING...?
NEXT WEEK.
I GUESS I'D BETTER ENJOY THIS VIEW WHILE I CAN.

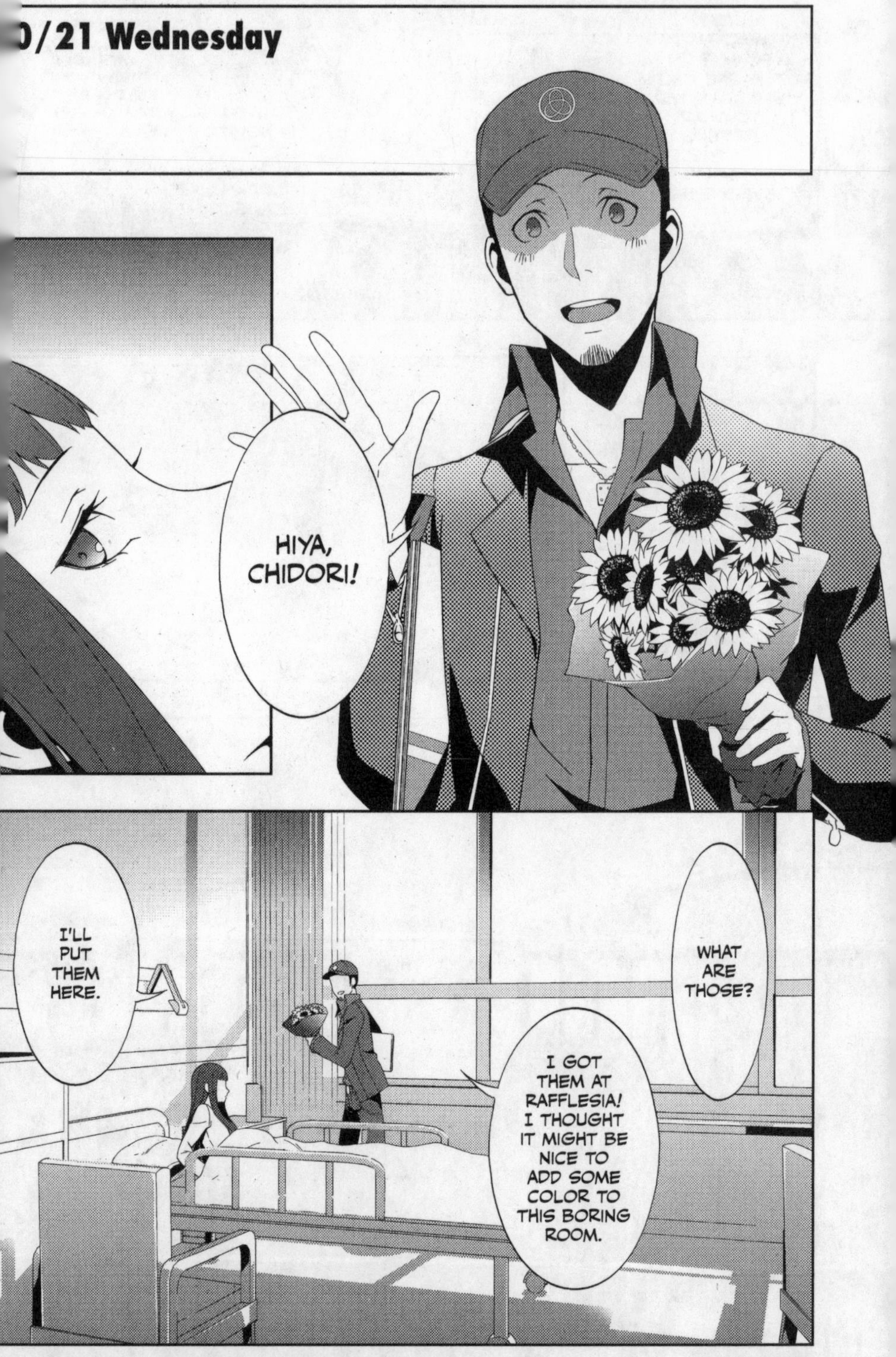
0/21 Wednesday
HIYA, CHIDORI!
WHAT ARE THOSE?
I GOT THEM AT RAFFLESIA! I THOUGHT IT MIGHT BE NICE TO ADD SOME COLOR TO THIS BORING ROOM.
I'LL PUT THEM HERE.

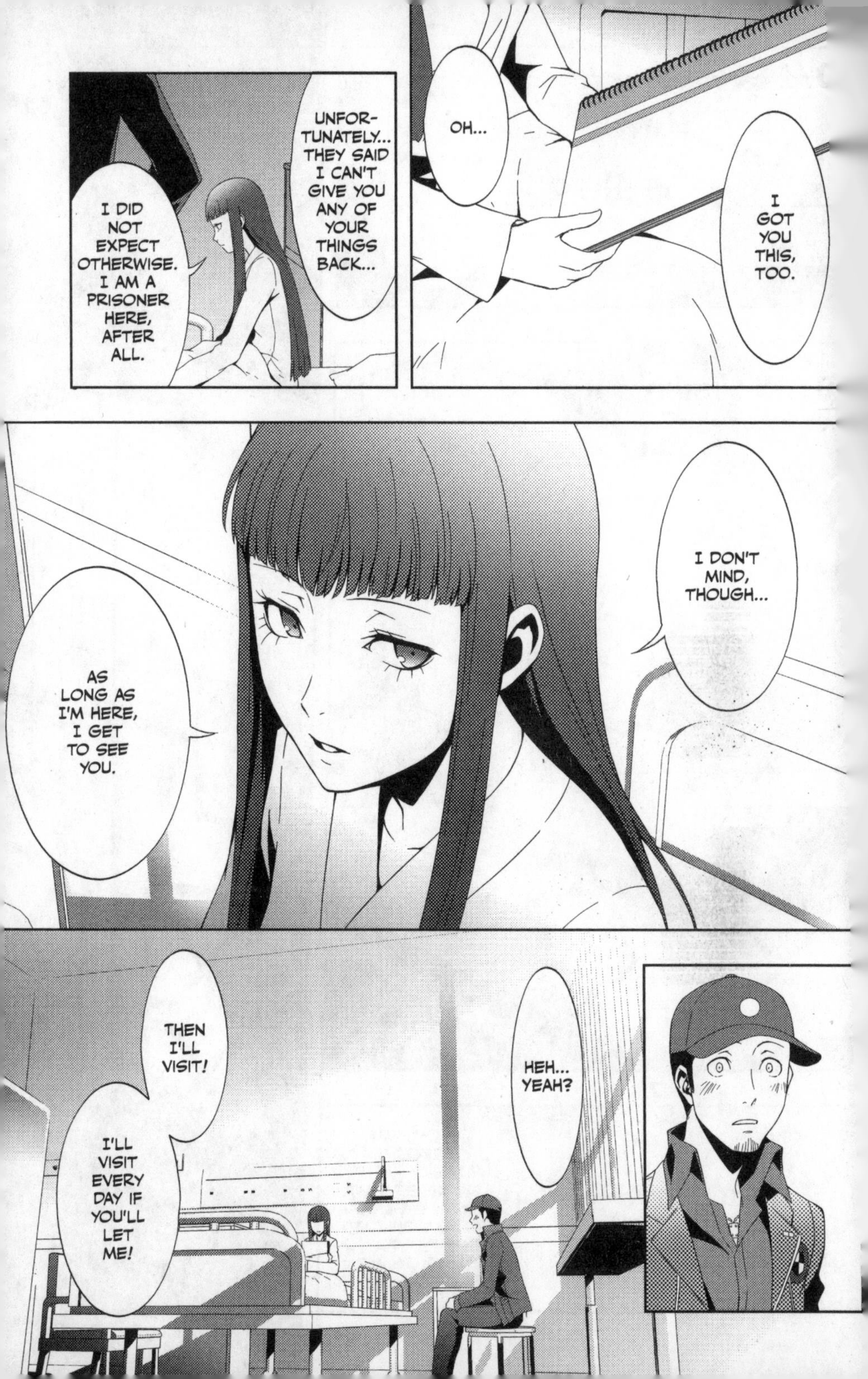
I GOT YOU THIS, TOO.
OH...
UNFOR-TUNATELY... THEY SAID I CAN'T GIVE YOU ANY OF YOUR THINGS BACK...
I DID NOT EXPECT OTHERWISE. I AM A PRISONER HERE, AFTER ALL.
I DON'T MIND, THOUGH...
AS LONG AS I'M HERE, I GET TO SEE YOU.
HEH... YEAH?
THEN I'LL VISIT!
I'LL VISIT EVERY DAY IF YOU'LL LET ME!

ATONEMENT...

0/25 Sunday

IF ONLY MY PERSONA POWERS HADN'T AWAKENED THAT DAY... MAYBE YOU GUYS WOULDN'T HAVE HAD TO GO THROUGH ALL OF THIS...

WHAT'S GOTTEN INTO YOU ALL OF A SUDDEN?

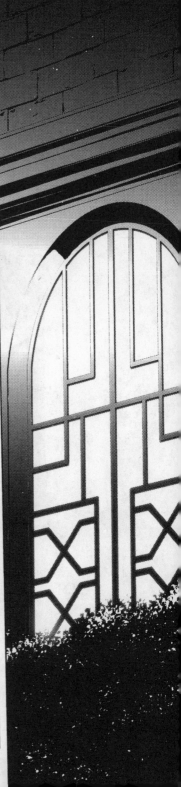

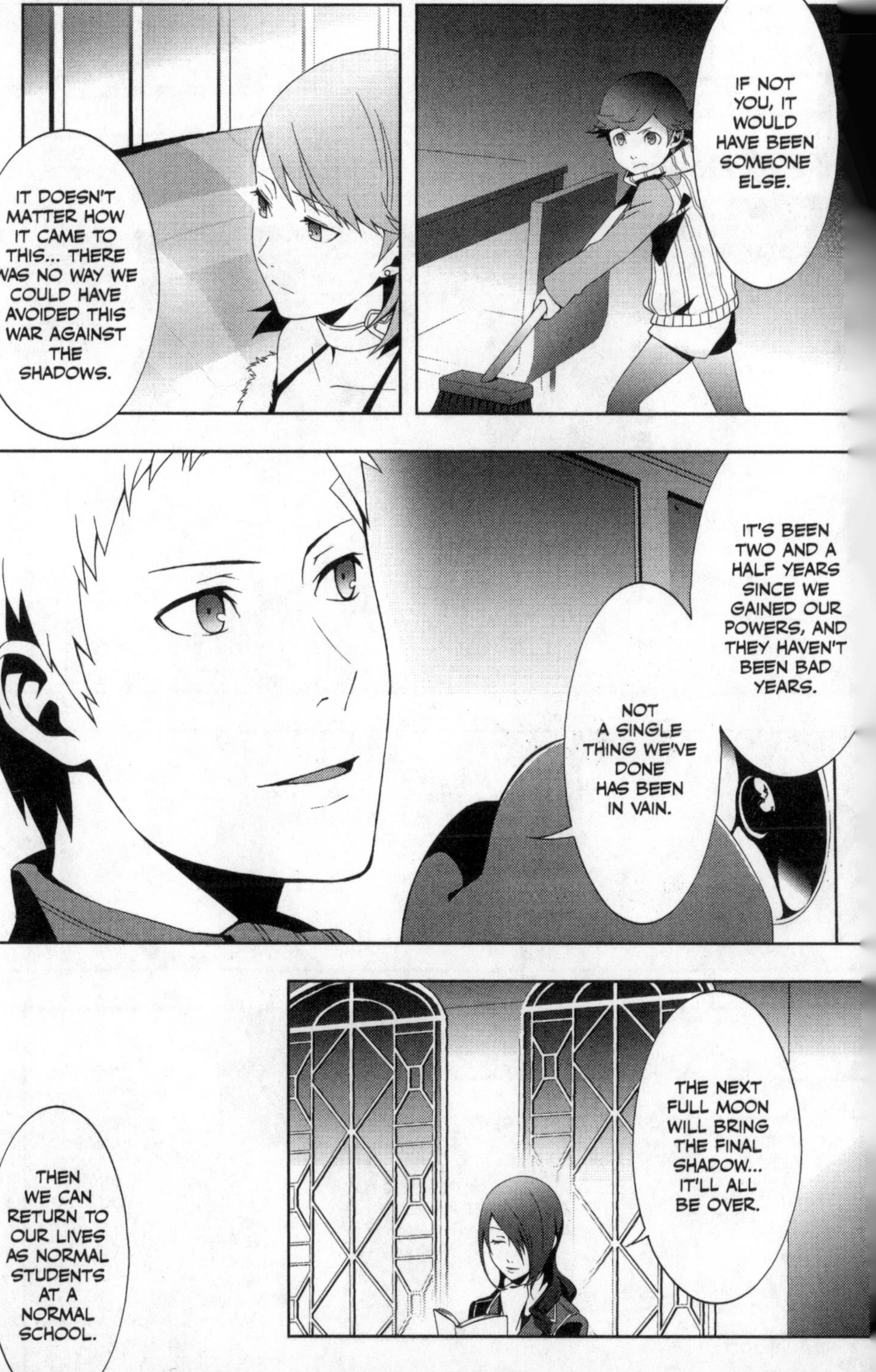
IF NOT YOU, IT WOULD HAVE BEEN SOMEONE ELSE.
IT DOESN'T MATTER HOW IT CAME TO THIS... THERE WAS NO WAY WE COULD HAVE AVOIDED THIS WAR AGAINST THE SHADOWS.
IT'S BEEN TWO AND A HALF YEARS SINCE WE GAINED OUR POWERS, AND THEY HAVEN'T BEEN BAD YEARS.
NOT A SINGLE THING WE'VE DONE HAS BEEN IN VAIN.
THE NEXT FULL MOON WILL BRING THE FINAL SHADOW... IT'LL ALL BE OVER.
THEN WE CAN RETURN TO OUR LIVES AS NORMAL STUDENTS AT A NORMAL SCHOOL.

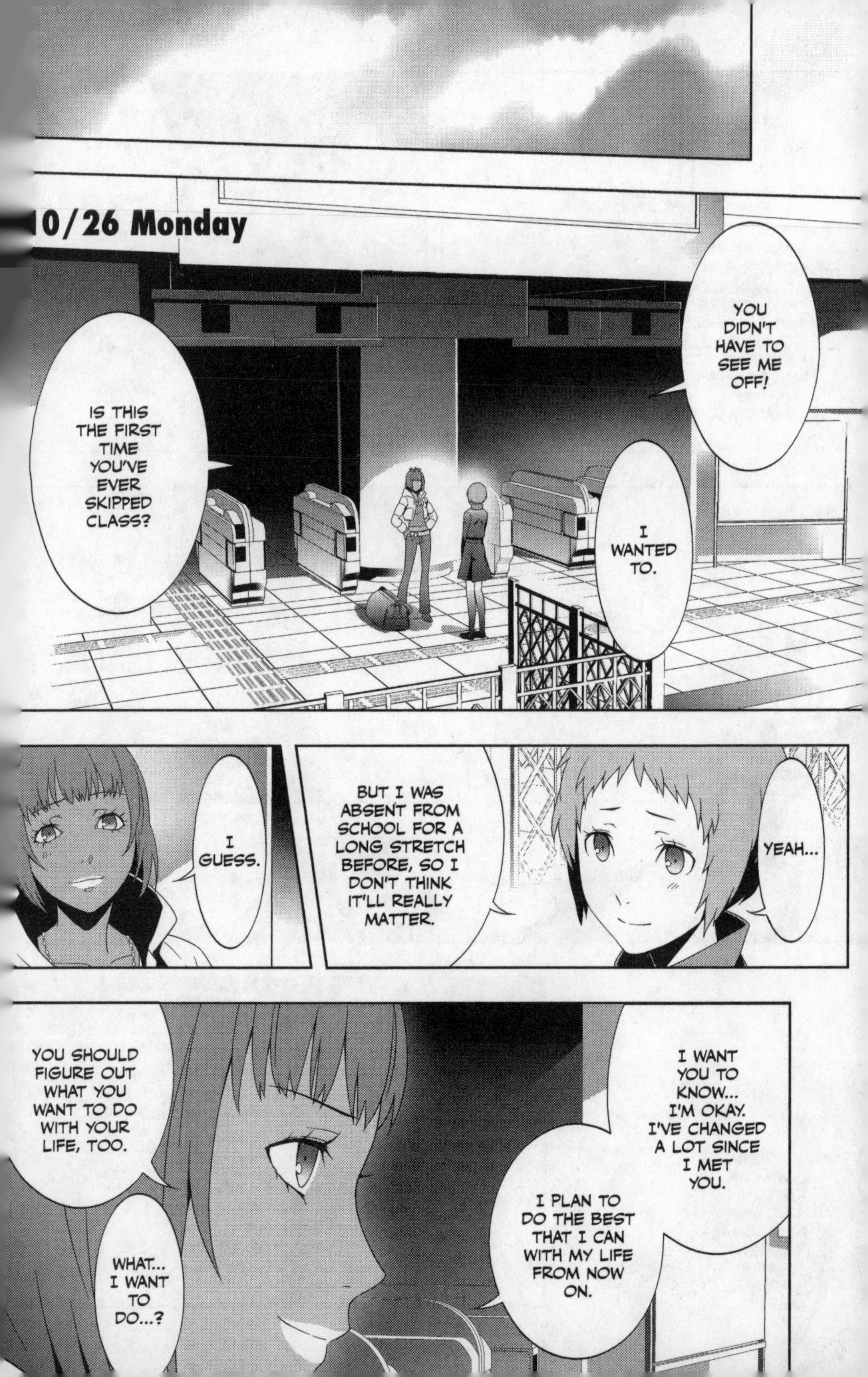
10/26 Monday
YOU DIDN'T HAVE TO SEE ME OFF!
I WANTED TO.
IS THIS THE FIRST TIME YOU'VE EVER SKIPPED CLASS?
YEAH...
BUT I WAS ABSENT FROM SCHOOL FOR A LONG STRETCH BEFORE, SO I DON'T THINK IT'LL REALLY MATTER.
I GUESS.
I WANT YOU TO KNOW... I'M OKAY. I'VE CHANGED A LOT SINCE I MET YOU.
I PLAN TO DO THE BEST THAT I CAN WITH MY LIFE FROM NOW ON.
YOU SHOULD FIGURE OUT WHAT YOU WANT TO DO WITH YOUR LIFE, TOO.
WHAT... I WANT TO DO...?

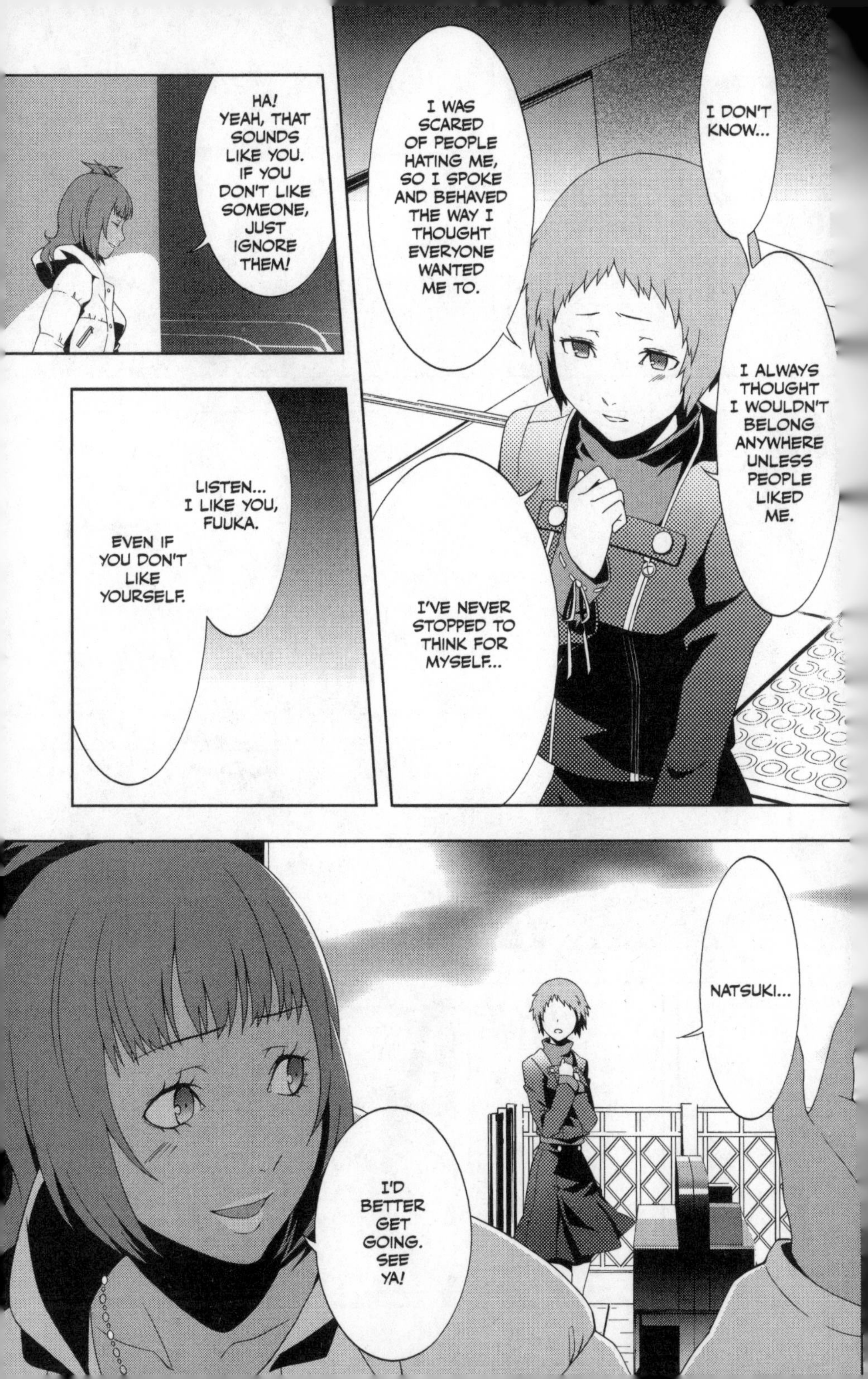
I DON'T KNOW...
I WAS SCARED OF PEOPLE HATING ME, SO I SPOKE AND BEHAVED THE WAY I THOUGHT EVERYONE WANTED ME TO.
I ALWAYS THOUGHT I WOULDN'T BELONG ANYWHERE UNLESS PEOPLE LIKED ME.
I'VE NEVER STOPPED TO THINK FOR MYSELF...
HA! YEAH, THAT SOUNDS LIKE YOU. IF YOU DON'T LIKE SOMEONE, JUST IGNORE THEM!
LISTEN... I LIKE YOU, FUUKA.
EVEN IF YOU DON'T LIKE YOURSELF.
NATSUKI...
I'D BETTER GET GOING. SEE YA!

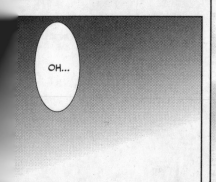

OH...

WAIT! I DIDN'T ASK HER FOR HER CONTACT INFO!

CHAK

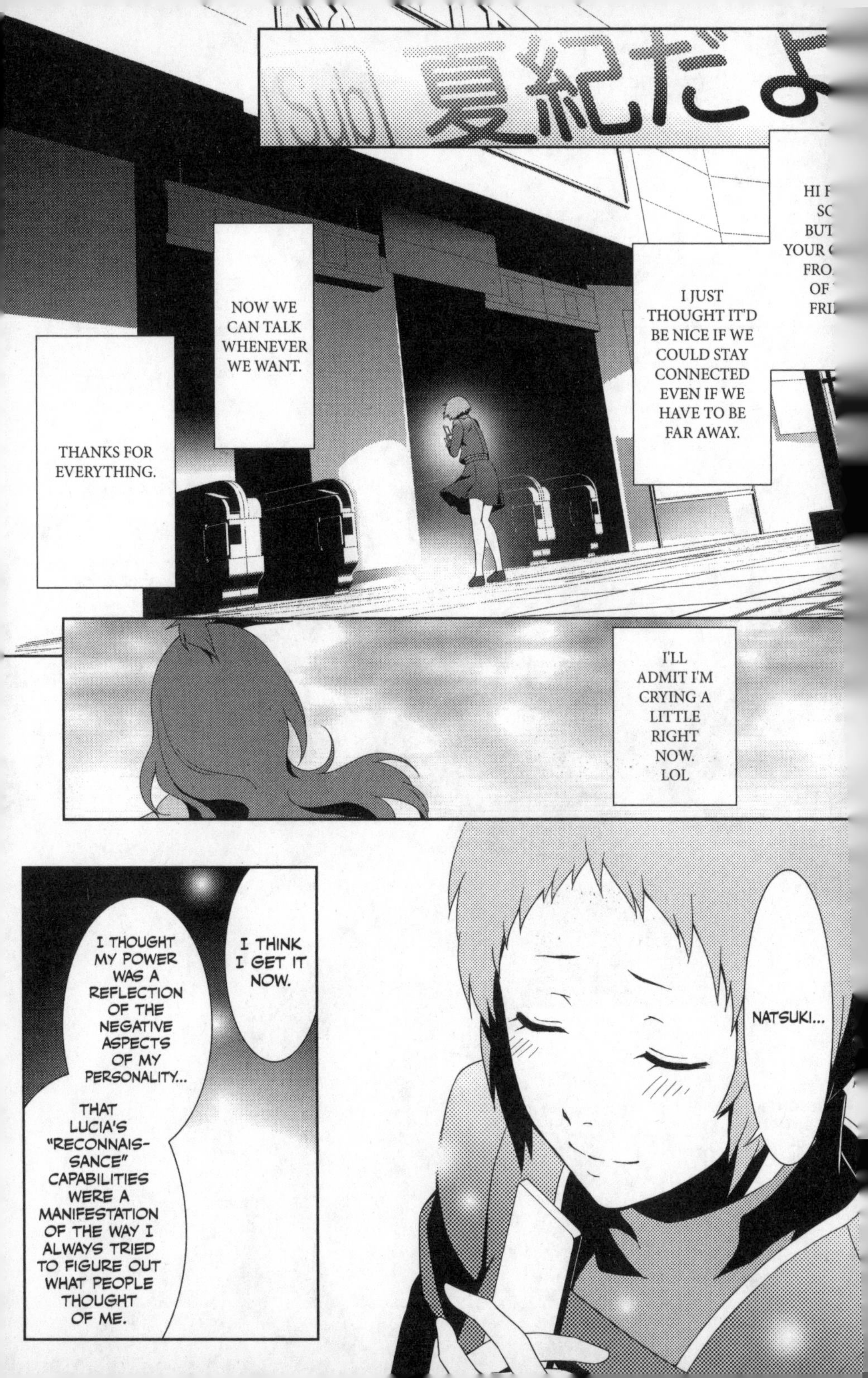
夏紀だよ
I JUST THOUGHT IT'D BE NICE IF WE COULD STAY CONNECTED EVEN IF WE HAVE TO BE FAR AWAY.
NOW WE CAN TALK WHENEVER WE WANT.
THANKS FOR EVERYTHING.
I'LL ADMIT I'M CRYING A LITTLE RIGHT NOW. LOL
NATSUKI...
I THINK I GET IT NOW.
I THOUGHT MY POWER WAS A REFLECTION OF THE NEGATIVE ASPECTS OF MY PERSONALITY...
THAT LUCIA'S "RECONNAIS-SANCE" CAPABILITIES WERE A MANIFESTATION OF THE WAY I ALWAYS TRIED TO FIGURE OUT WHAT PEOPLE THOUGHT OF ME.

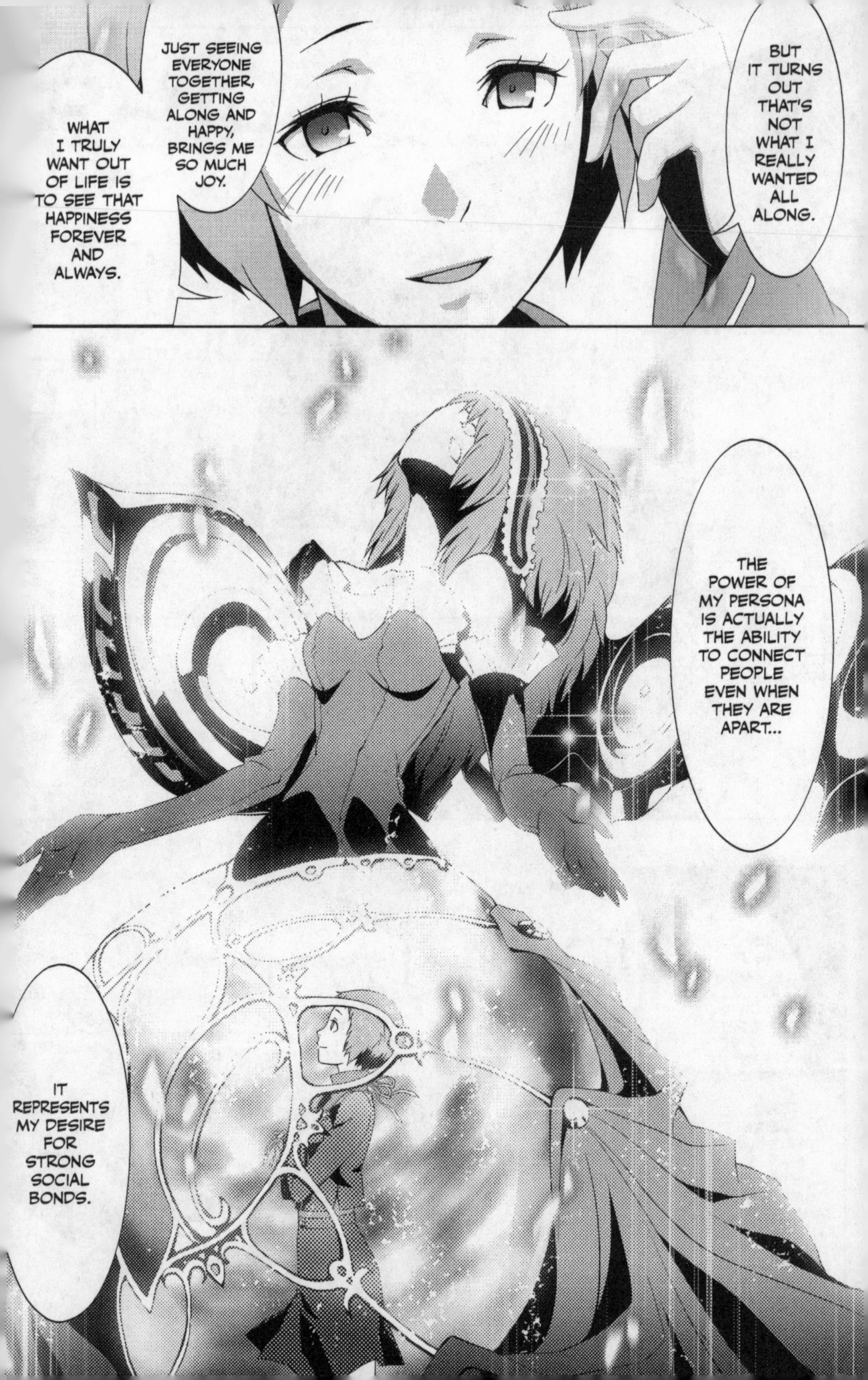
BUT IT TURNS OUT THAT'S NOT WHAT I REALLY WANTED ALL ALONG.
JUST SEEING EVERYONE TOGETHER, GETTING ALONG AND HAPPY, BRINGS ME SO MUCH JOY.
WHAT I TRULY WANT OUT OF LIFE IS TO SEE THAT HAPPINESS FOREVER AND ALWAYS.
THE POWER OF MY PERSONA IS ACTUALLY THE ABILITY TO CONNECT PEOPLE EVEN WHEN THEY ARE APART...
IT REPRESENTS MY DESIRE FOR STRONG SOCIAL BONDS.

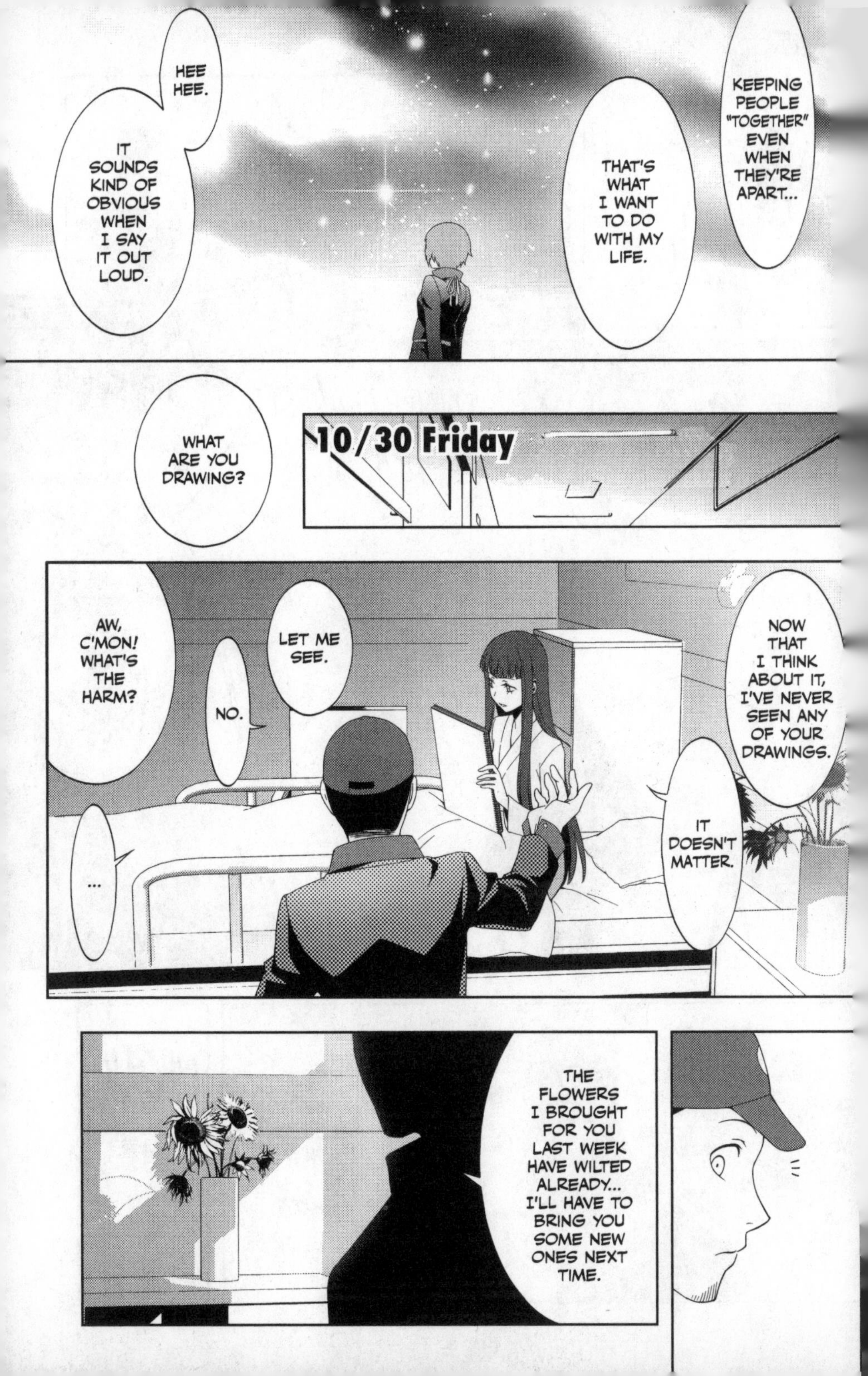
KEEPING PEOPLE "TOGETHER" EVEN WHEN THEY'RE APART...
THAT'S WHAT I WANT TO DO WITH MY LIFE.
HEE HEE.
IT SOUNDS KIND OF OBVIOUS WHEN I SAY IT OUT LOUD.
10/30 Friday
WHAT ARE YOU DRAWING?
NOW THAT I THINK ABOUT IT, I'VE NEVER SEEN ANY OF YOUR DRAWINGS.
IT DOESN'T MATTER.
LET ME SEE.
NO.
AW, C'MON! WHAT'S THE HARM?
...
THE FLOWERS I BROUGHT FOR YOU LAST WEEK HAVE WILTED ALREADY... I'LL HAVE TO BRING YOU SOME NEW ONES NEXT TIME.

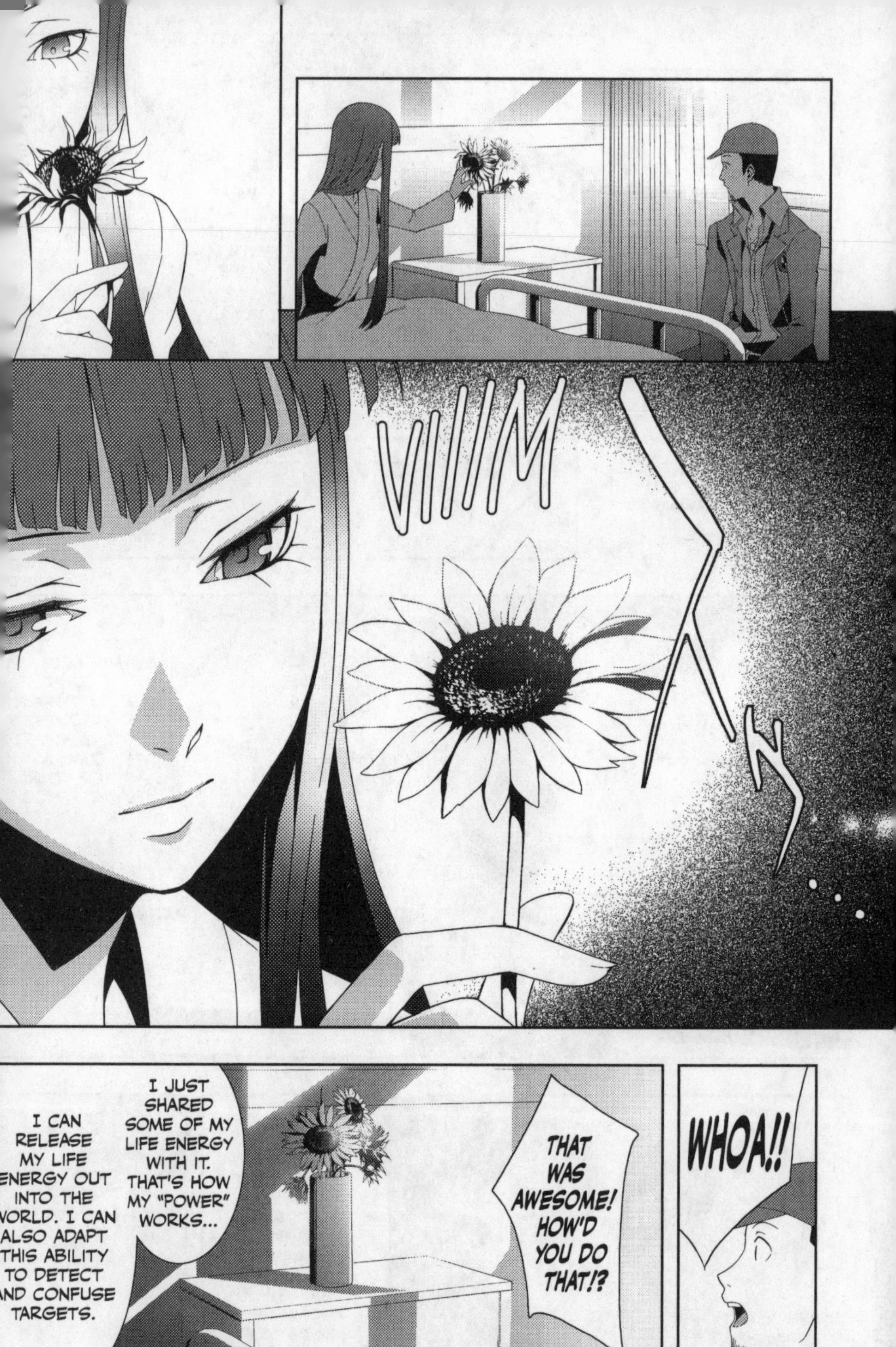
VIIIM
WHOA!!
THAT WAS AWESOME! HOW'D YOU DO THAT!?
I JUST SHARED SOME OF MY LIFE ENERGY WITH IT. THAT'S HOW MY "POWER" WORKS...
I CAN RELEASE MY LIFE ENERGY OUT INTO THE WORLD. I CAN ALSO ADAPT THIS ABILITY TO DETECT AND CONFUSE TARGETS.

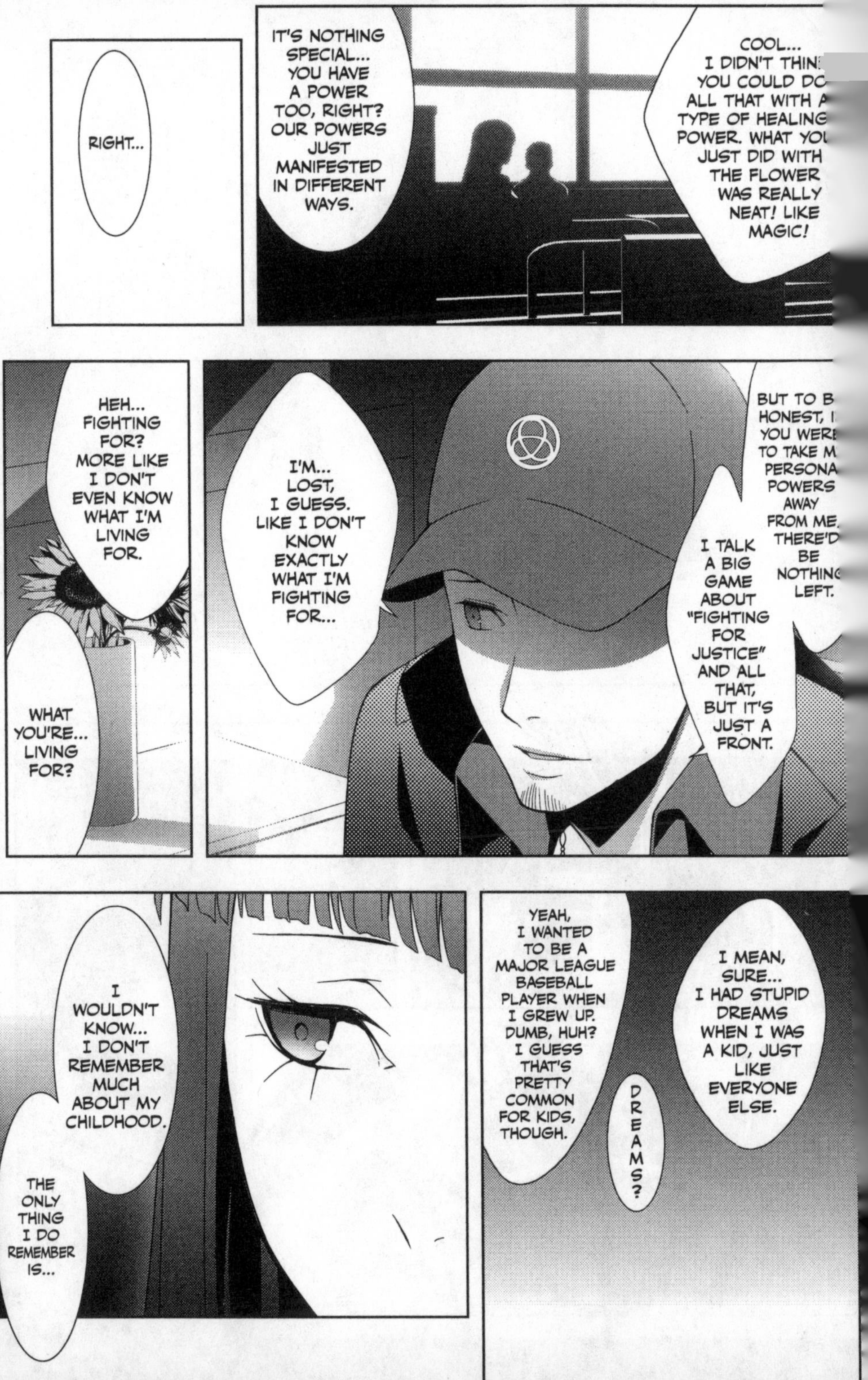
COOL... I DIDN'T THIN YOU COULD DO ALL THAT WITH A TYPE OF HEALING POWER. WHAT YOU JUST DID WITH THE FLOWER WAS REALLY NEAT! LIKE MAGIC!
IT'S NOTHING SPECIAL... YOU HAVE A POWER TOO, RIGHT? OUR POWERS JUST MANIFESTED IN DIFFERENT WAYS.
RIGHT...
BUT TO B HONEST, I YOU WERE TO TAKE M PERSONA POWERS AWAY FROM ME, THERE'D BE NOTHING LEFT.
I TALK A BIG GAME ABOUT "FIGHTING FOR JUSTICE" AND ALL THAT, BUT IT'S JUST A FRONT.
I'M... LOST, I GUESS. LIKE I DON'T KNOW EXACTLY WHAT I'M FIGHTING FOR...
HEH... FIGHTING FOR? MORE LIKE I DON'T EVEN KNOW WHAT I'M LIVING FOR.
WHAT YOU'RE... LIVING FOR?
I MEAN, SURE... I HAD STUPID DREAMS WHEN I WAS A KID, JUST LIKE EVERYONE ELSE.
YEAH, I WANTED TO BE A MAJOR LEAGUE BASEBALL PLAYER WHEN I GREW UP. DUMB, HUH? I GUESS THAT'S PRETTY COMMON FOR KIDS, THOUGH.
DREAMS?
I WOULDN'T KNOW... I DON'T REMEMBER MUCH ABOUT MY CHILDHOOD.
THE ONLY THING I DO REMEMBER IS...

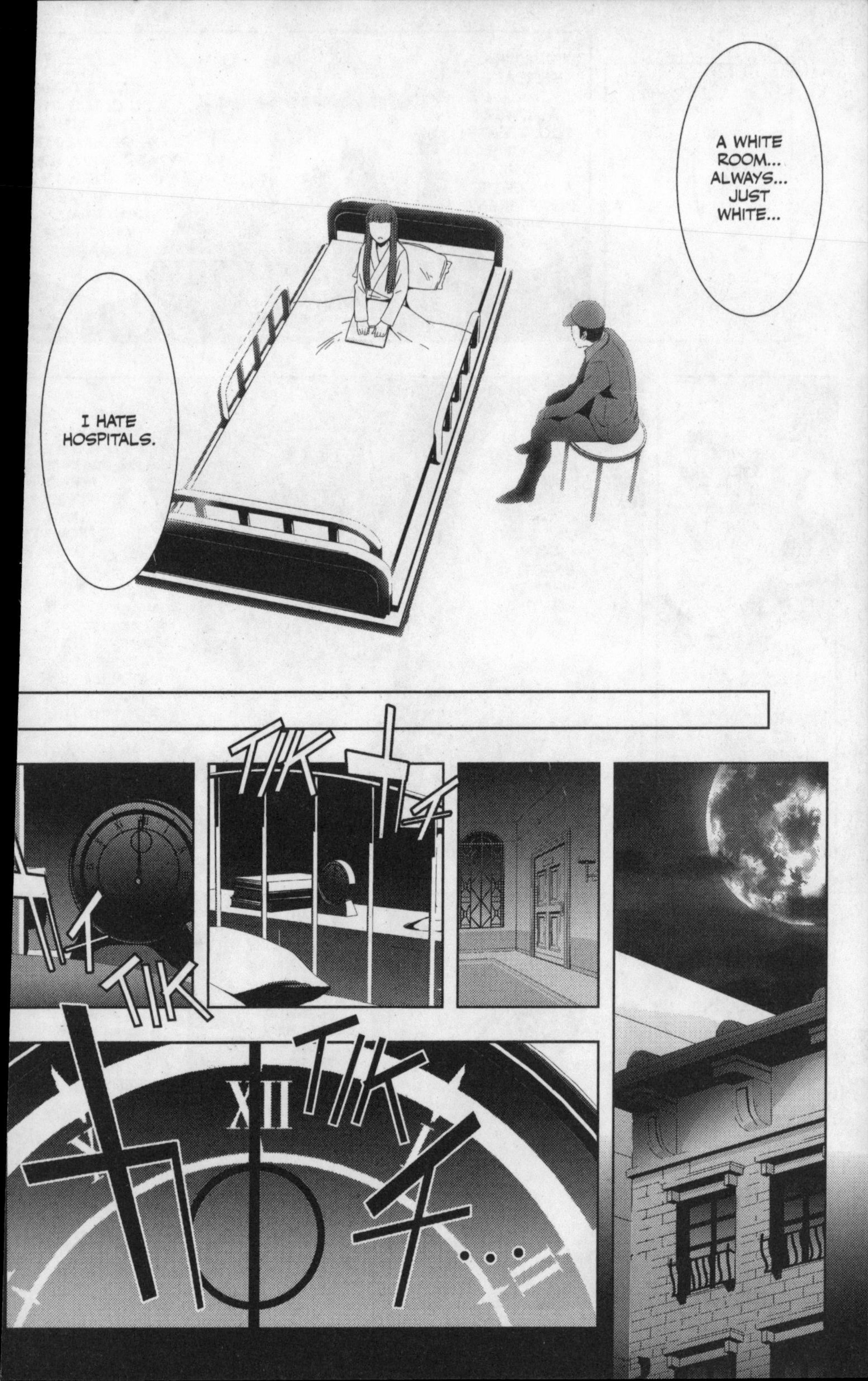
A WHITE ROOM... ALWAYS... JUST WHITE...
I HATE HOSPITALS.
TIK
TIK
TIK

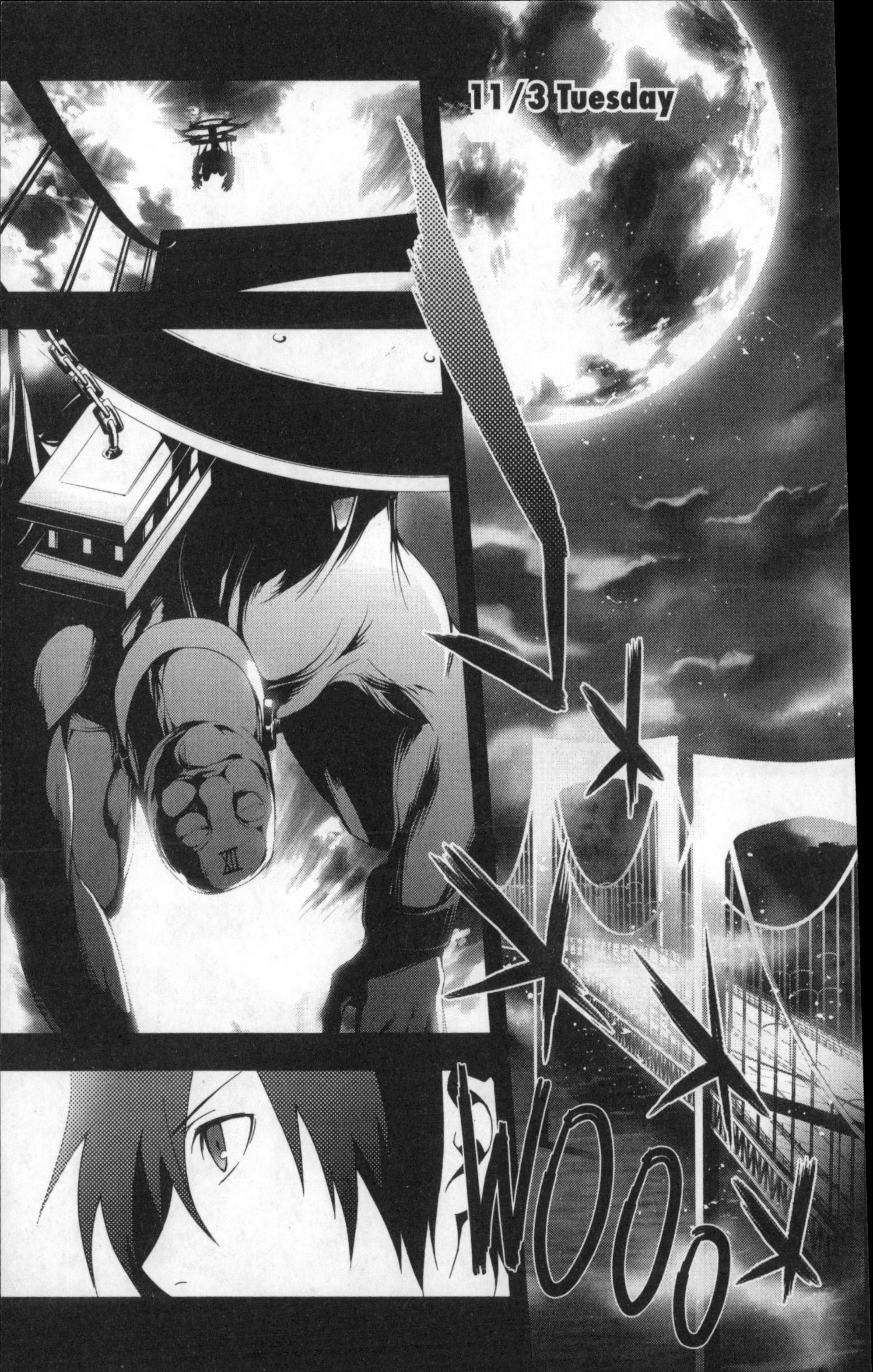
11/3 Tuesday
WOOO

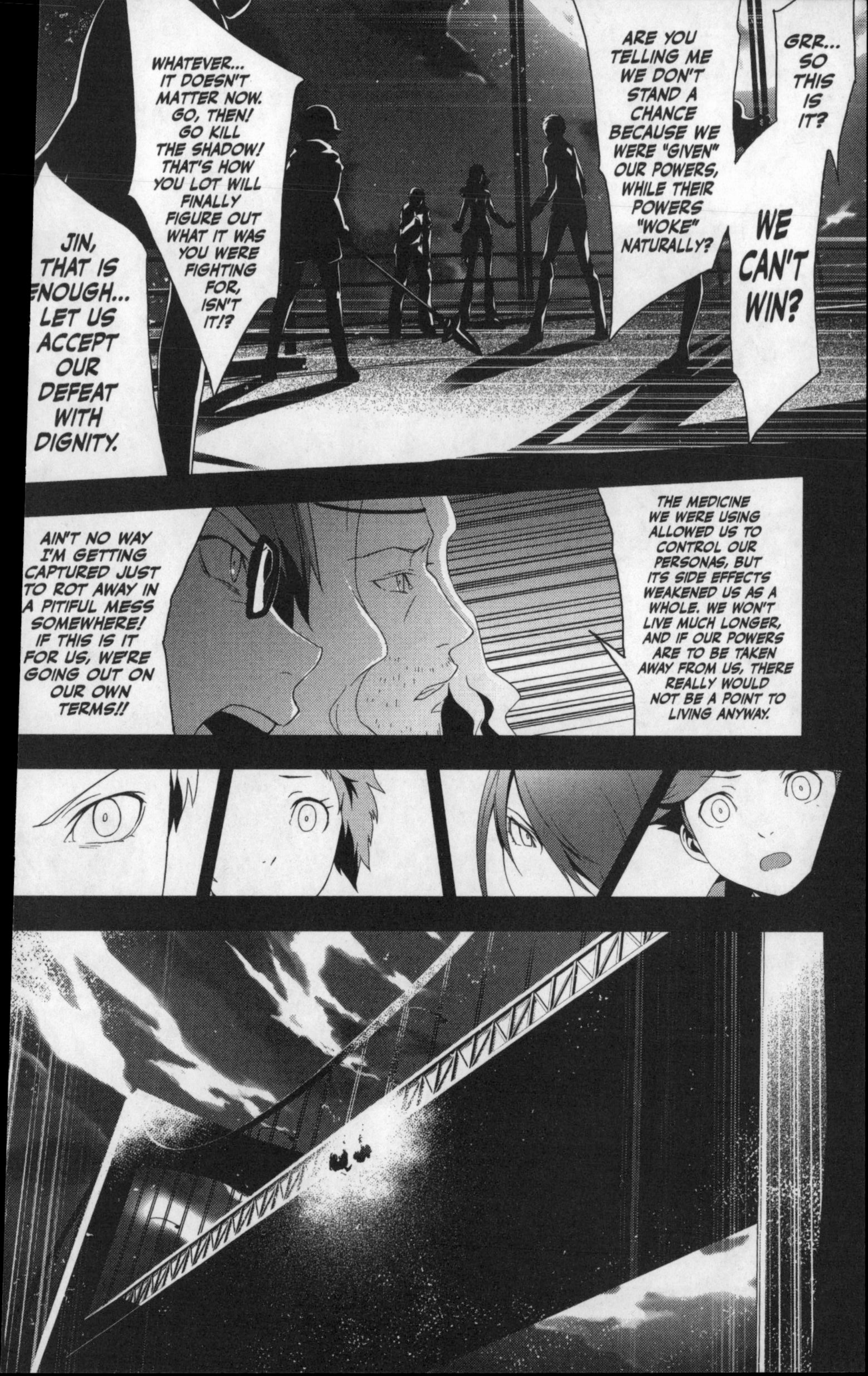
GRR... SO THIS IS IT?
WE CAN'T WIN?
ARE YOU TELLING ME WE DON'T STAND A CHANCE BECAUSE WE WERE "GIVEN" OUR POWERS, WHILE THEIR POWERS "WOKE" NATURALLY?
WHATEVER... IT DOESN'T MATTER NOW. GO, THEN! GO KILL THE SHADOW! THAT'S HOW YOU LOT WILL FINALLY FIGURE OUT WHAT IT WAS YOU WERE FIGHTING FOR, ISN'T IT!?
JIN, THAT IS ENOUGH... LET US ACCEPT OUR DEFEAT WITH DIGNITY.
THE MEDICINE WE WERE USING ALLOWED US TO CONTROL OUR PERSONAS, BUT ITS SIDE EFFECTS WEAKENED US AS A WHOLE. WE WON'T LIVE MUCH LONGER, AND IF OUR POWERS ARE TO BE TAKEN AWAY FROM US, THERE REALLY WOULD NOT BE A POINT TO LIVING ANYWAY.
AIN'T NO WAY I'M GETTING CAPTURED JUST TO ROT AWAY IN A PITIFUL MESS SOMEWHERE! IF THIS IS IT FOR US, WE'RE GOING OUT ON OUR OWN TERMS!!

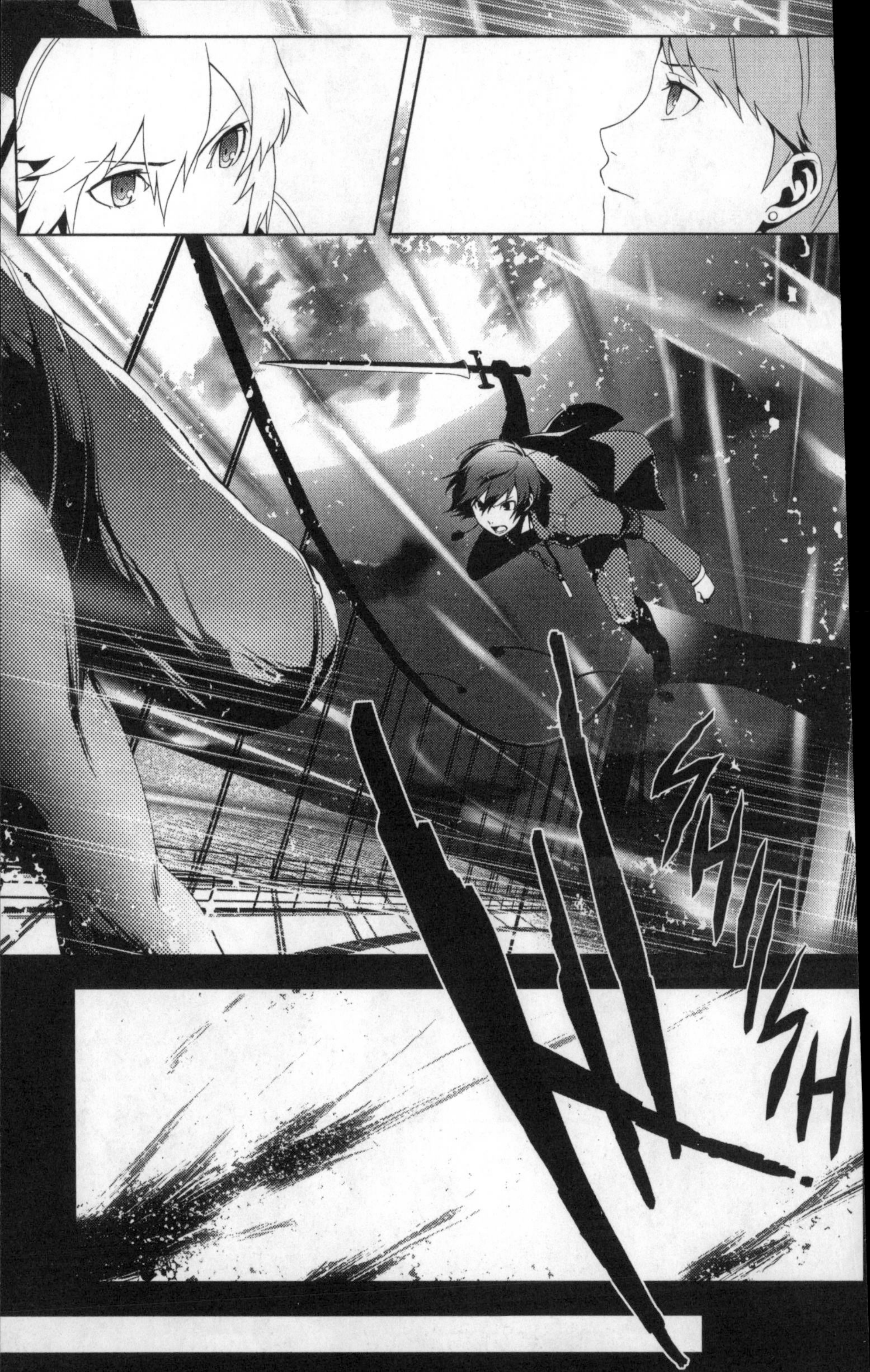
SHIIISH

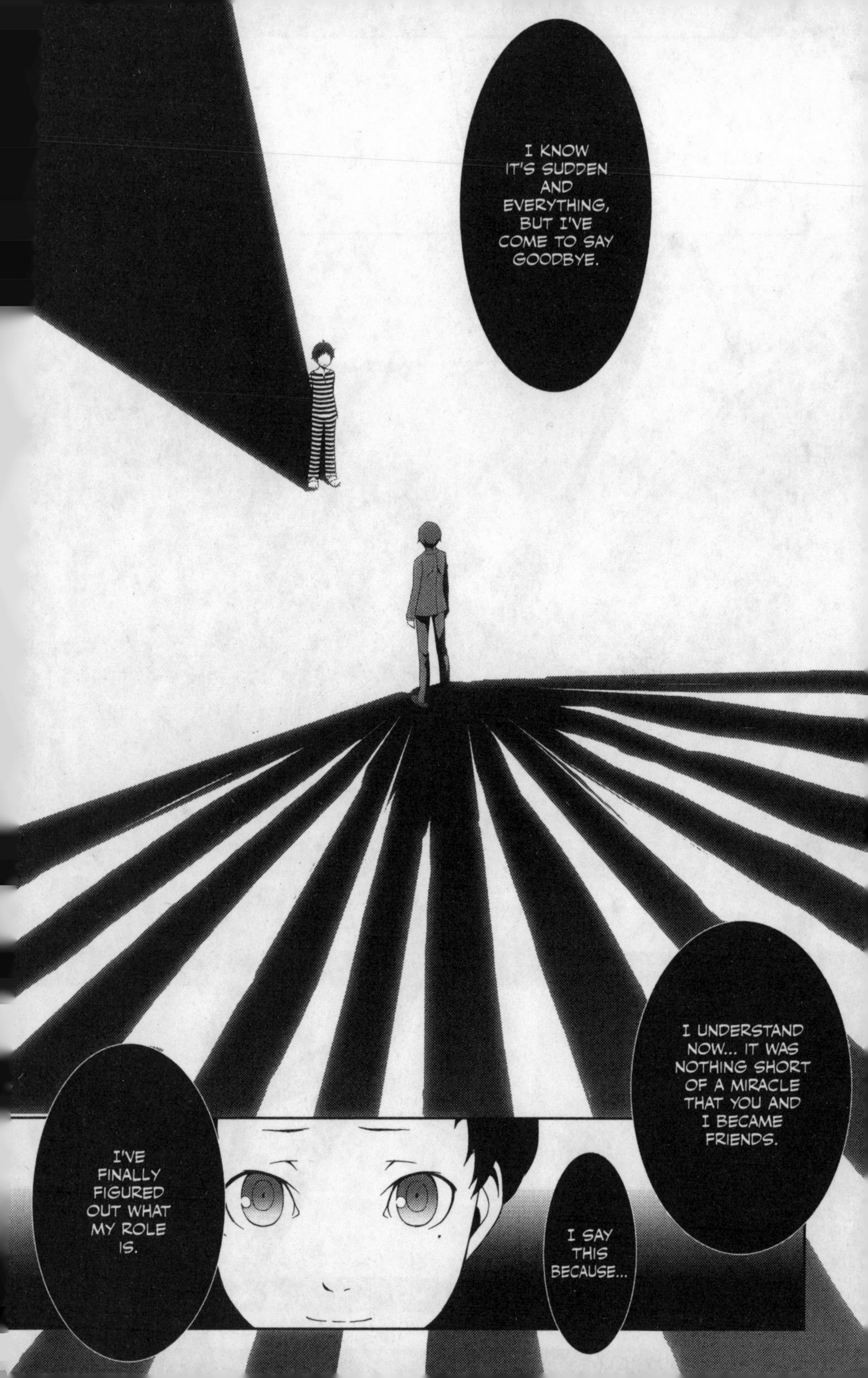
I KNOW IT'S SUDDEN AND EVERYTHING, BUT I'VE COME TO SAY GOODBYE.
I UNDERSTAND NOW... IT WAS NOTHING SHORT OF A MIRACLE THAT YOU AND I BECAME FRIENDS.
I SAY THIS BECAUSE...
I'VE FINALLY FIGURED OUT WHAT MY ROLE IS.

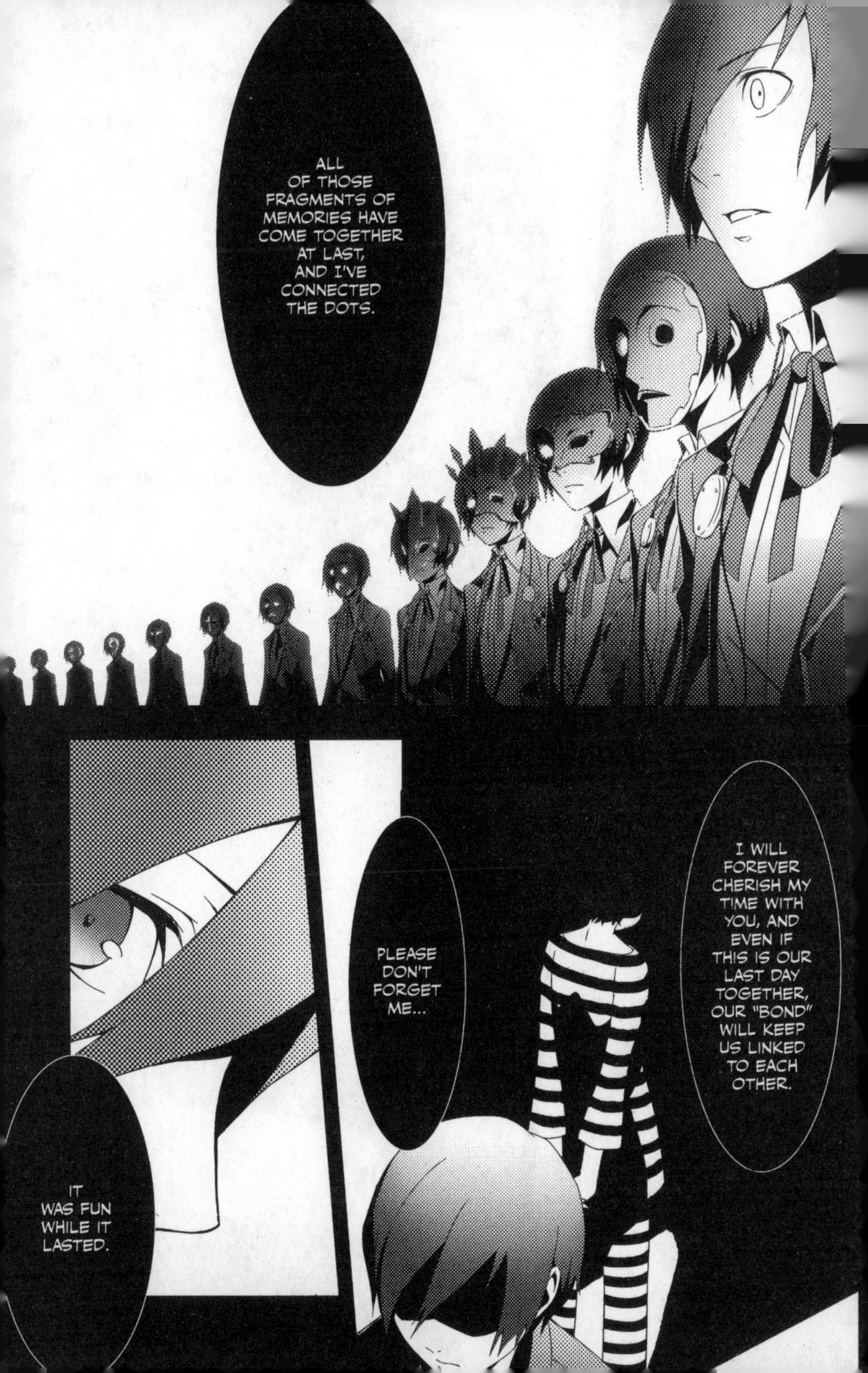
ALL OF THOSE FRAGMENTS OF MEMORIES HAVE COME TOGETHER AT LAST, AND I'VE CONNECTED THE DOTS.
I WILL FOREVER CHERISH MY TIME WITH YOU, AND EVEN IF THIS IS OUR LAST DAY TOGETHER, OUR "BOND" WILL KEEP US LINKED TO EACH OTHER.
PLEASE DON'T FORGET ME...
IT WAS FUN WHILE IT LASTED.

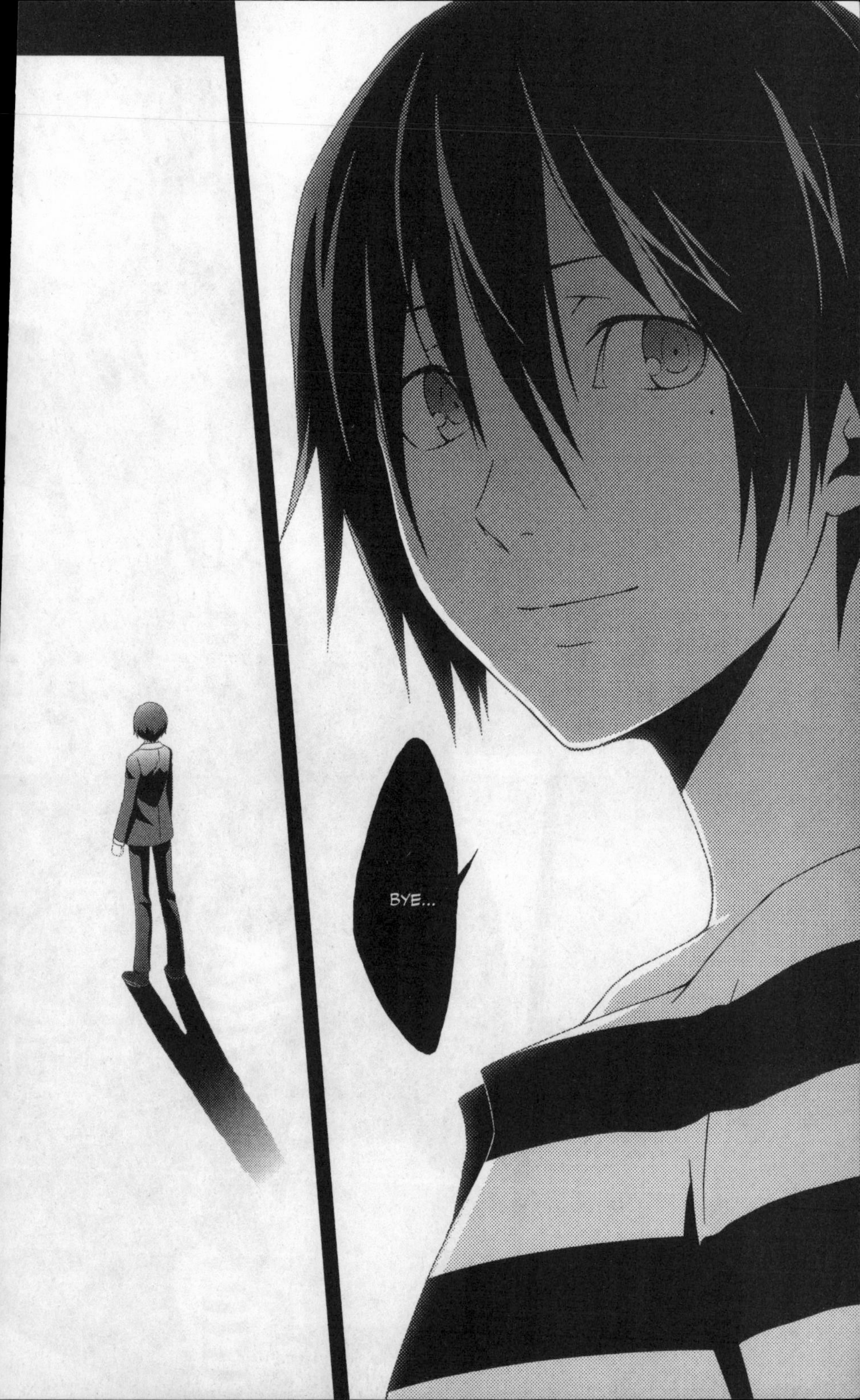
BYE...

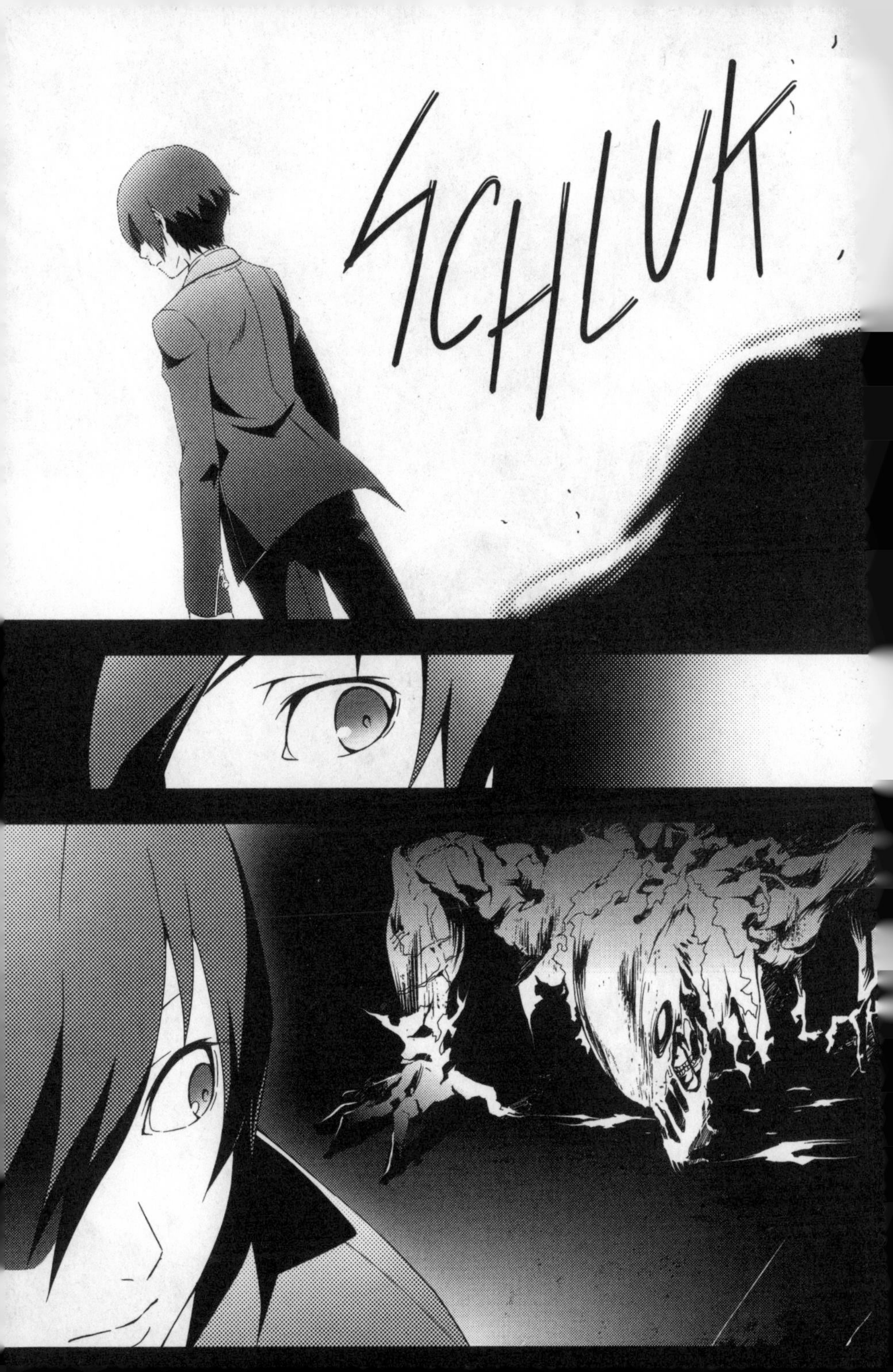
SCHLUK

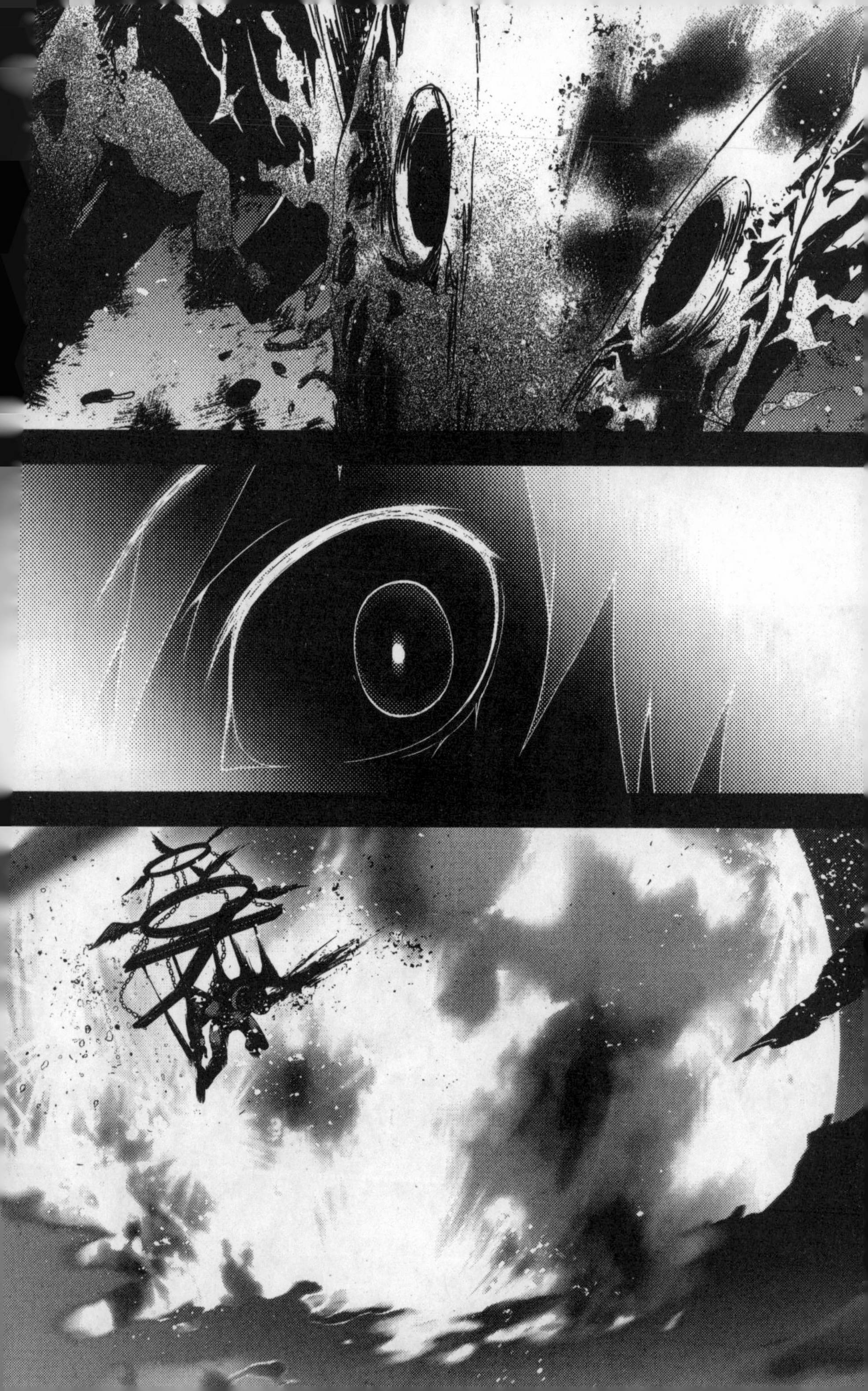

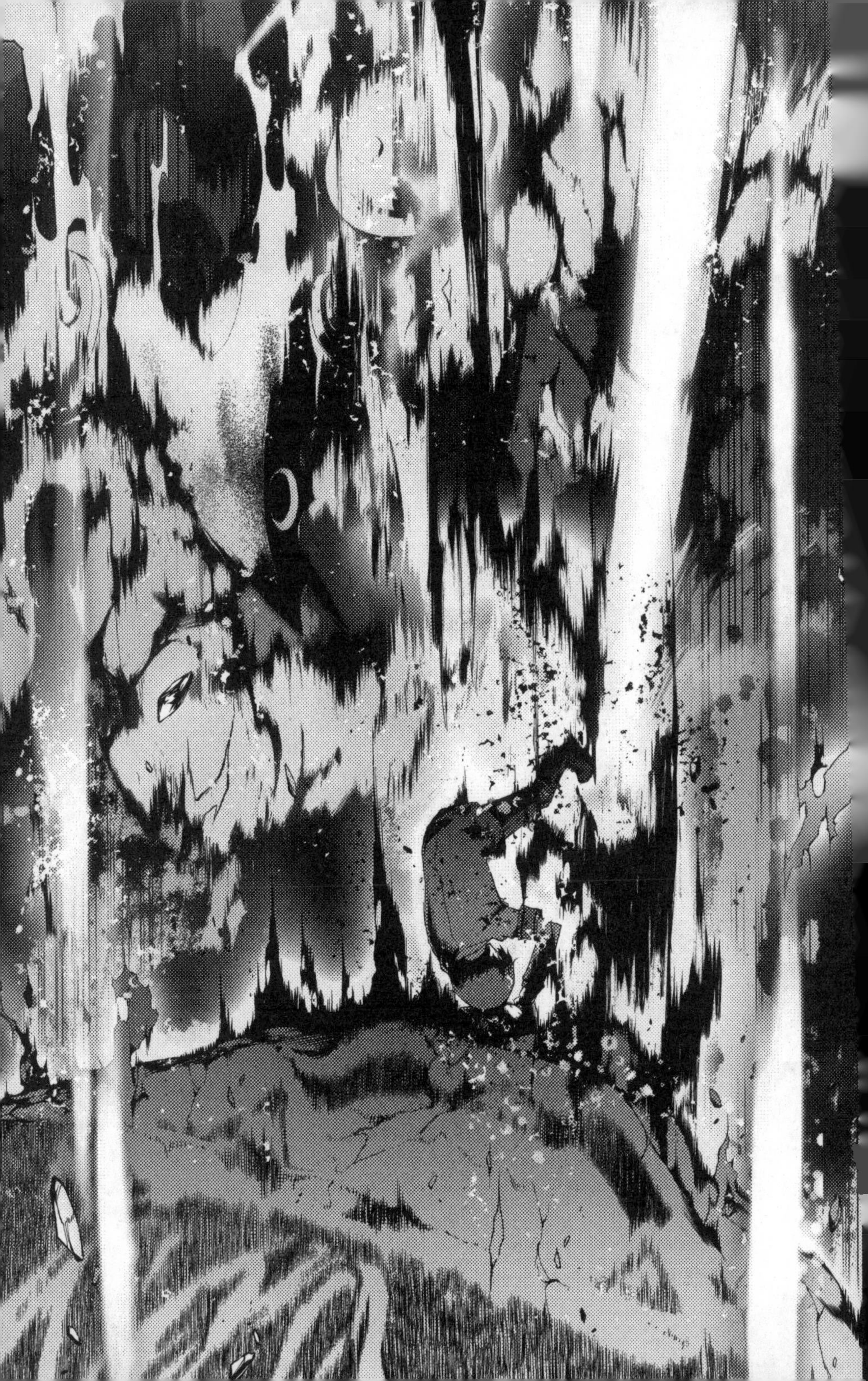

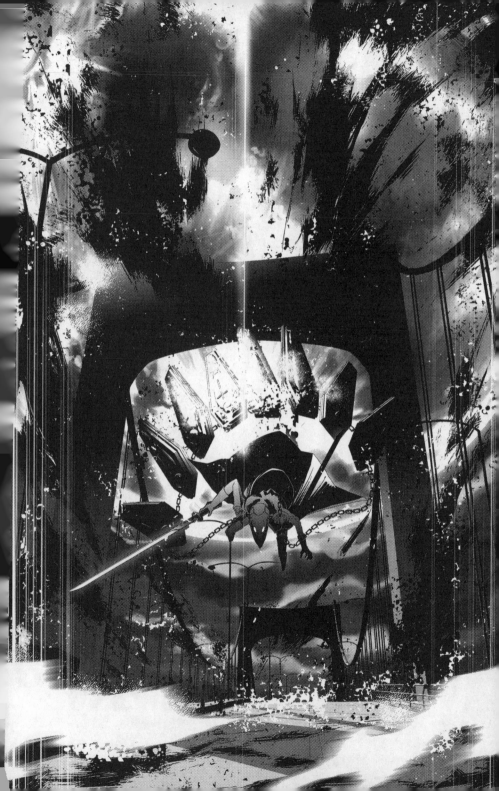

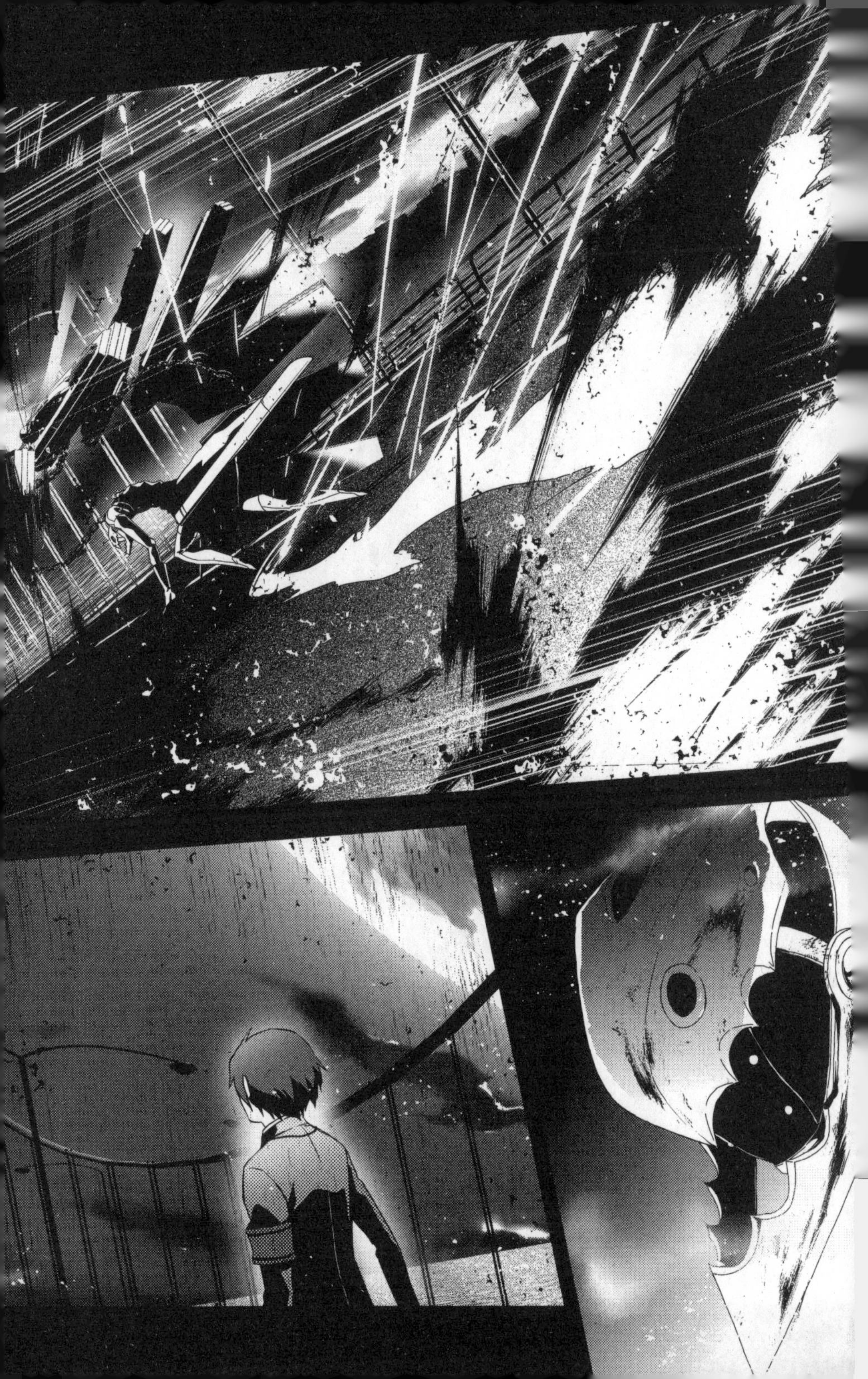

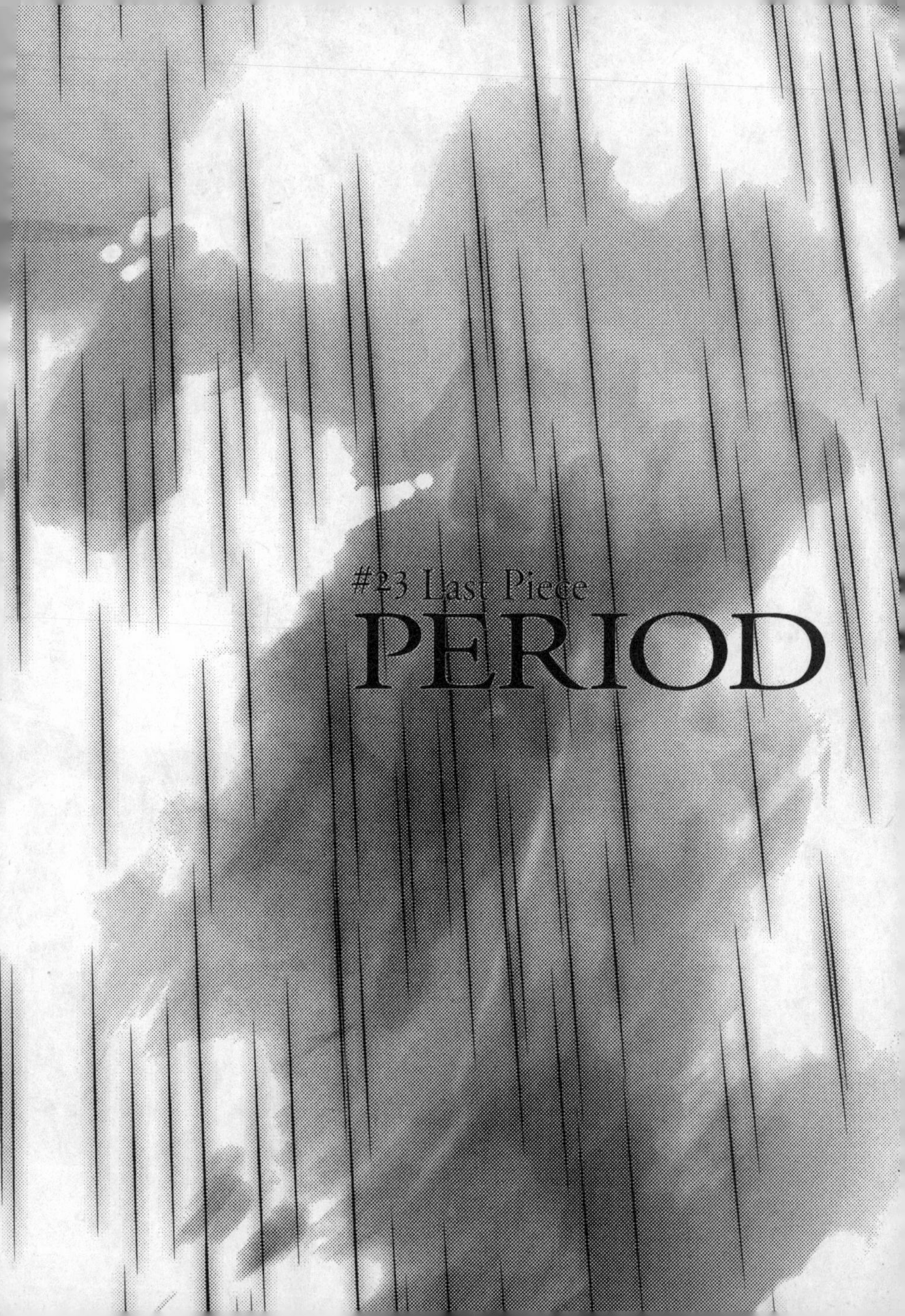
#23 Last Piece
PERIOD

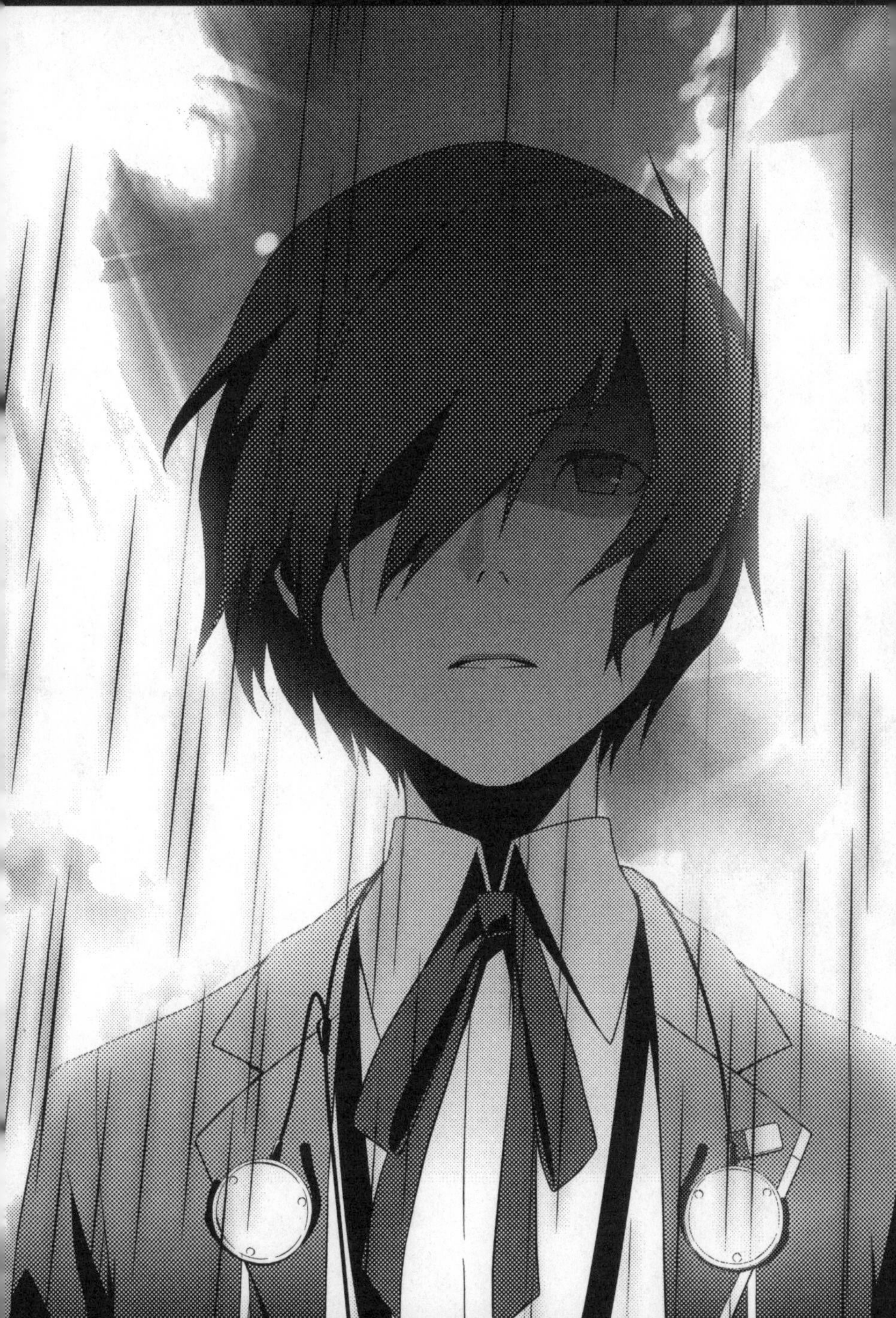

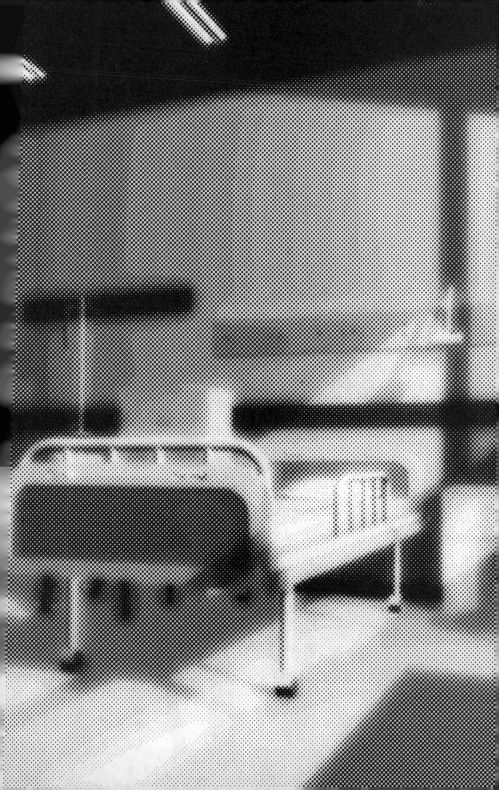

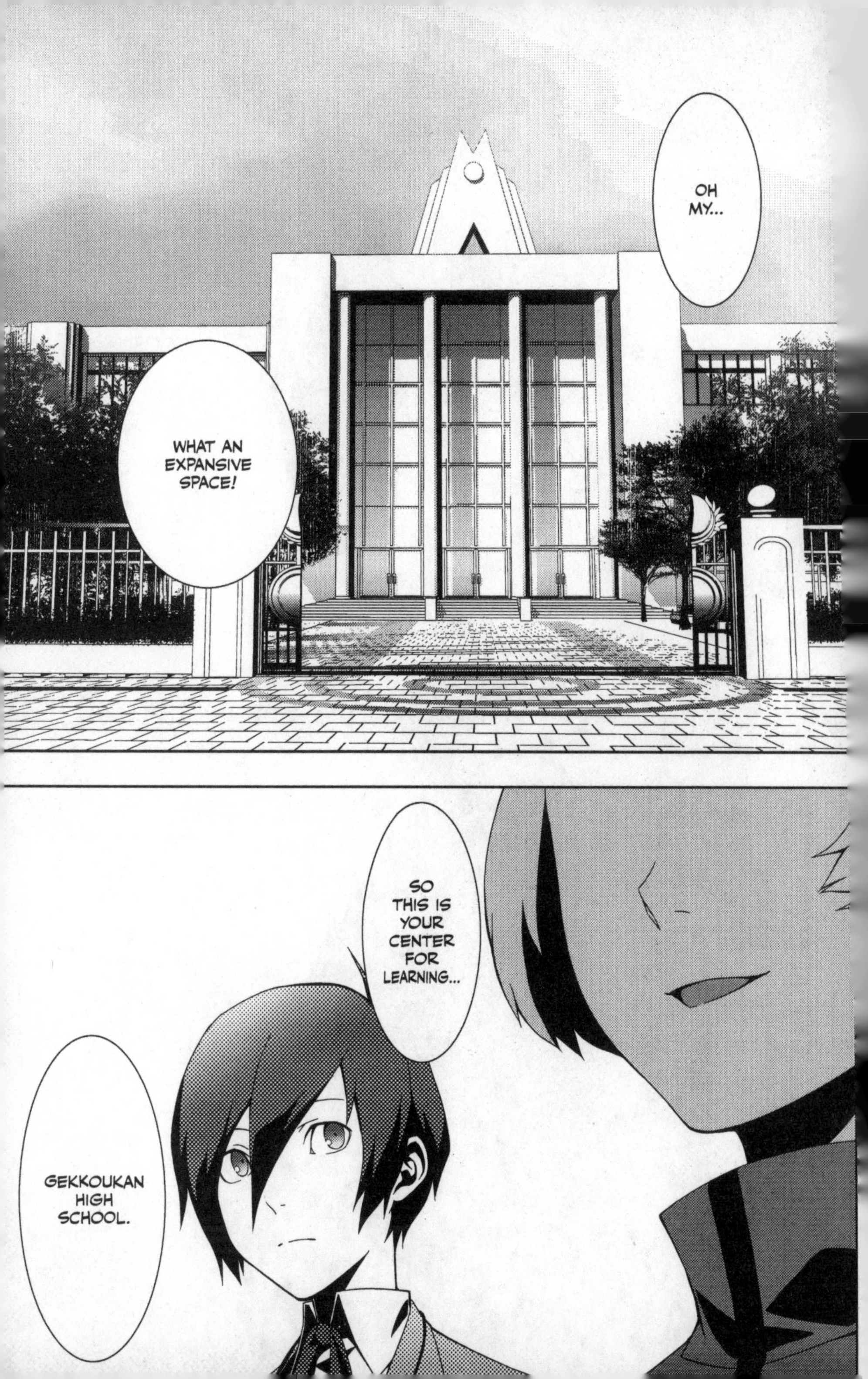
OH MY...
WHAT AN EXPANSIVE SPACE!
SO THIS IS YOUR CENTER FOR LEARNING...
GEKKOUKAN HIGH SCHOOL.

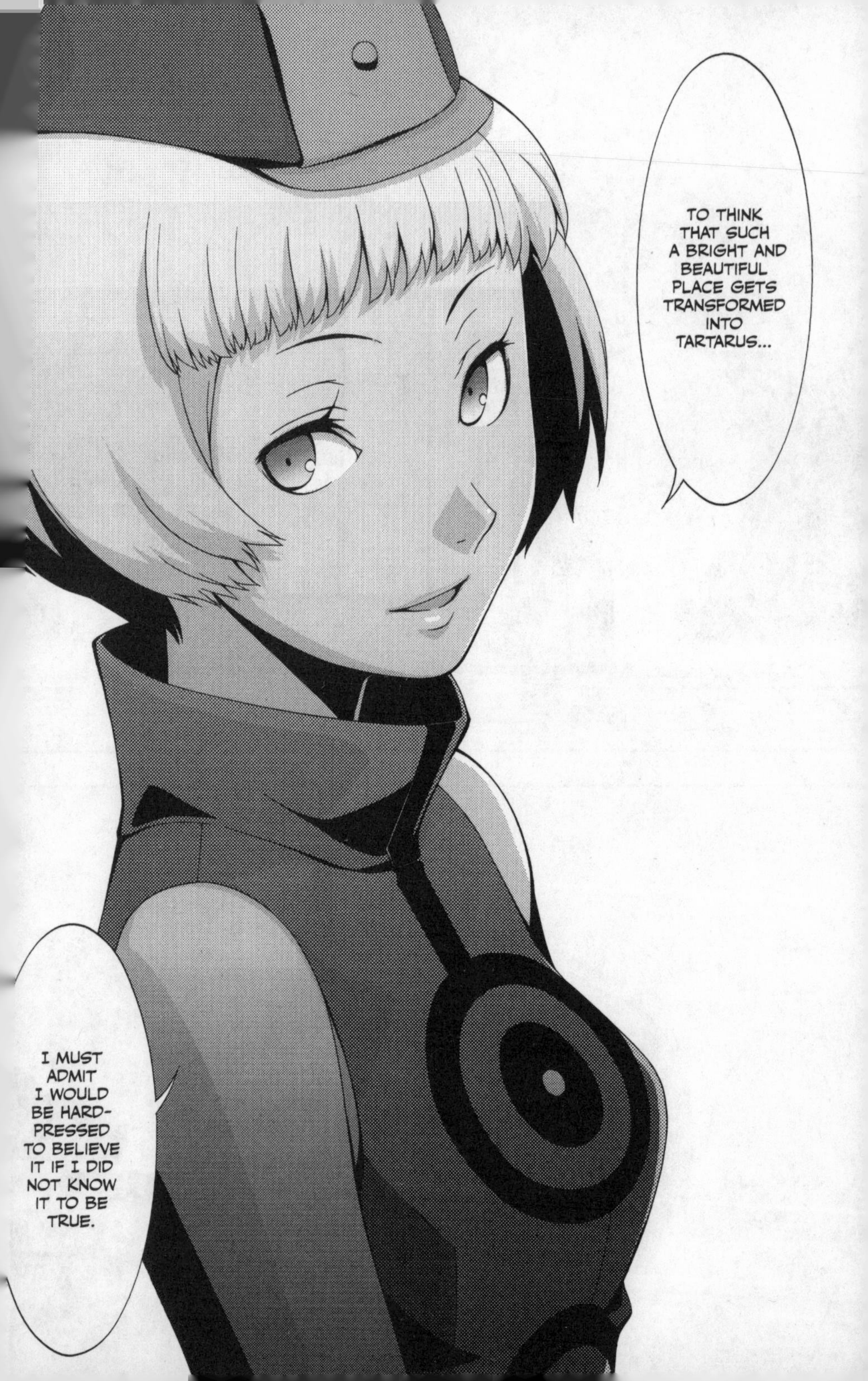
TO THINK THAT SUCH A BRIGHT AND BEAUTIFUL PLACE GETS TRANSFORMED INTO TARTARUS...
I MUST ADMIT I WOULD BE HARD-PRESSED TO BELIEVE IT IF I DID NOT KNOW IT TO BE TRUE.

#24 Perspective:04
Recursion

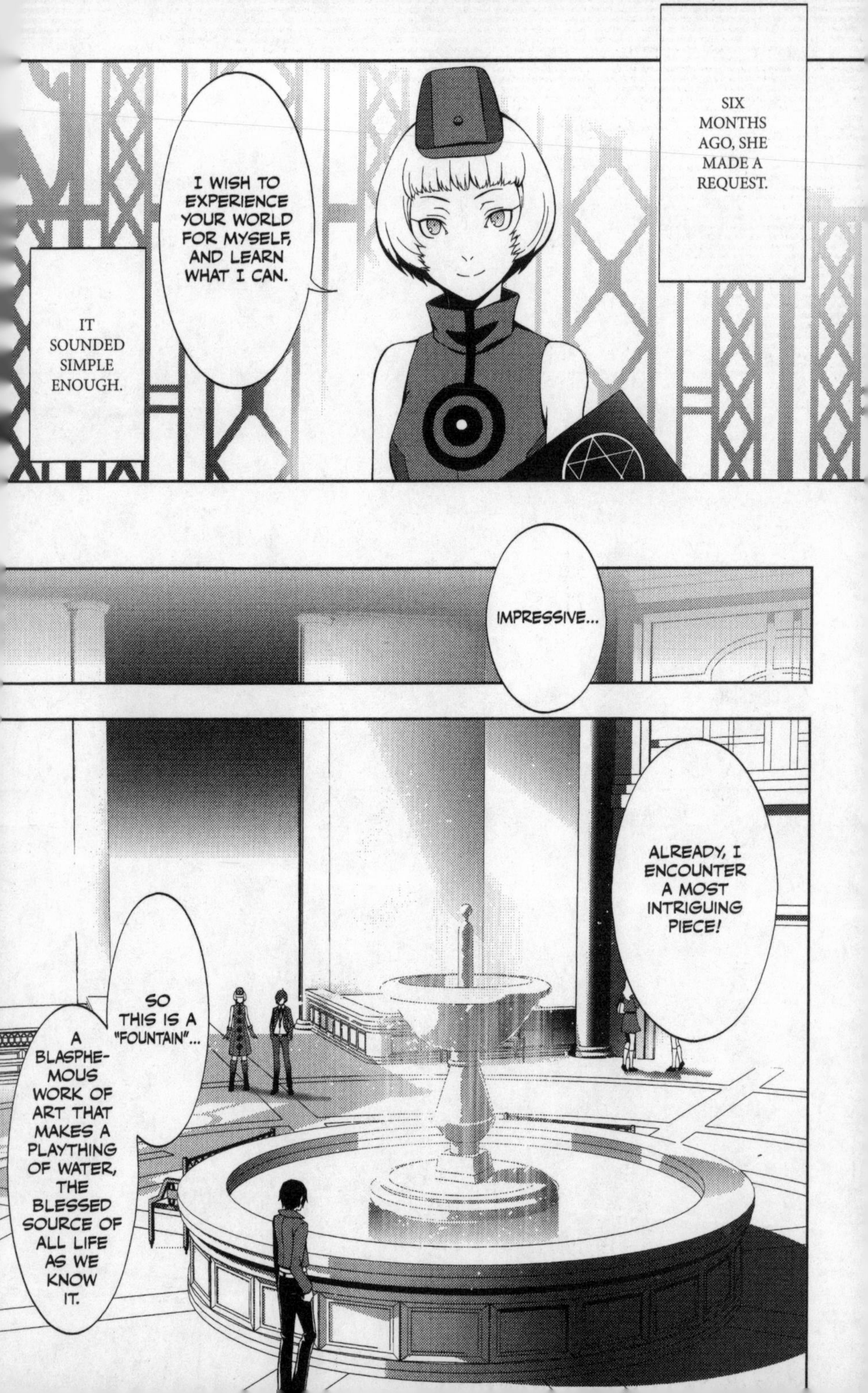
SIX MONTHS AGO, SHE MADE A REQUEST.
I WISH TO EXPERIENCE YOUR WORLD FOR MYSELF, AND LEARN WHAT I CAN.
IT SOUNDED SIMPLE ENOUGH.
IMPRESSIVE...
ALREADY, I ENCOUNTER A MOST INTRIGUING PIECE!
SO THIS IS A "FOUNTAIN"...
A BLASPHE-MOUS WORK OF ART THAT MAKES A PLAYTHING OF WATER, THE BLESSED SOURCE OF ALL LIFE AS WE KNOW IT.

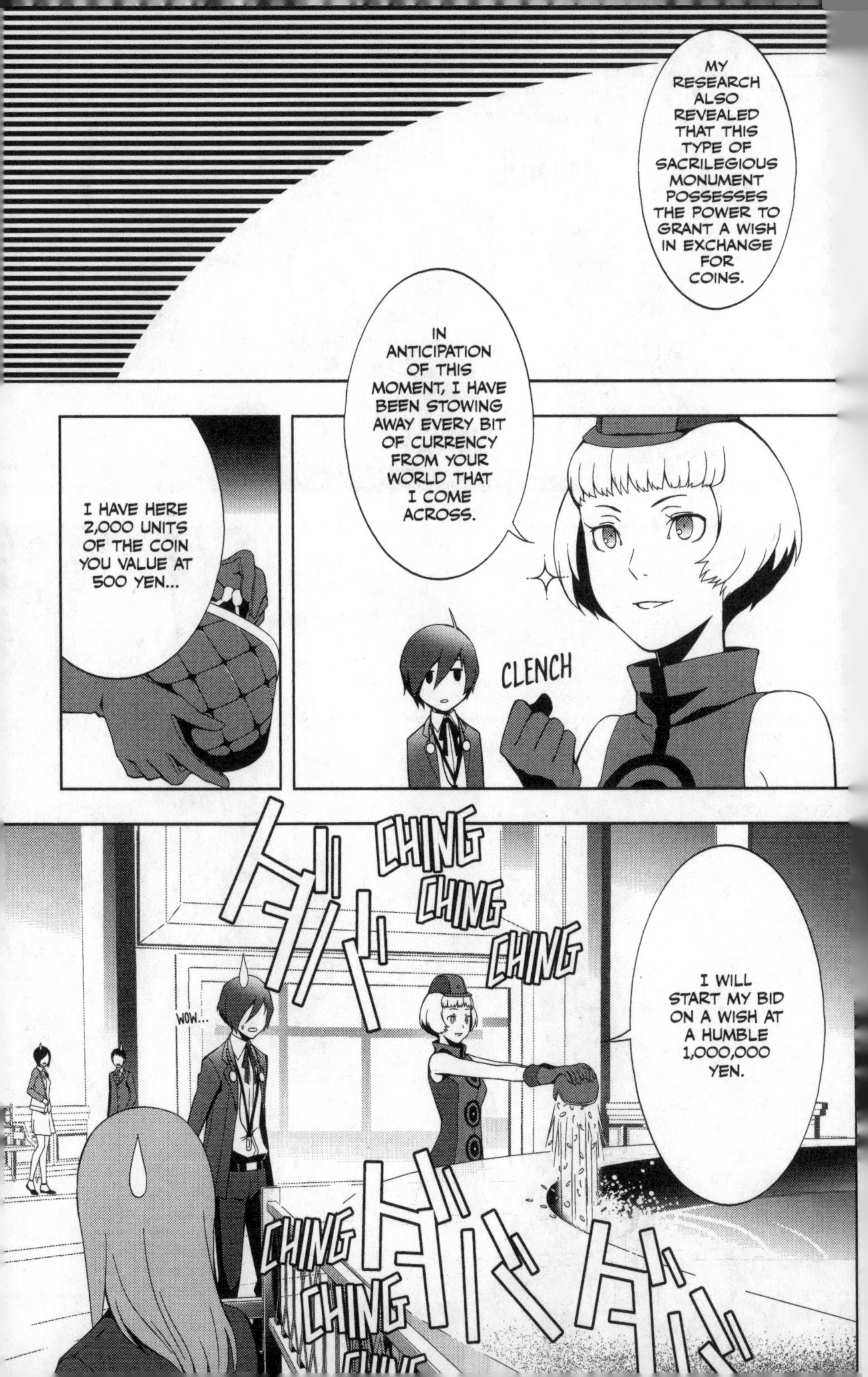
MY RESEARCH ALSO REVEALED THAT THIS TYPE OF SACRILEGIOUS MONUMENT POSSESSES THE POWER TO GRANT A WISH IN EXCHANGE FOR COINS.
IN ANTICIPATION OF THIS MOMENT, I HAVE BEEN STOWING AWAY EVERY BIT OF CURRENCY FROM YOUR WORLD THAT I COME ACROSS.
CLENCH
I HAVE HERE 2,000 UNITS OF THE COIN YOU VALUE AT 500 YEN...
I WILL START MY BID ON A WISH AT A HUMBLE 1,000,000 YEN.
CHING
CHING
CHING
WOW...
CHING
CHING

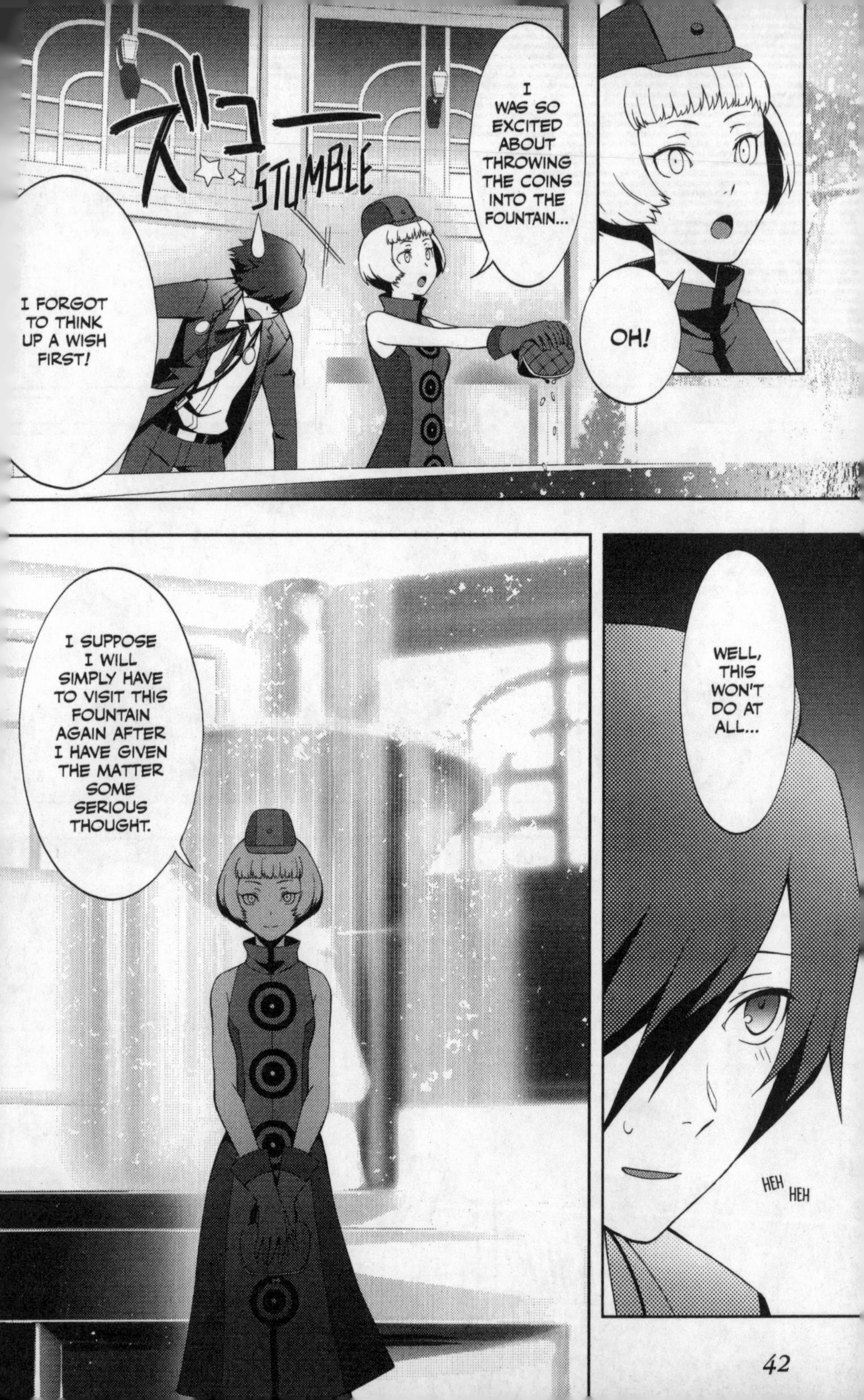
OH!
I WAS SO EXCITED ABOUT THROWING THE COINS INTO THE FOUNTAIN...
ズコー
STUMBLE
I FORGOT TO THINK UP A WISH FIRST!
WELL, THIS WON'T DO AT ALL...
HEH HEH
I SUPPOSE I WILL SIMPLY HAVE TO VISIT THIS FOUNTAIN AGAIN AFTER I HAVE GIVEN THE MATTER SOME SERIOUS THOUGHT.

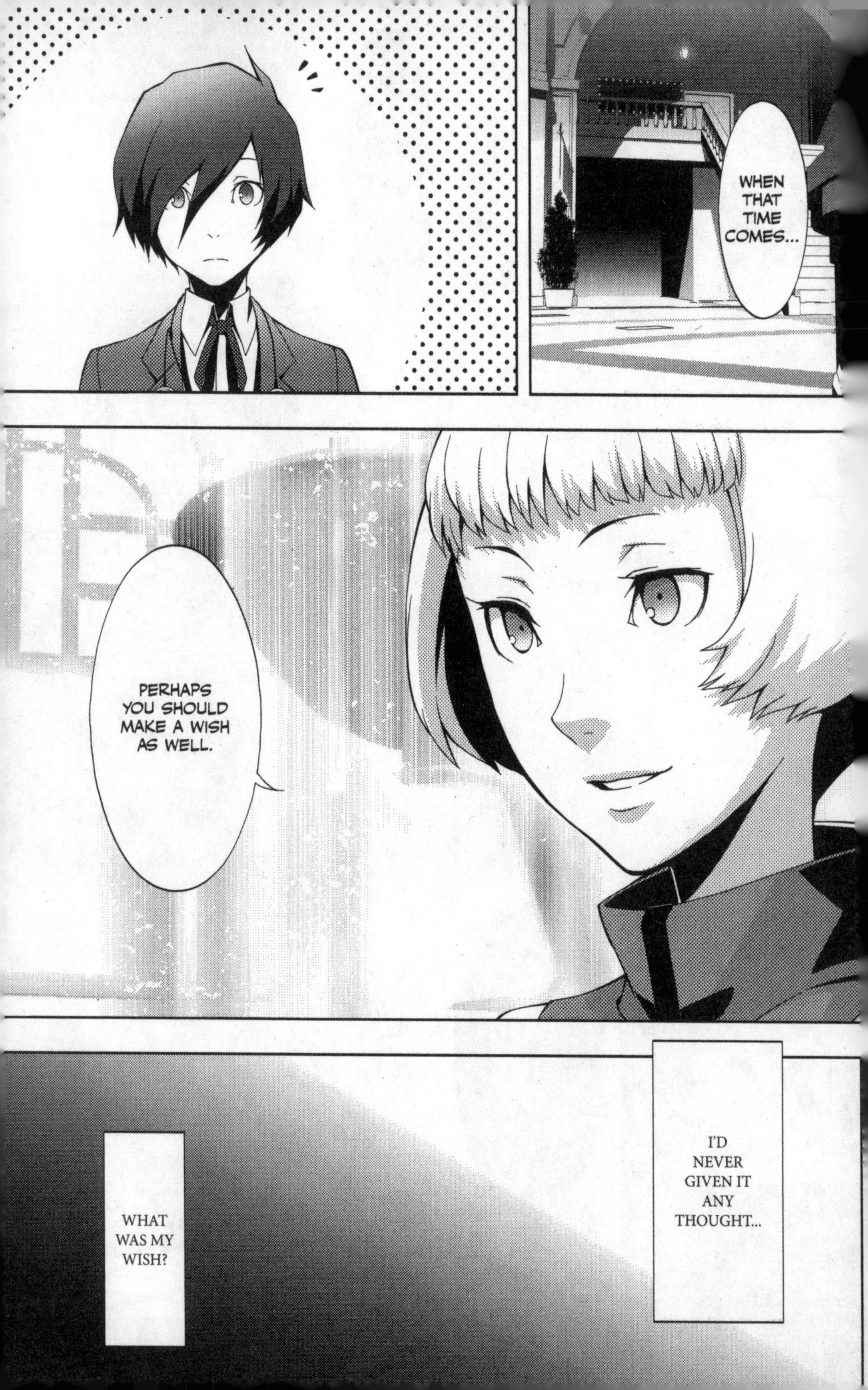
WHEN THAT TIME COMES...
PERHAPS YOU SHOULD MAKE A WISH AS WELL.
I'D NEVER GIVEN IT ANY THOUGHT...
WHAT WAS MY WISH?

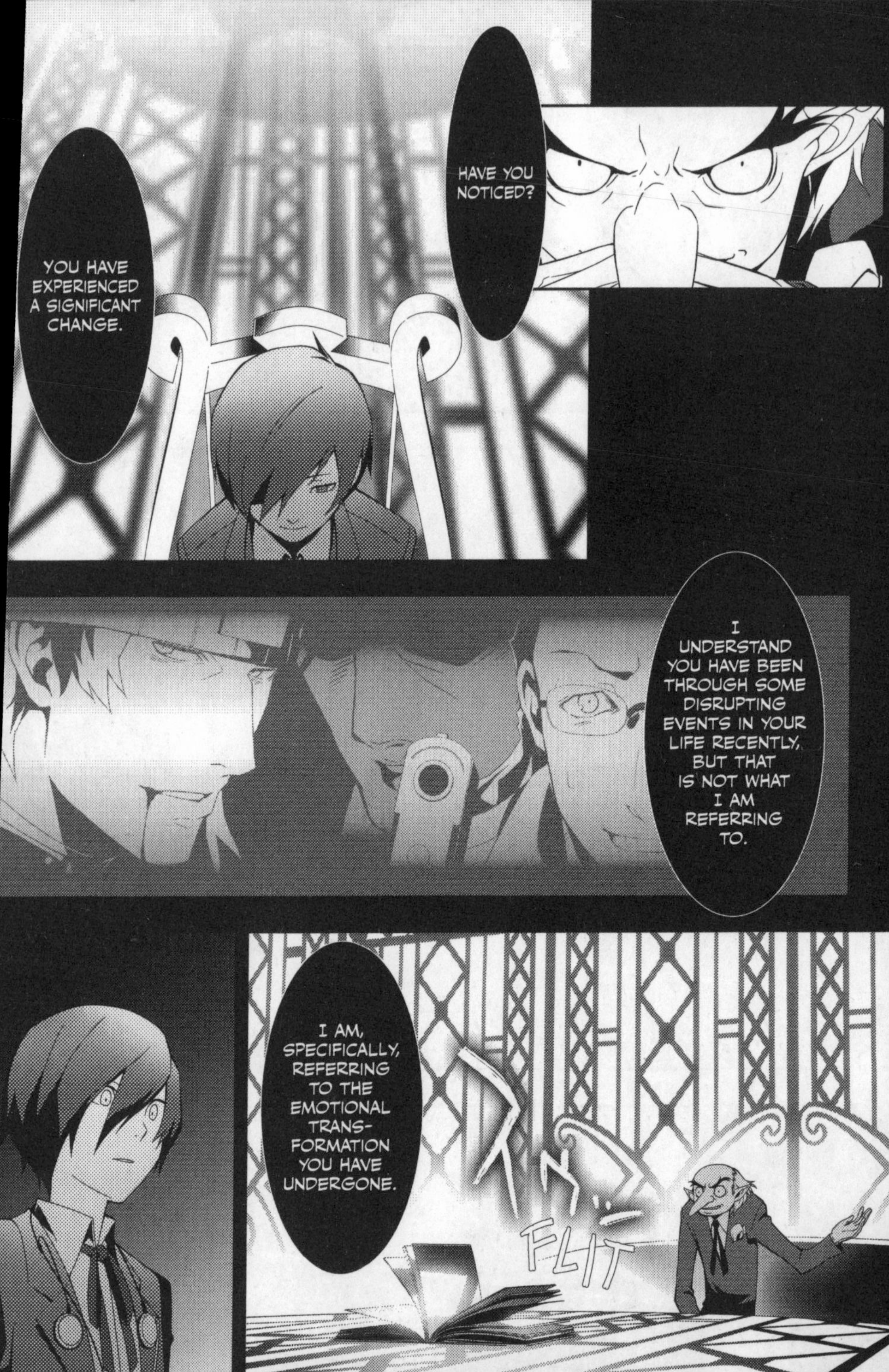
HAVE YOU NOTICED?
YOU HAVE EXPERIENCED A SIGNIFICANT CHANGE.
I UNDERSTAND YOU HAVE BEEN THROUGH SOME DISRUPTING EVENTS IN YOUR LIFE RECENTLY, BUT THAT IS NOT WHAT I AM REFERRING TO.
I AM, SPECIFICALLY, REFERRING TO THE EMOTIONAL TRANS-FORMATION YOU HAVE UNDERGONE.
FLIT

THE CONTRACT YOU SIGNED READS AS FOLLOWS:

"I AGREE TO ACCEPT ANY AND ALL CONSEQUENCES ARISING FROM THE CHOICES THAT I MAKE."

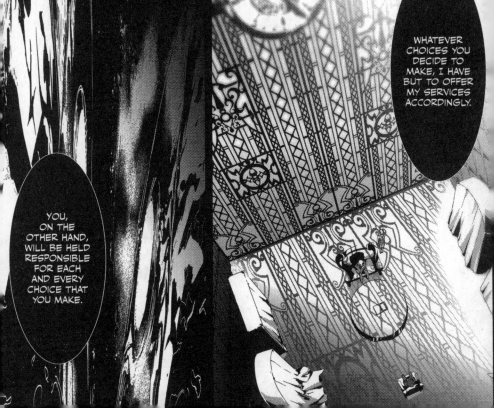

WHATEVER CHOICES YOU DECIDE TO MAKE, I HAVE BUT TO OFFER MY SERVICES ACCORDINGLY.

YOU, ON THE OTHER HAND, WILL BE HELD RESPONSIBLE FOR EACH AND EVERY CHOICE THAT YOU MAKE.

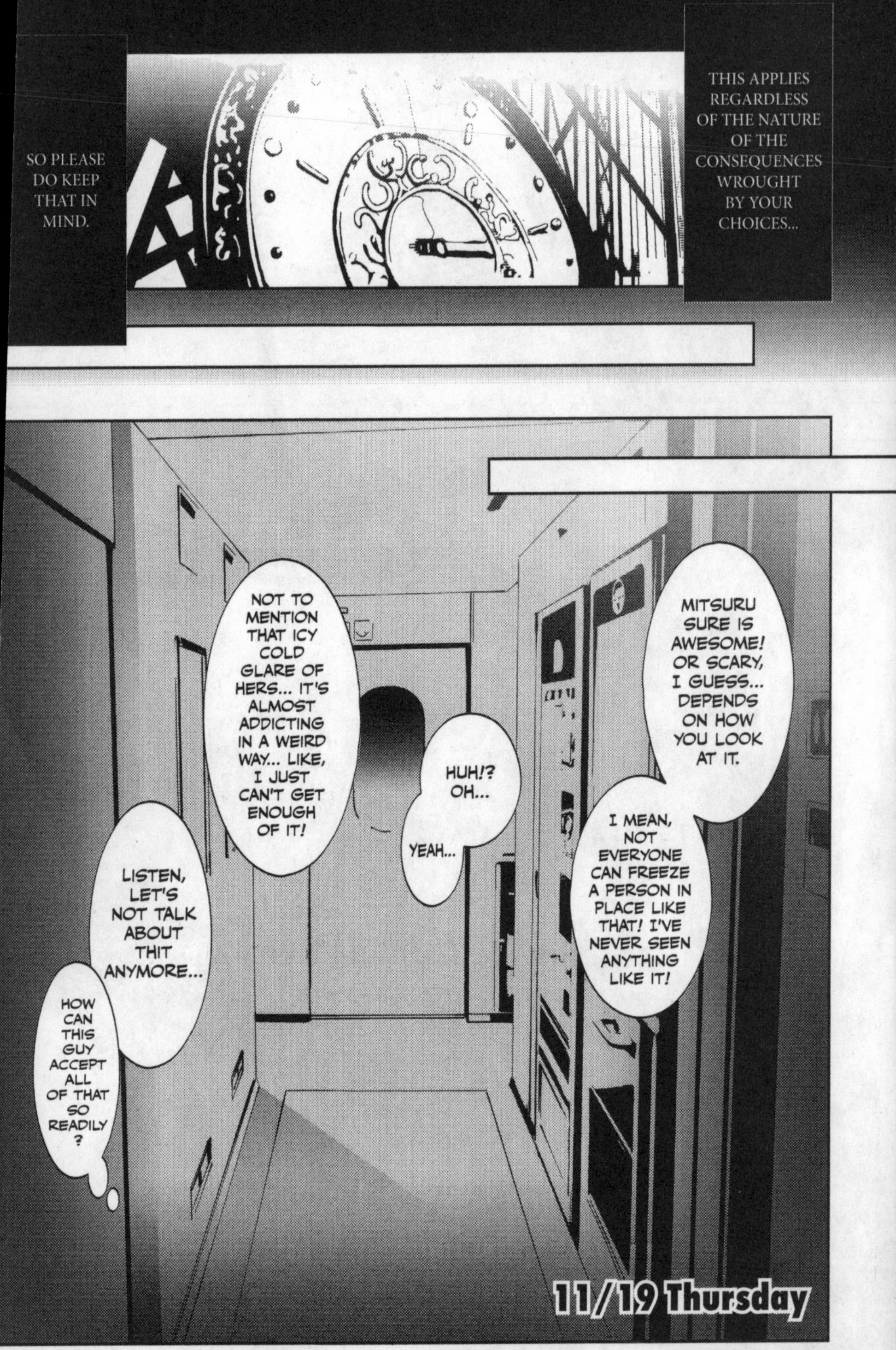
THIS APPLIES REGARDLESS OF THE NATURE OF THE CONSEQUENCES WROUGHT BY YOUR CHOICES...
SO PLEASE DO KEEP THAT IN MIND.
MITSURU SURE IS AWESOME! OR SCARY, I GUESS... DEPENDS ON HOW YOU LOOK AT IT.
I MEAN, NOT EVERYONE CAN FREEZE A PERSON IN PLACE LIKE THAT! I'VE NEVER SEEN ANYTHING LIKE IT!
HUH!? OH...
YEAH...
NOT TO MENTION THAT ICY COLD GLARE OF HERS... IT'S ALMOST ADDICTING IN A WEIRD WAY... LIKE, I JUST CAN'T GET ENOUGH OF IT!
LISTEN, LET'S NOT TALK ABOUT THIT ANYMORE...
HOW CAN THIS GUY ACCEPT ALL OF THAT SO READILY?
11/19 Thursday

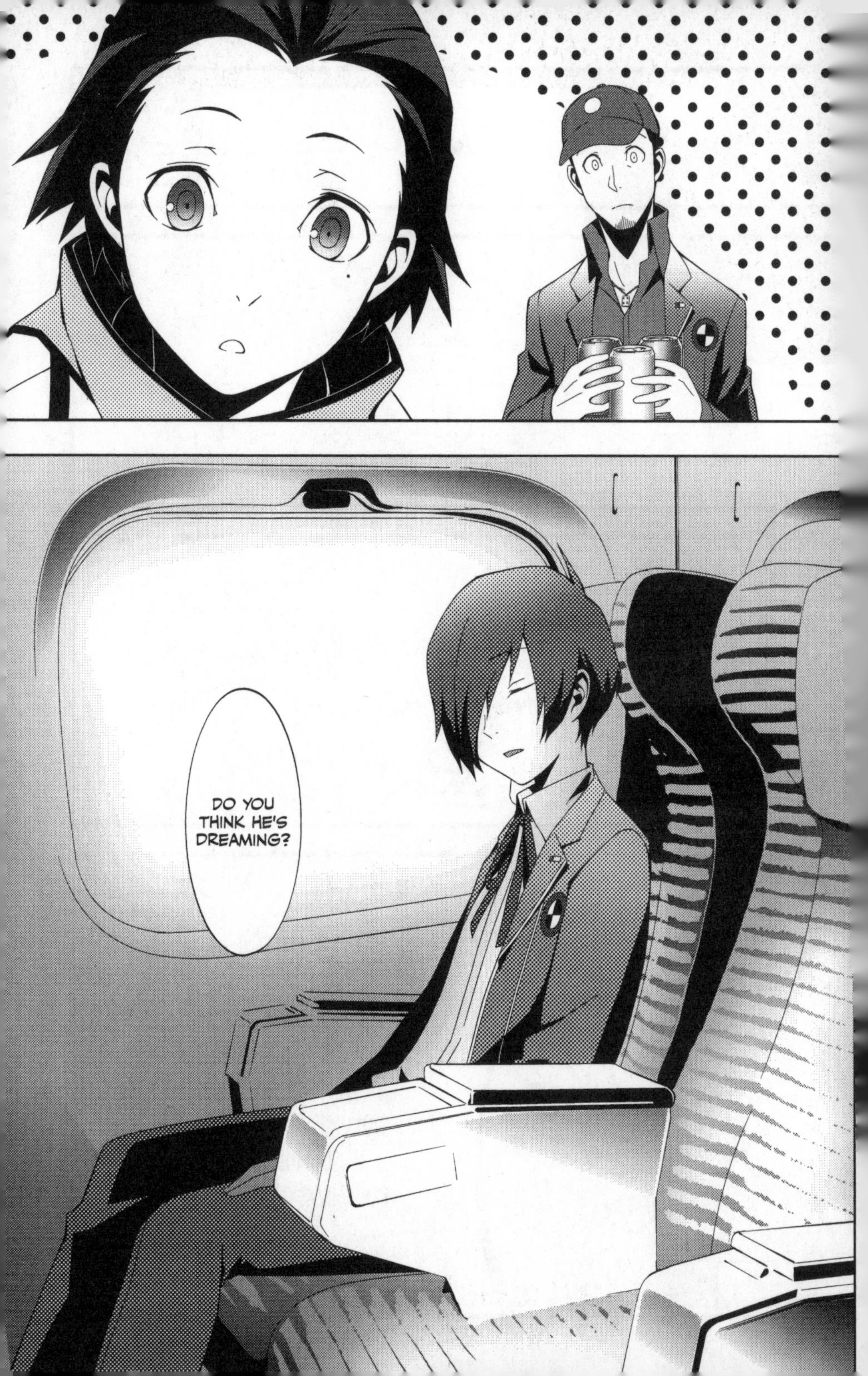
DO YOU THINK HE'S DREAMING?

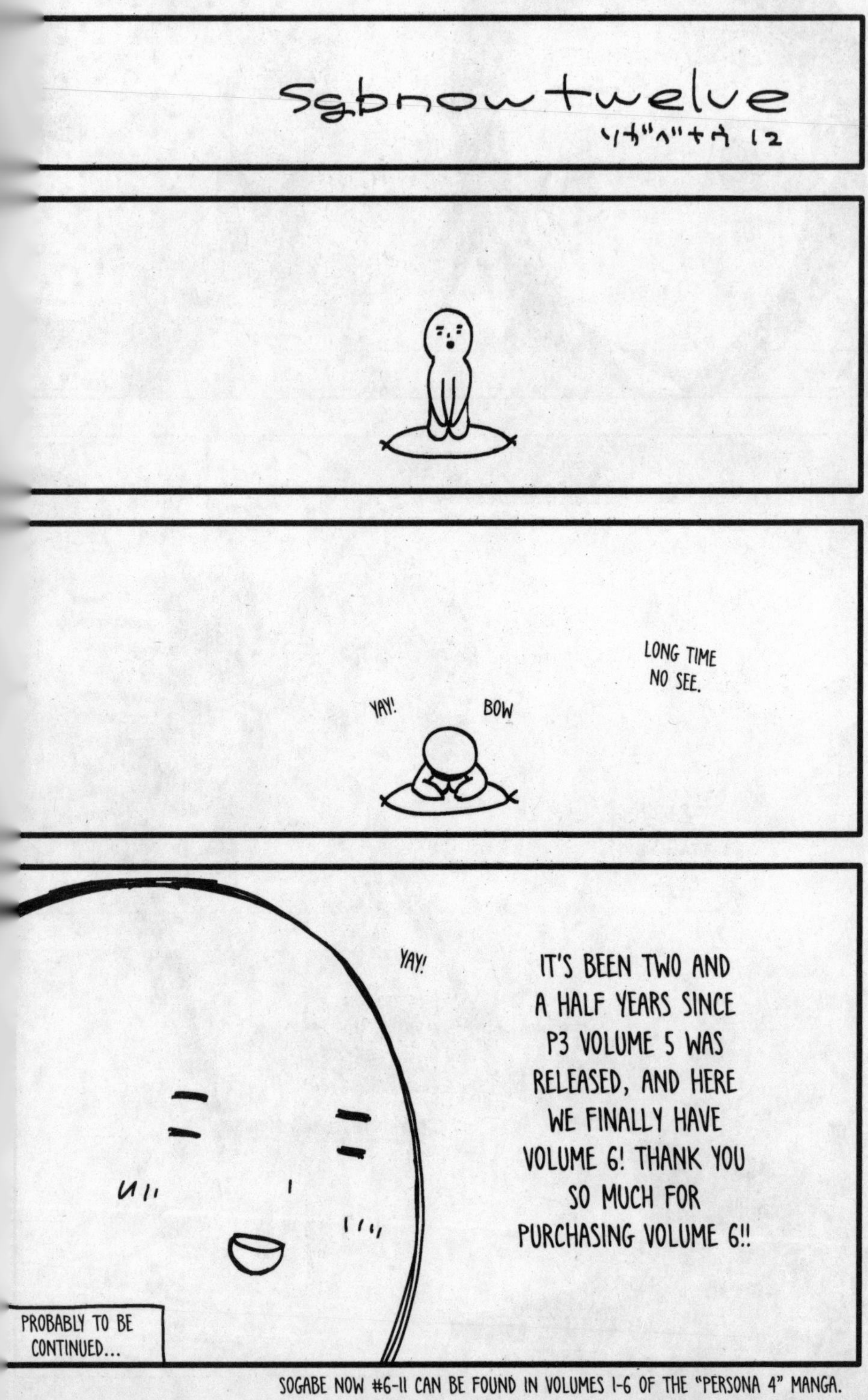
sgbnowtwelve
ソガベナウ 12
LONG TIME NO SEE.
BOW
YAY!
IT'S BEEN TWO AND A HALF YEARS SINCE P3 VOLUME 5 WAS RELEASED, AND HERE WE FINALLY HAVE VOLUME 6! THANK YOU SO MUCH FOR PURCHASING VOLUME 6!!
YAY!
PROBABLY TO BE CONTINUED...

SOGABE NOW #6-11 CAN BE FOUND IN VOLUMES 1-6 OF THE "PERSONA 4" MANGA.

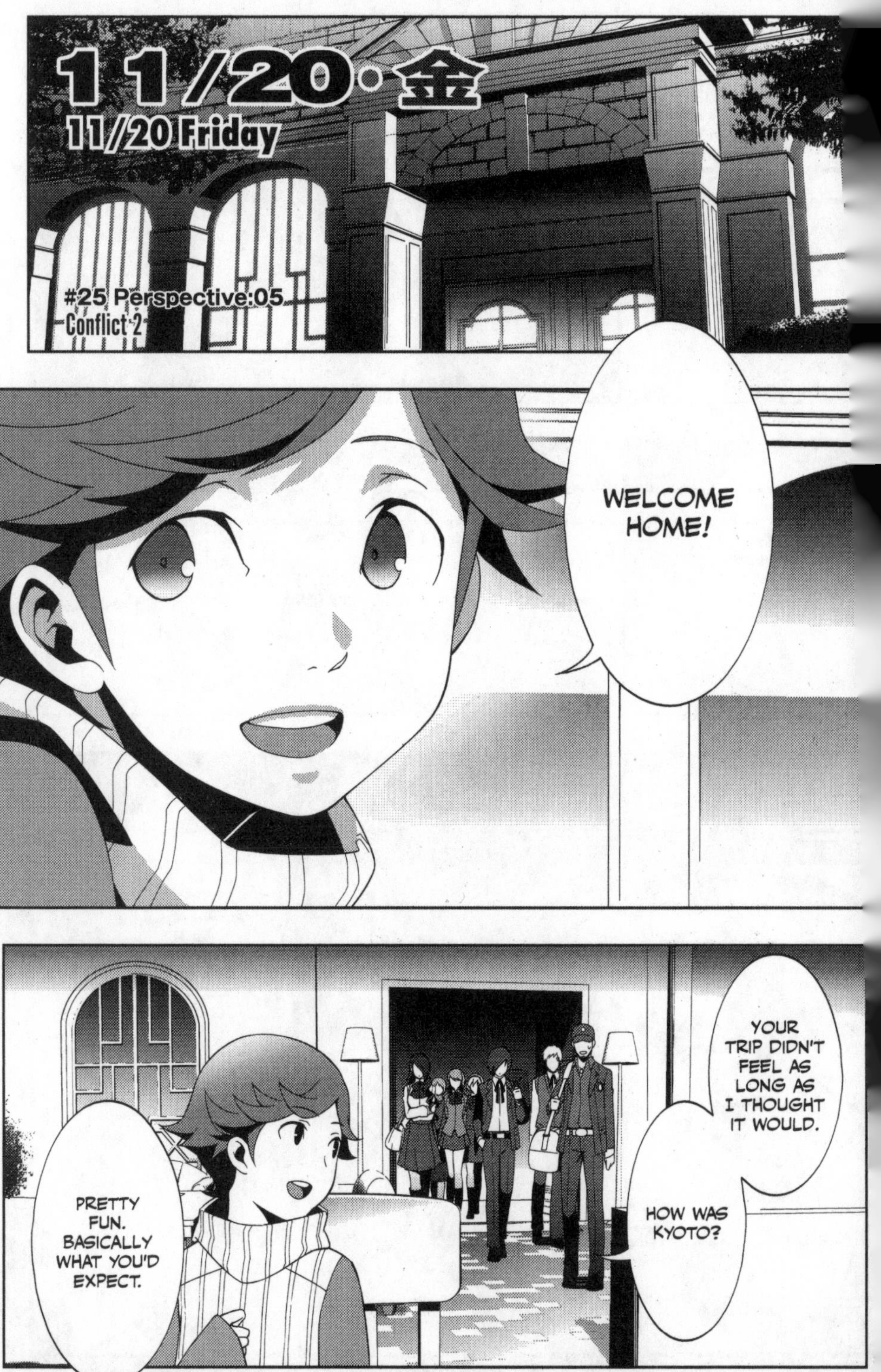
11/20・金
11/20 Friday
#25 Perspective:05
Conflict 2
WELCOME HOME!
YOUR TRIP DIDN'T FEEL AS LONG AS I THOUGHT IT WOULD.
HOW WAS KYOTO?
PRETTY FUN. BASICALLY WHAT YOU'D EXPECT.

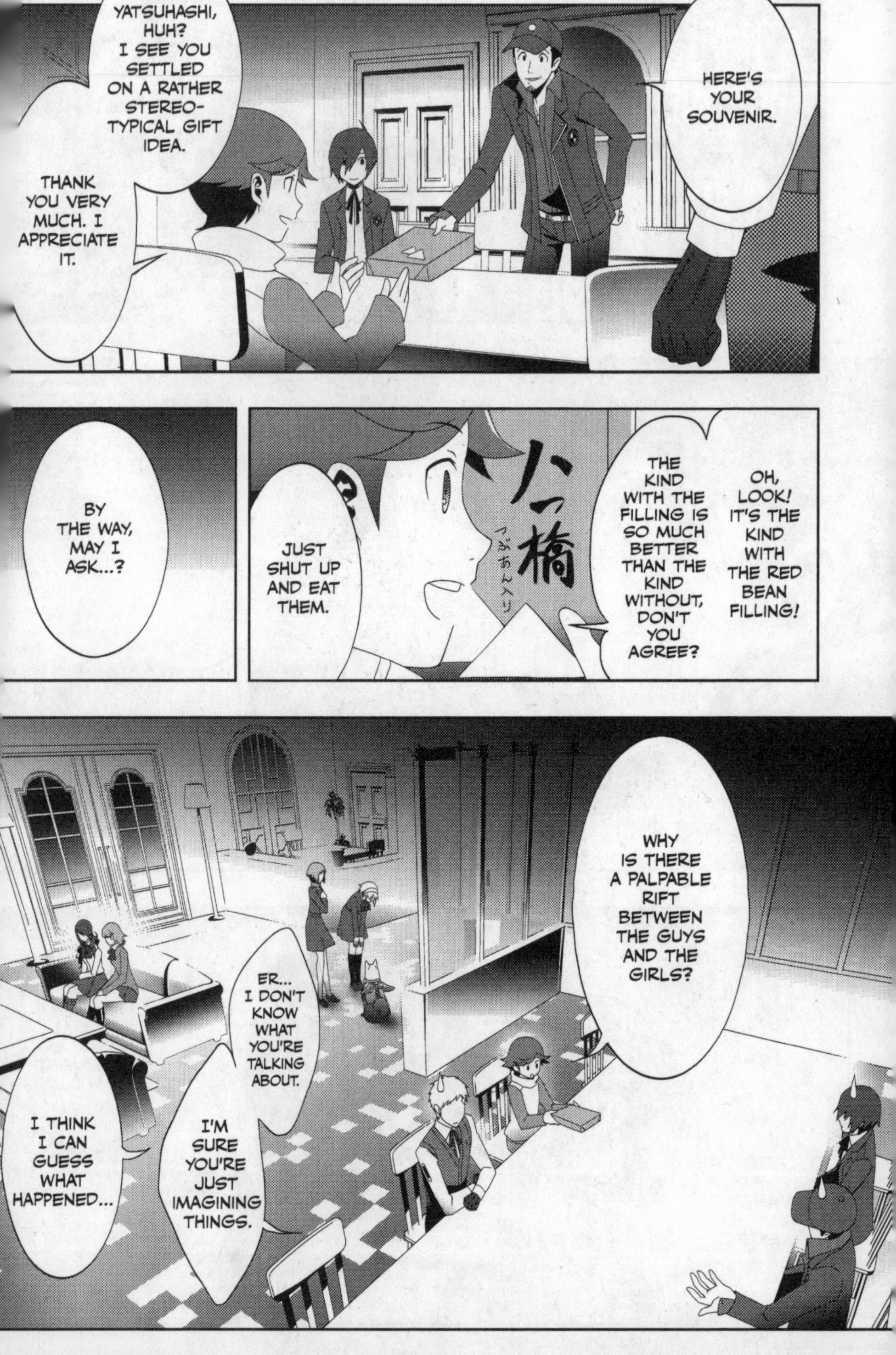
HERE'S YOUR SOUVENIR.
RAW YATSUHASHI, HUH? I SEE YOU SETTLED ON A RATHER STEREO-TYPICAL GIFT IDEA.
THANK YOU VERY MUCH. I APPRECIATE IT.
OH, LOOK! IT'S THE KIND WITH THE RED BEAN FILLING!
THE KIND WITH THE FILLING IS SO MUCH BETTER THAN THE KIND WITHOUT, DON'T YOU AGREE?
八ッ橋
つぶあん入り
JUST SHUT UP AND EAT THEM.
BY THE WAY, MAY I ASK...?
WHY IS THERE A PALPABLE RIFT BETWEEN THE GUYS AND THE GIRLS?
ER... I DON'T KNOW WHAT YOU'RE TALKING ABOUT.
I'M SURE YOU'RE JUST IMAGINING THINGS.
I THINK I CAN GUESS WHAT HAPPENED...

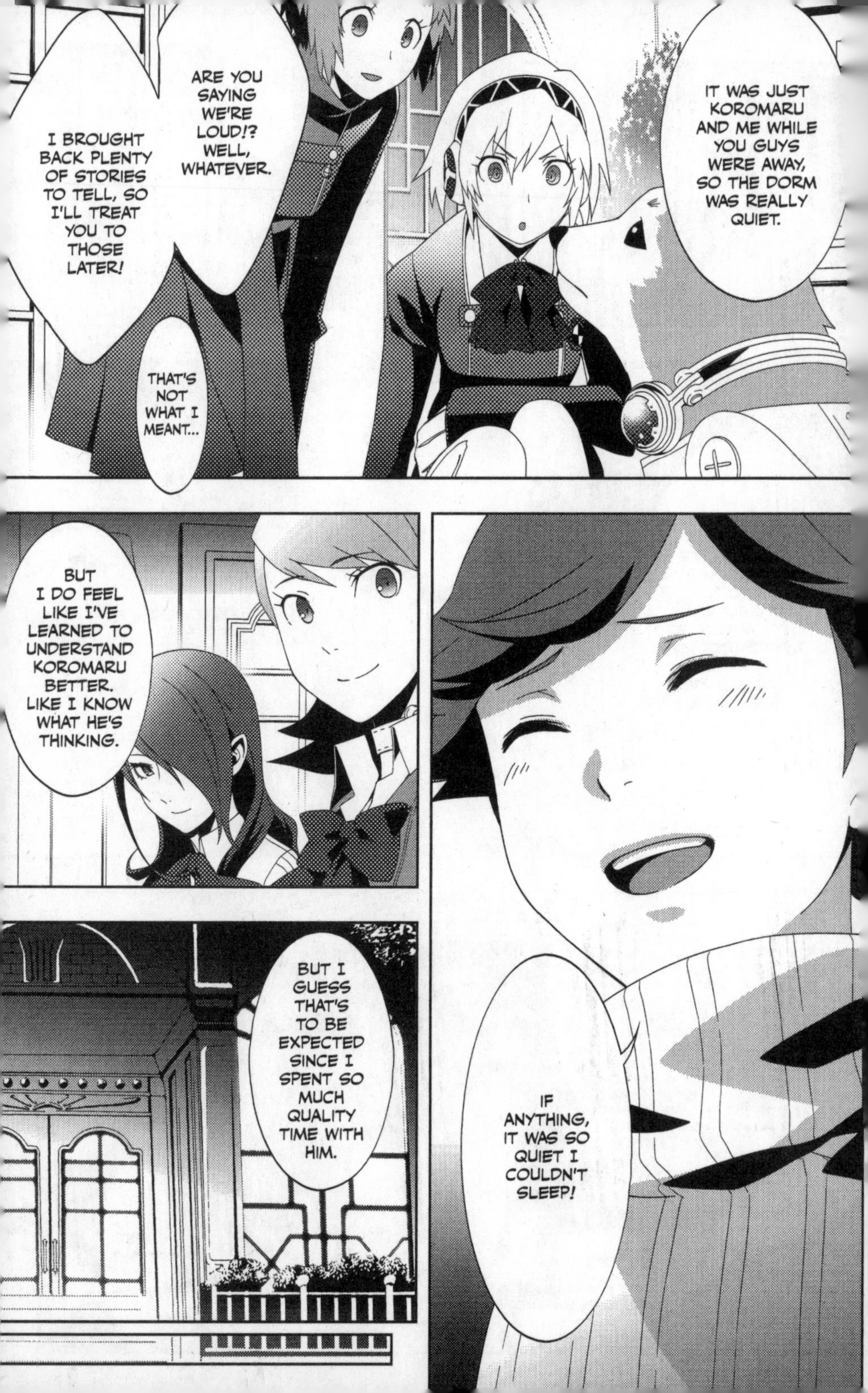
IT WAS JUST KOROMARU AND ME WHILE YOU GUYS WERE AWAY, SO THE DORM WAS REALLY QUIET.
ARE YOU SAYING WE'RE LOUD!? WELL, WHATEVER.
I BROUGHT BACK PLENTY OF STORIES TO TELL, SO I'LL TREAT YOU TO THOSE LATER!
THAT'S NOT WHAT I MEANT...
IF ANYTHING, IT WAS SO QUIET I COULDN'T SLEEP!
BUT I DO FEEL LIKE I'VE LEARNED TO UNDERSTAND KOROMARU BETTER. LIKE I KNOW WHAT HE'S THINKING.
BUT I GUESS THAT'S TO BE EXPECTED SINCE I SPENT SO MUCH QUALITY TIME WITH HIM.

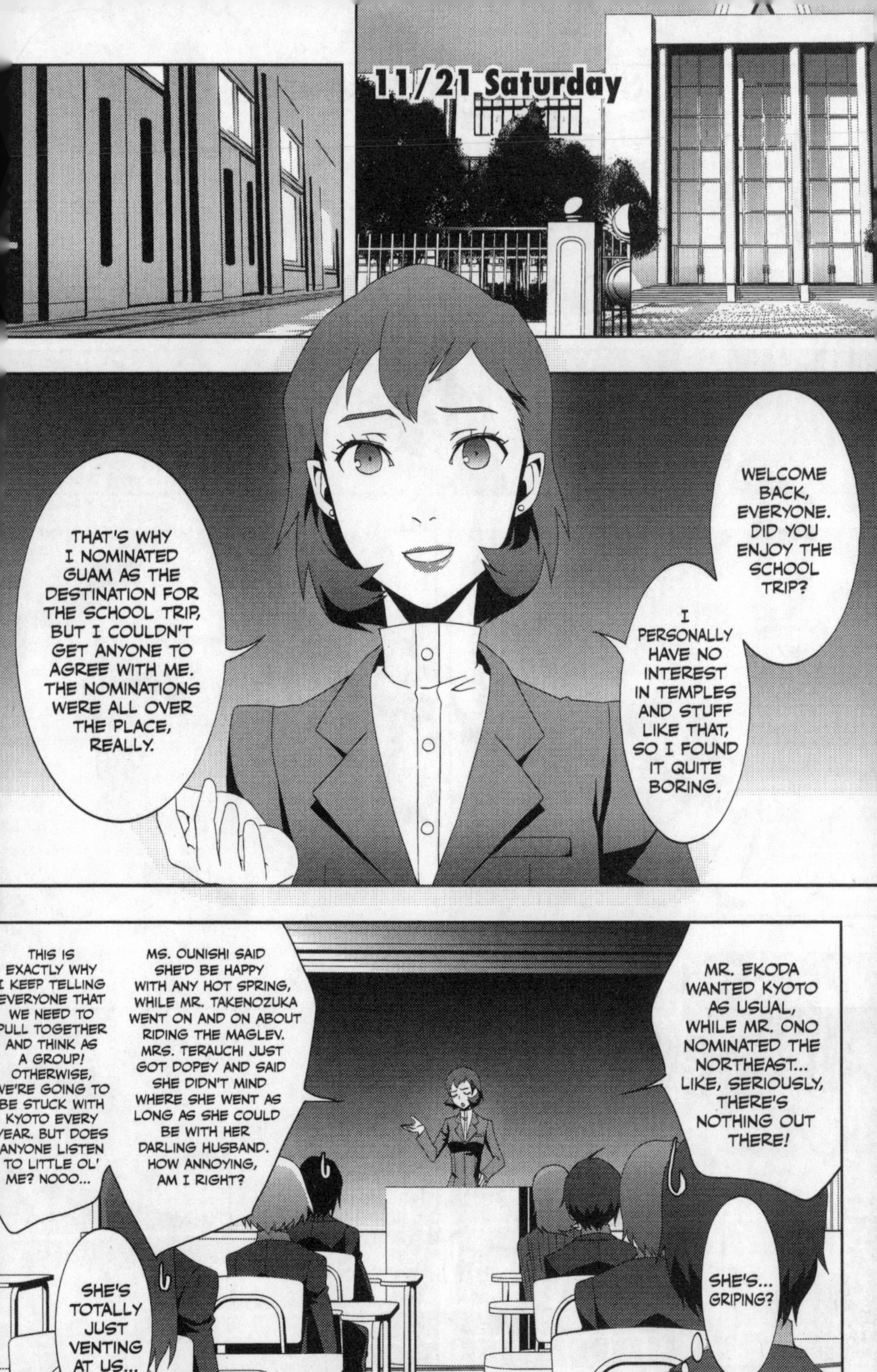
11/21 Saturday
WELCOME BACK, EVERYONE. DID YOU ENJOY THE SCHOOL TRIP?
I PERSONALLY HAVE NO INTEREST IN TEMPLES AND STUFF LIKE THAT, SO I FOUND IT QUITE BORING.
THAT'S WHY I NOMINATED GUAM AS THE DESTINATION FOR THE SCHOOL TRIP, BUT I COULDN'T GET ANYONE TO AGREE WITH ME. THE NOMINATIONS WERE ALL OVER THE PLACE, REALLY.
MR. EKODA WANTED KYOTO AS USUAL, WHILE MR. ONO NOMINATED THE NORTHEAST... LIKE, SERIOUSLY, THERE'S NOTHING OUT THERE!
MS. OUNISHI SAID SHE'D BE HAPPY WITH ANY HOT SPRING, WHILE MR. TAKENOZUKA WENT ON AND ON ABOUT RIDING THE MAGLEV. MRS. TERAUCHI JUST GOT DOPEY AND SAID SHE DIDN'T MIND WHERE SHE WENT AS LONG AS SHE COULD BE WITH HER DARLING HUSBAND. HOW ANNOYING, AM I RIGHT?
THIS IS EXACTLY WHY I KEEP TELLING EVERYONE THAT WE NEED TO PULL TOGETHER AND THINK AS A GROUP! OTHERWISE, WE'RE GOING TO BE STUCK WITH KYOTO EVERY YEAR. BUT DOES ANYONE LISTEN TO LITTLE OL' ME? NOOO...
SHE'S... GRIPING?
SHE'S TOTALLY JUST VENTING AT US...

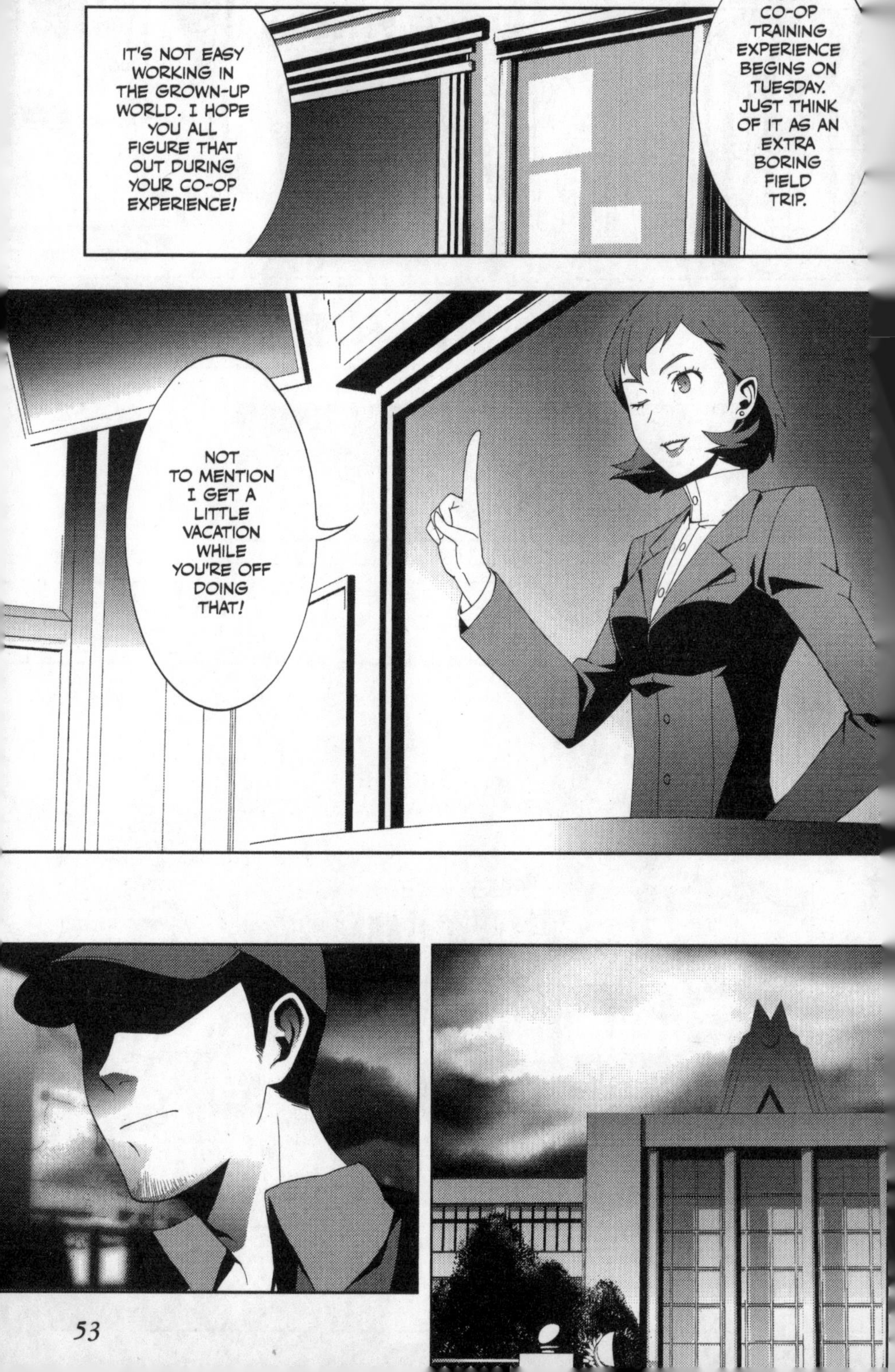
YOUR CO-OP TRAINING EXPERIENCE BEGINS ON TUESDAY. JUST THINK OF IT AS AN EXTRA BORING FIELD TRIP.
IT'S NOT EASY WORKING IN THE GROWN-UP WORLD. I HOPE YOU ALL FIGURE THAT OUT DURING YOUR CO-OP EXPERIENCE!
NOT TO MENTION I GET A LITTLE VACATION WHILE YOU'RE OFF DOING THAT!

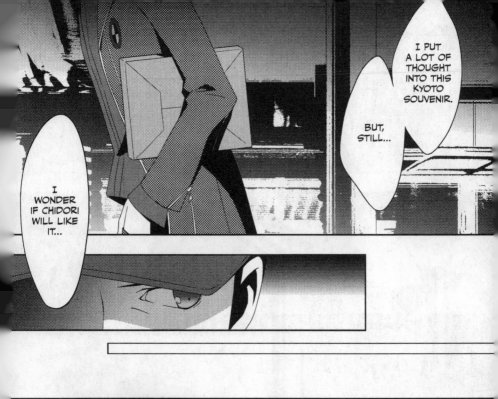

I PUT A LOT OF THOUGHT INTO THIS KYOTO SOUVENIR.

BUT, STILL...

I WONDER IF CHIDORI WILL LIKE IT...

11/7 Saturday

HI, CHIDORI. SORRY I DIDN'T COME FOR A LITTLE WHILE... I HAD A LOT GOING ON.

...

HM...? WHAT'S WRONG?

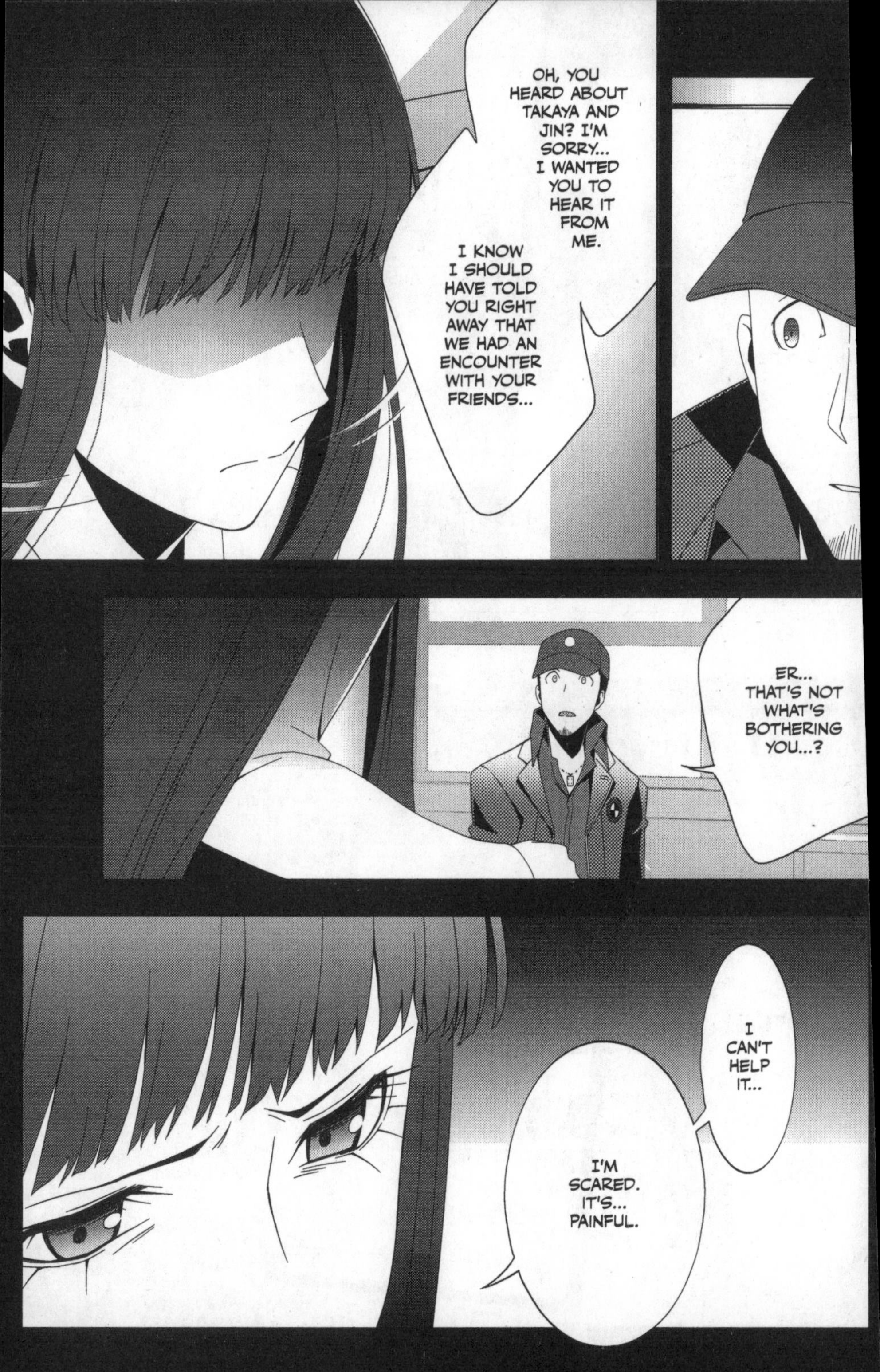
OH, YOU HEARD ABOUT TAKAYA AND JIN? I'M SORRY... I WANTED YOU TO HEAR IT FROM ME.
I KNOW I SHOULD HAVE TOLD YOU RIGHT AWAY THAT WE HAD AN ENCOUNTER WITH YOUR FRIENDS...
ER... THAT'S NOT WHAT'S BOTHERING YOU...?
I CAN'T HELP IT...
I'M SCARED. IT'S... PAINFUL.

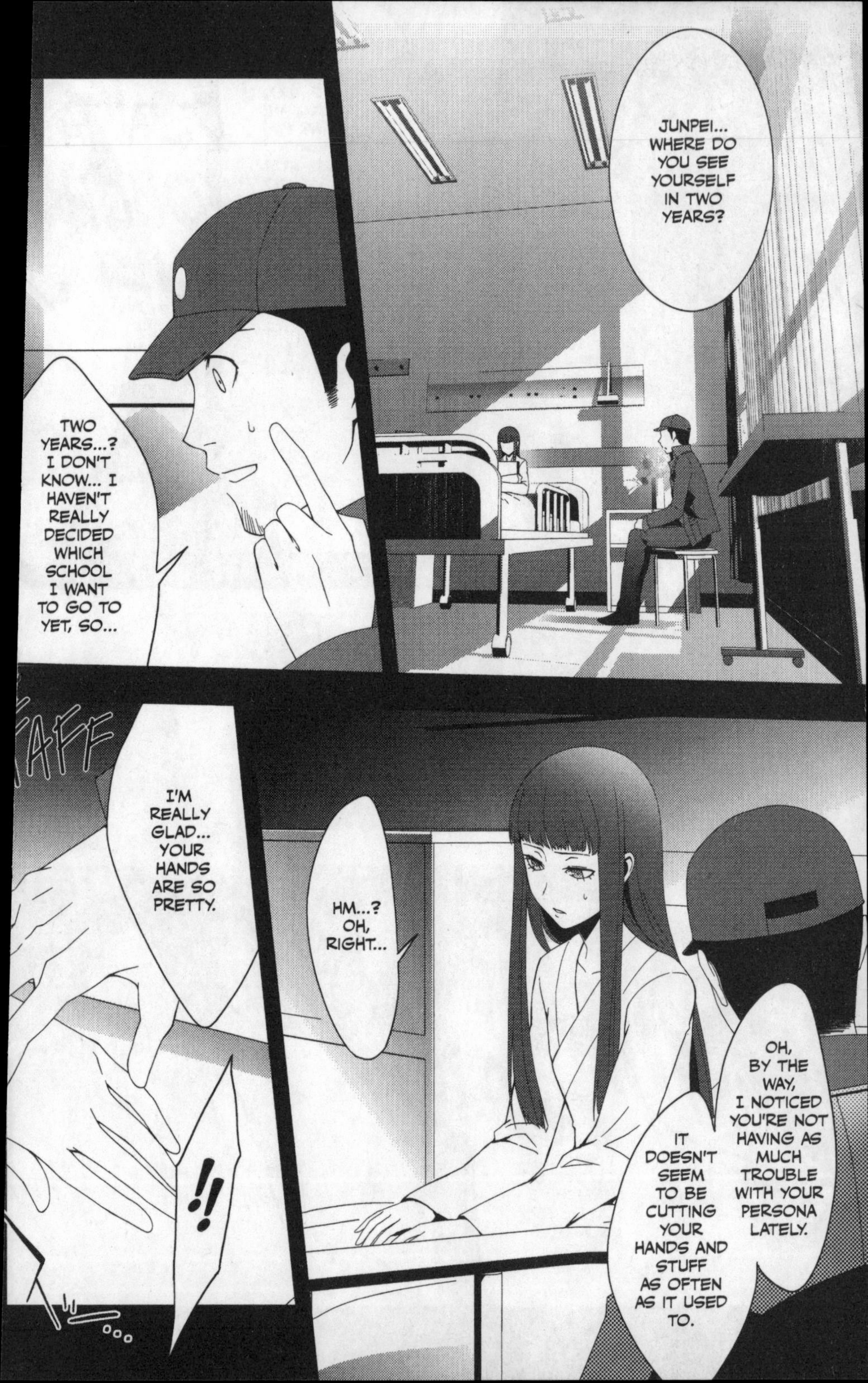
JUNPEI... WHERE DO YOU SEE YOURSELF IN TWO YEARS?
TWO YEARS...? I DON'T KNOW... I HAVEN'T REALLY DECIDED WHICH SCHOOL I WANT TO GO TO YET, SO...
OH, BY THE WAY, I NOTICED YOU'RE NOT HAVING AS MUCH TROUBLE WITH YOUR PERSONA LATELY.
IT DOESN'T SEEM TO BE CUTTING YOUR HANDS AND STUFF AS OFTEN AS IT USED TO.
HM...? OH, RIGHT...
I'M REALLY GLAD... YOUR HANDS ARE SO PRETTY.
!!

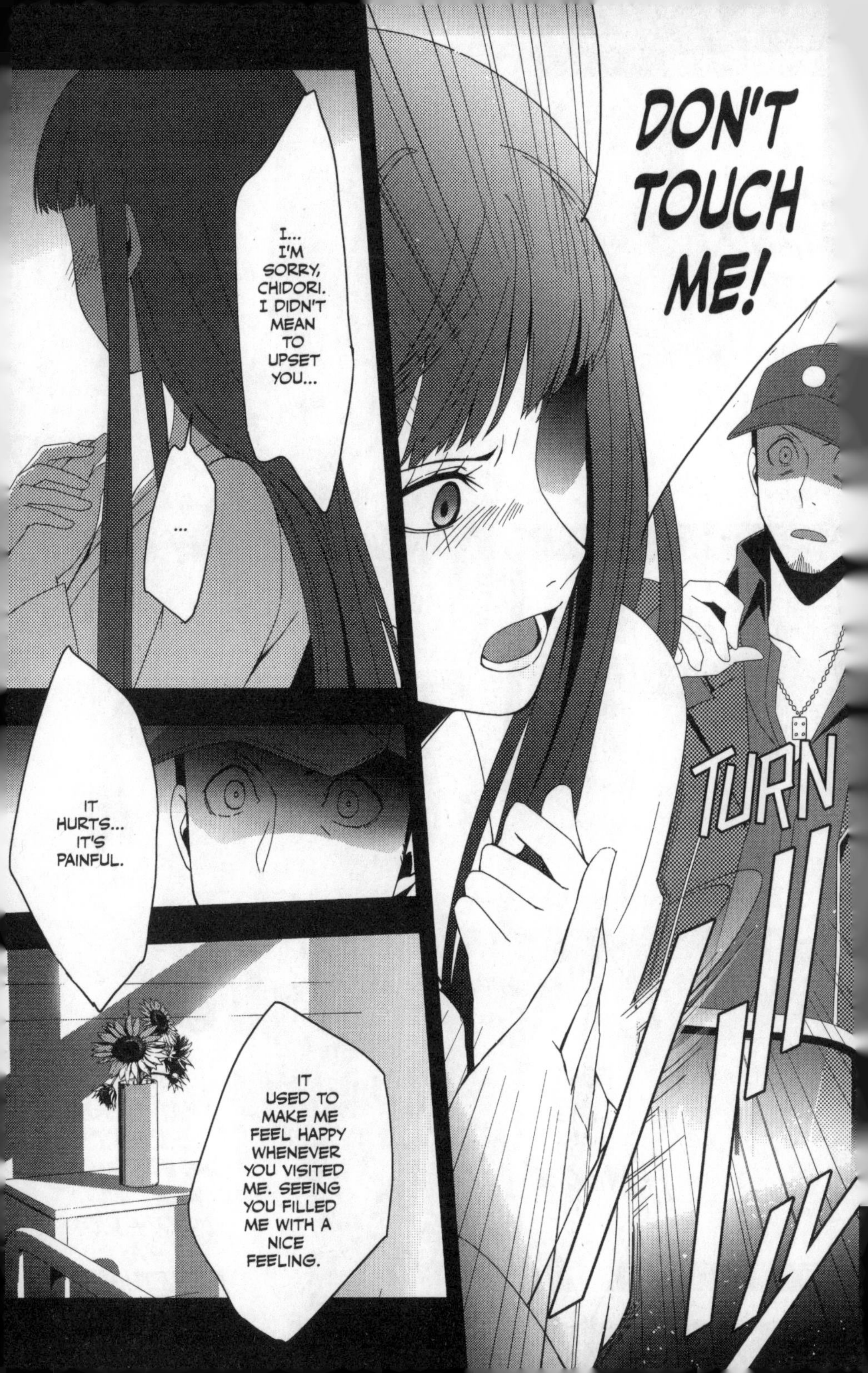
DON'T TOUCH ME!
TURN
I... I'M SORRY, CHIDORI. I DIDN'T MEAN TO UPSET YOU...
...
IT HURTS... IT'S PAINFUL.
IT USED TO MAKE ME FEEL HAPPY WHENEVER YOU VISITED ME. SEEING YOU FILLED ME WITH A NICE FEELING.

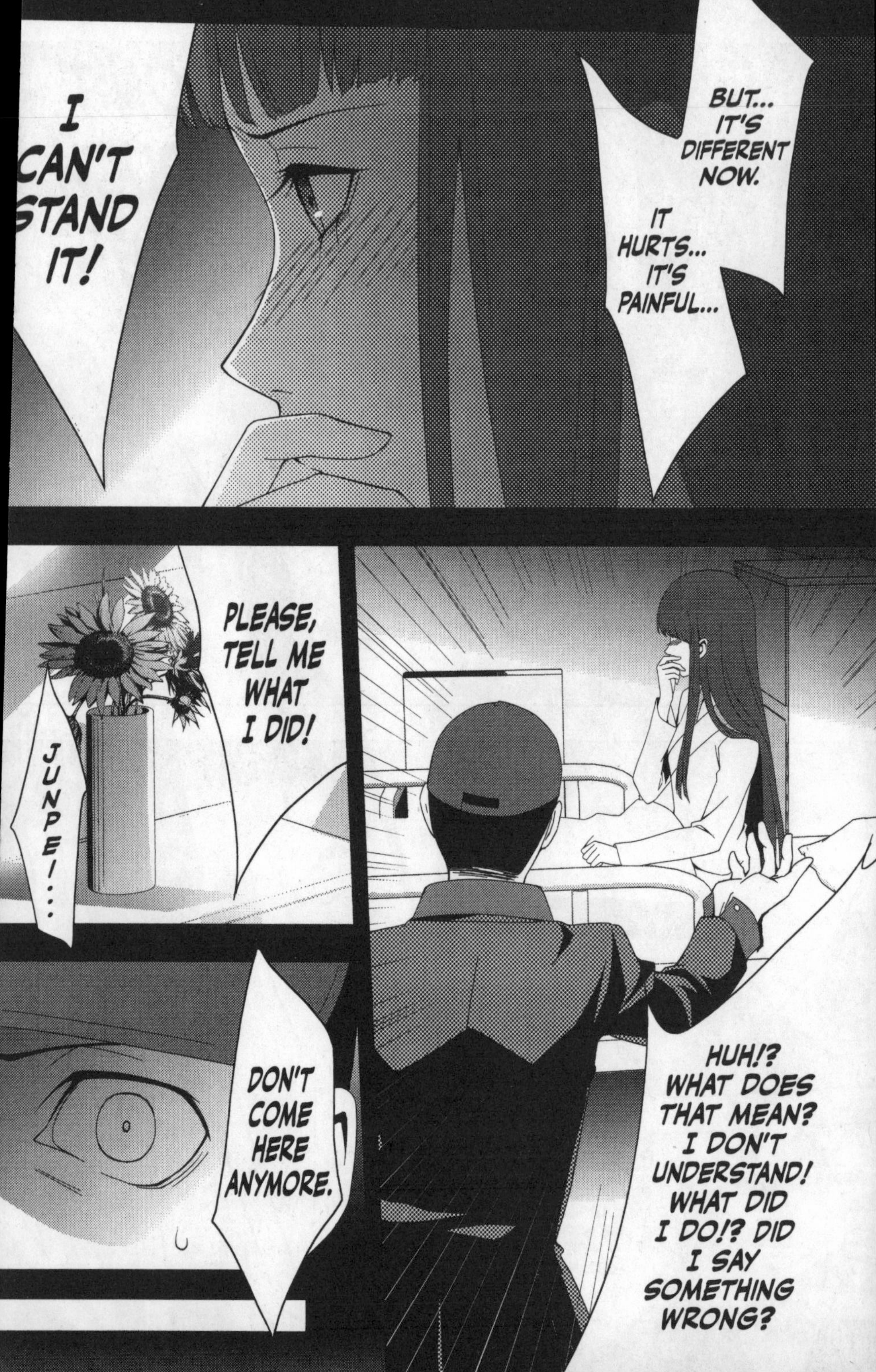
BUT... IT'S DIFFERENT NOW.
IT HURTS... IT'S PAINFUL...
I CAN'T STAND IT!
HUH!? WHAT DOES THAT MEAN? I DON'T UNDERSTAND! WHAT DID I DO!? DID I SAY SOMETHING WRONG?
PLEASE, TELL ME WHAT I DID!
JUNPEI!...
DON'T COME HERE ANYMORE.

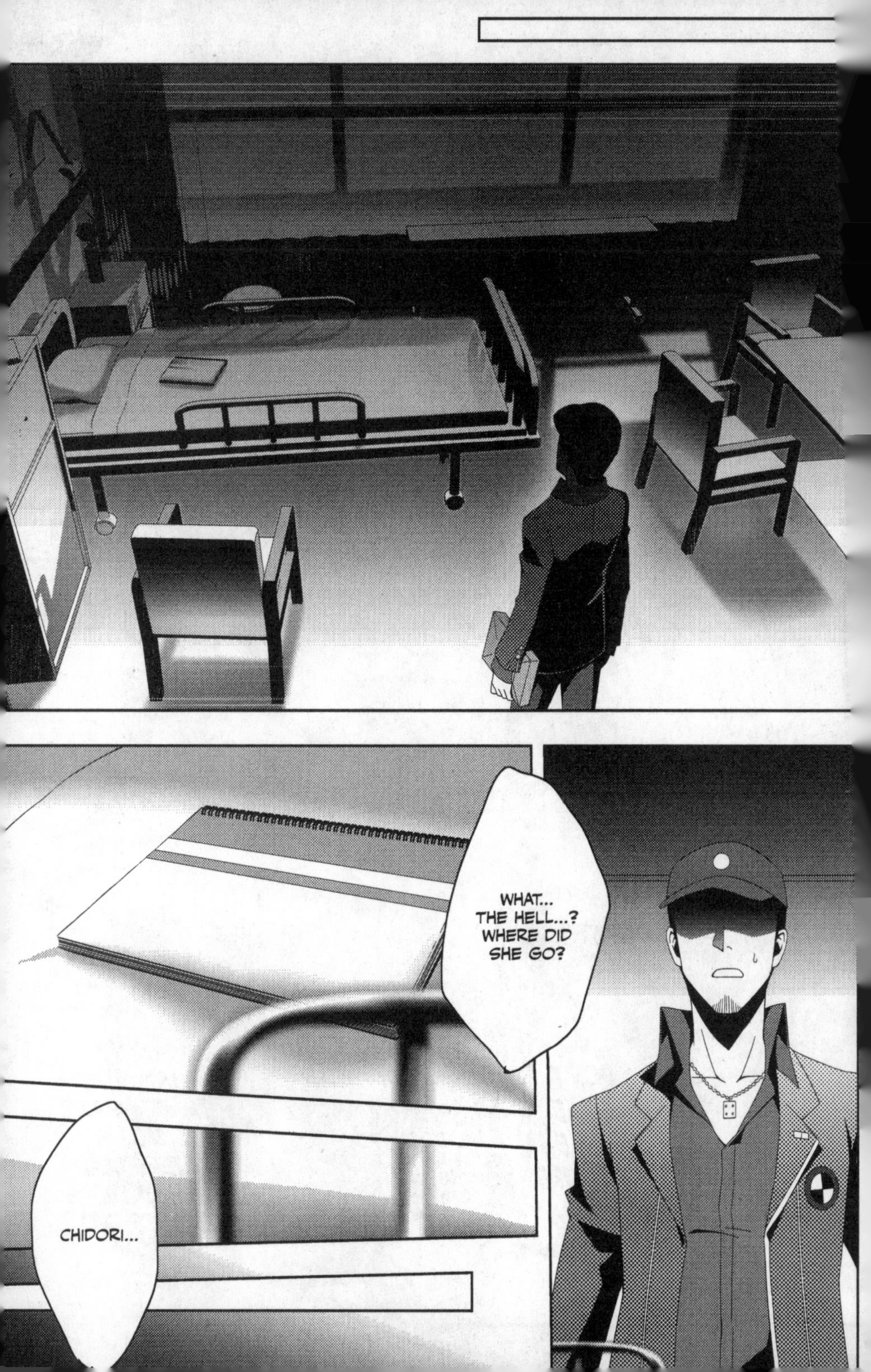
WHAT... THE HELL...? WHERE DID SHE GO?
CHIDORI...

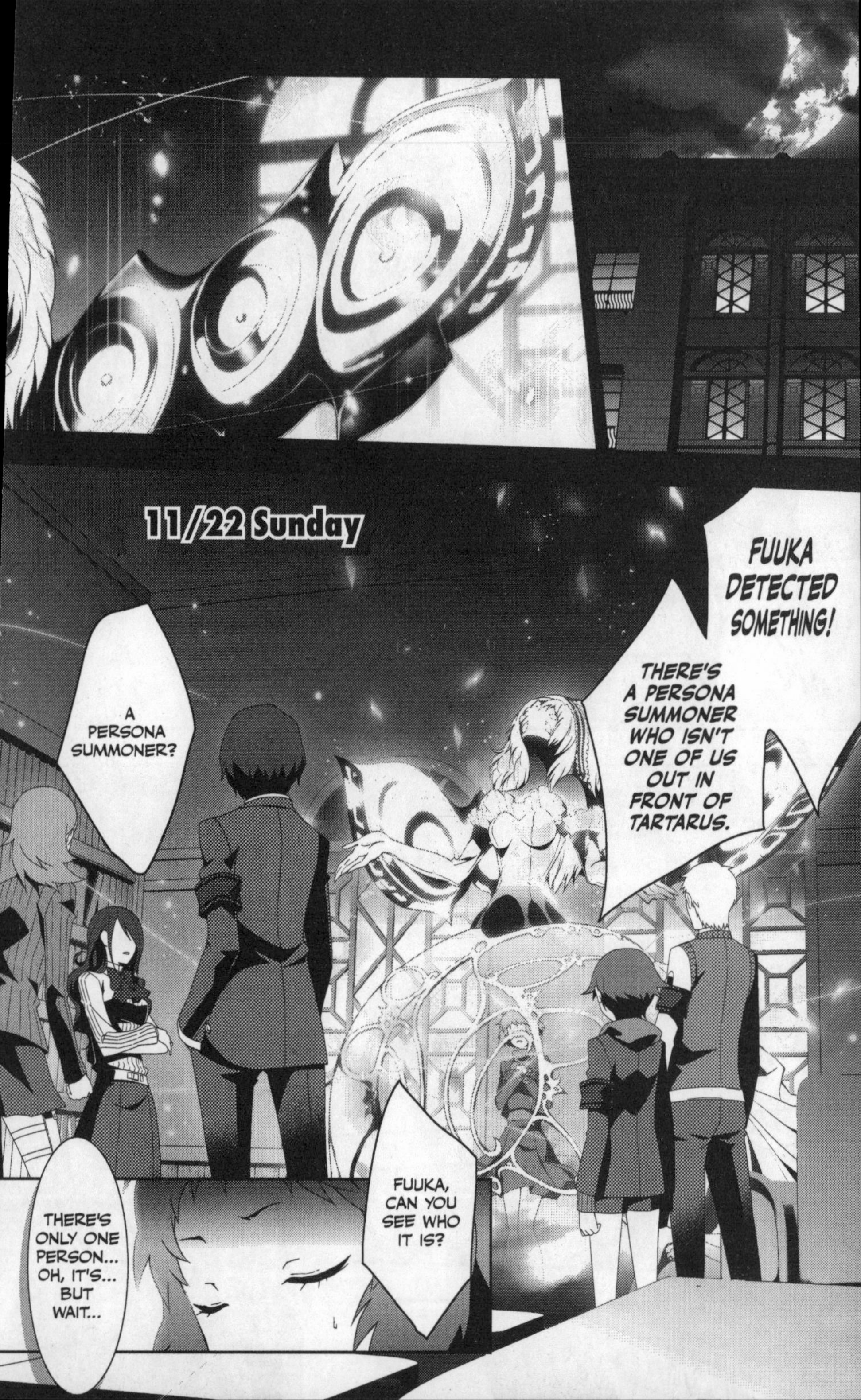
11/22 Sunday
FUUKA DETECTED SOMETHING!
THERE'S A PERSONA SUMMONER WHO ISN'T ONE OF US OUT IN FRONT OF TARTARUS.
A PERSONA SUMMONER?
FUUKA, CAN YOU SEE WHO IT IS?
THERE'S ONLY ONE PERSON... OH, IT'S... BUT WAIT...

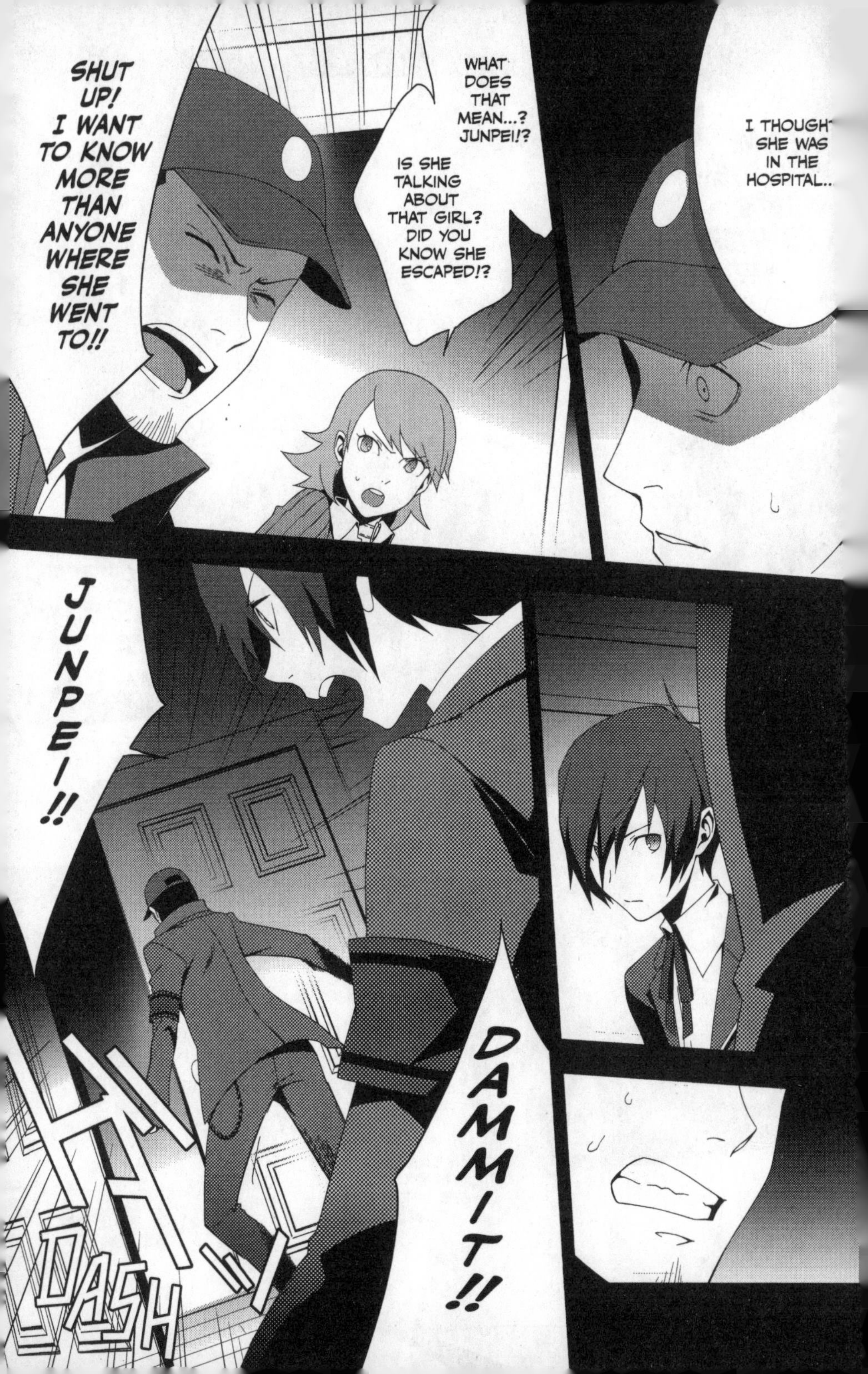
I THOUGHT SHE WAS IN THE HOSPITAL...
WHAT DOES THAT MEAN...? JUNPEI!?
IS SHE TALKING ABOUT THAT GIRL? DID YOU KNOW SHE ESCAPED!?
SHUT UP! I WANT TO KNOW MORE THAN ANYONE WHERE SHE WENT TO!!
DAMMIT!!
JUNPEI!!
DASH

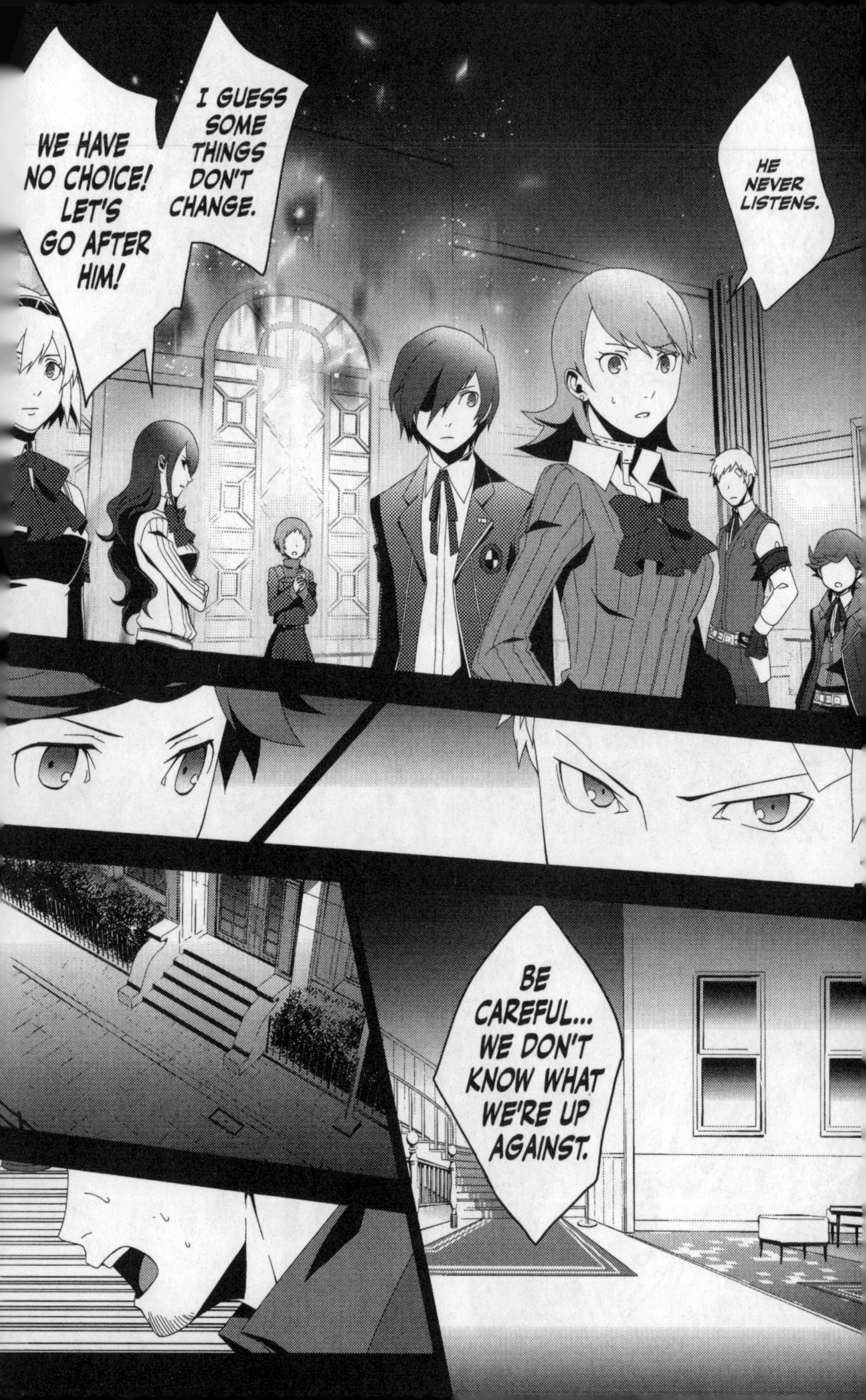
HE NEVER LISTENS.
I GUESS SOME THINGS DON'T CHANGE.
WE HAVE NO CHOICE! LET'S GO AFTER HIM!
BE CAREFUL... WE DON'T KNOW WHAT WE'RE UP AGAINST.

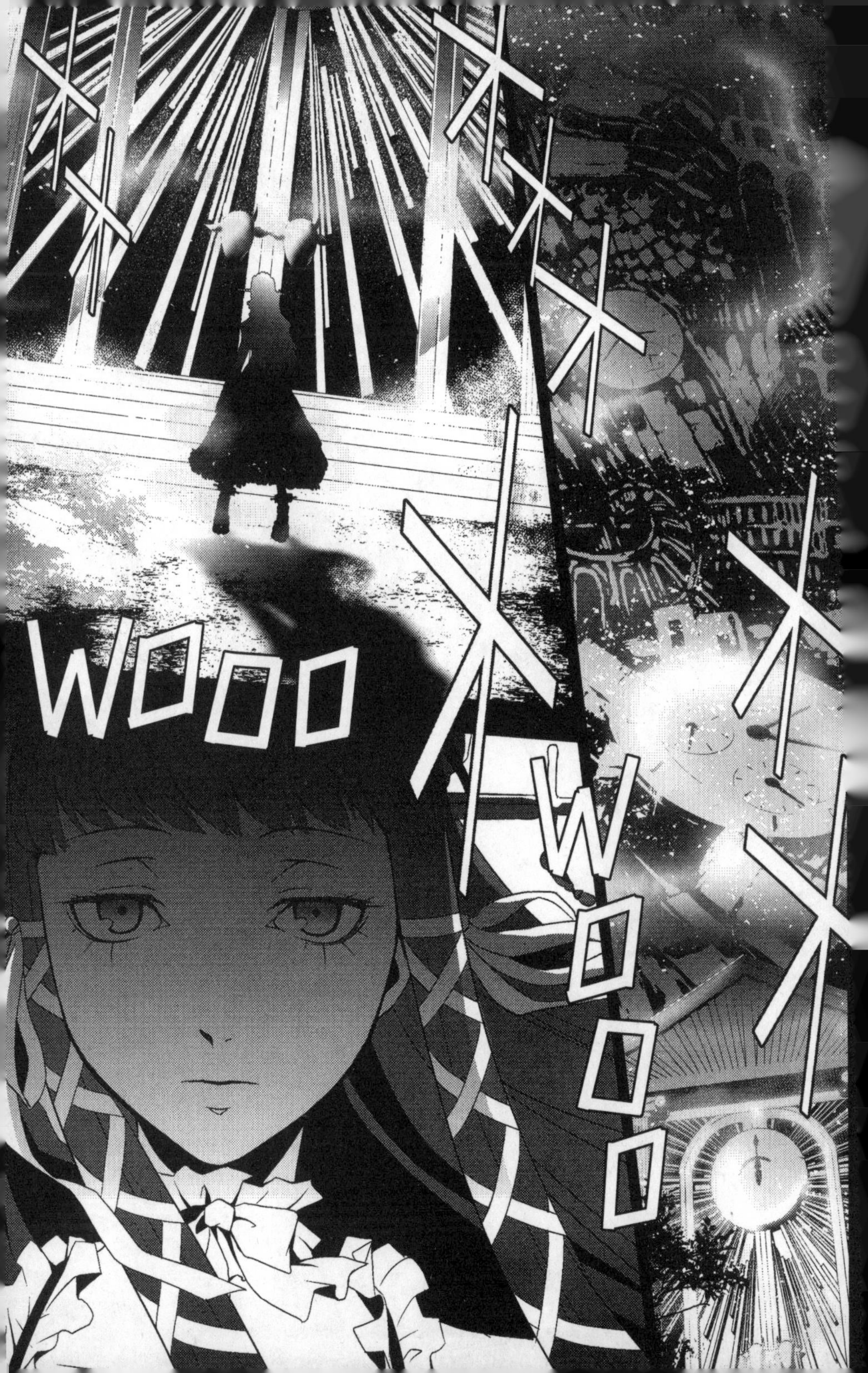
WOOO
WOOO

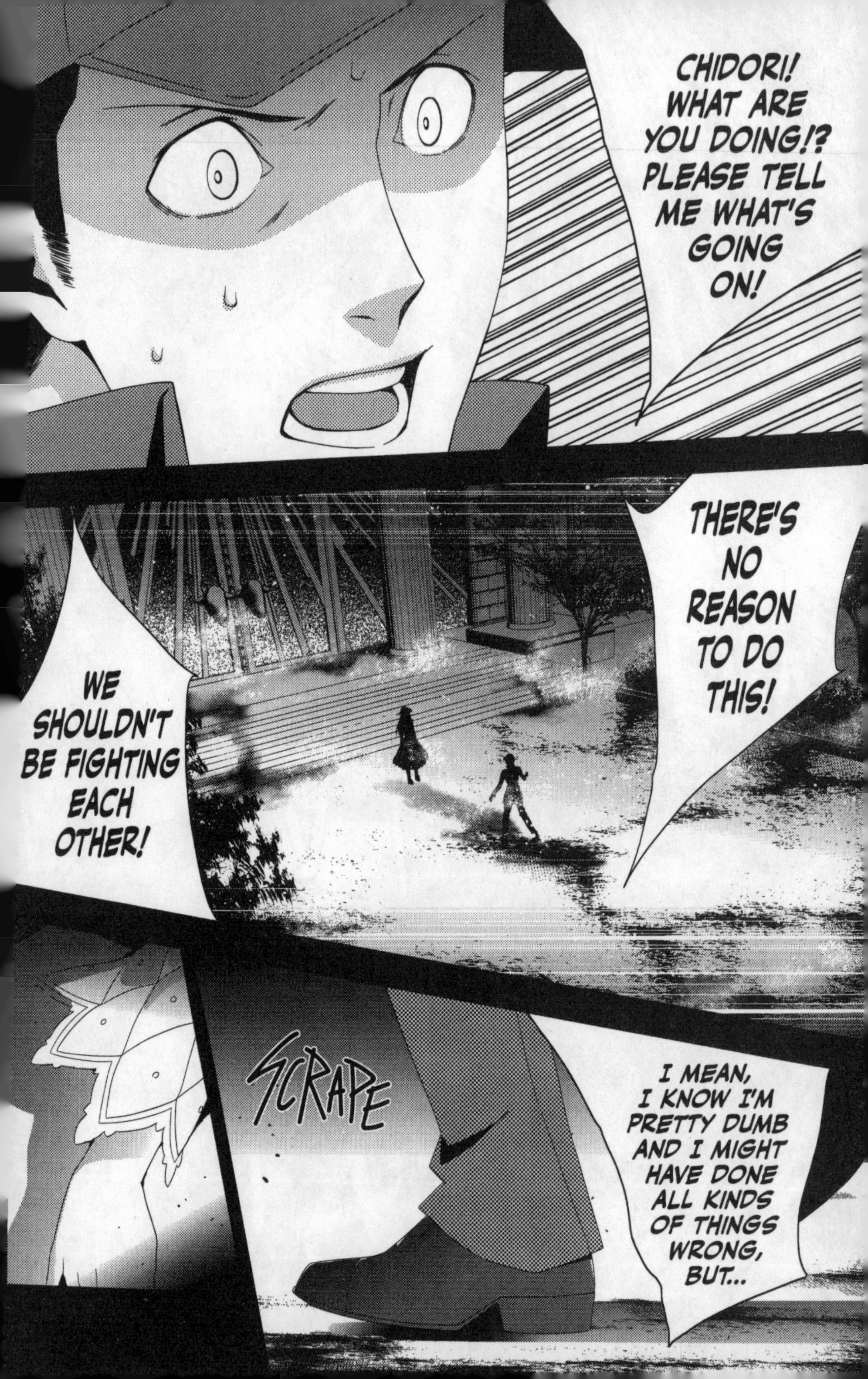
CHIDORI! WHAT ARE YOU DOING!? PLEASE TELL ME WHAT'S GOING ON!
THERE'S NO REASON TO DO THIS!
WE SHOULDN'T BE FIGHTING EACH OTHER!
I MEAN, I KNOW I'M PRETTY DUMB AND I MIGHT HAVE DONE ALL KINDS OF THINGS WRONG, BUT...
SCRAPE

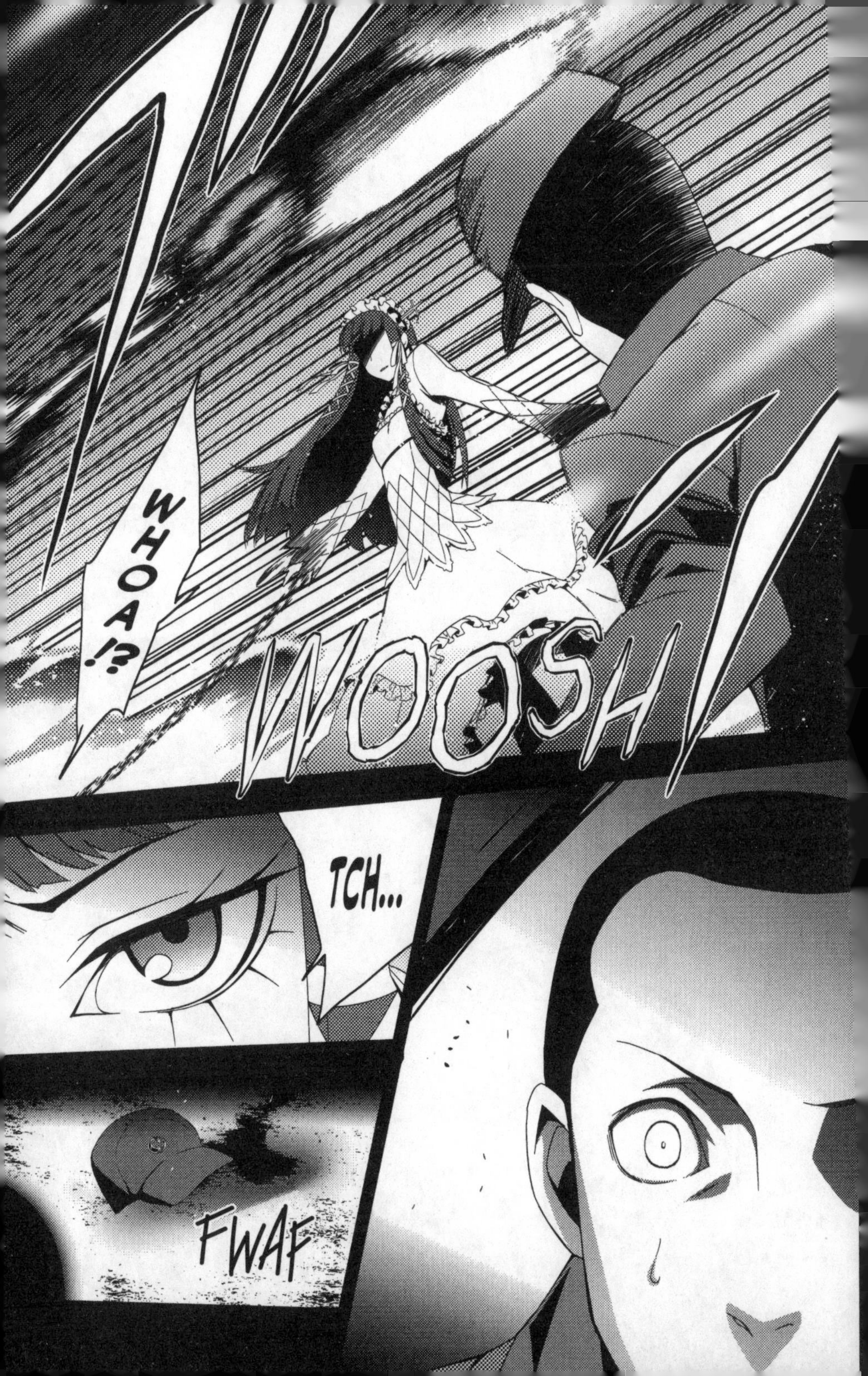
WHOA!?
WOOSH
TCH...
FWAF

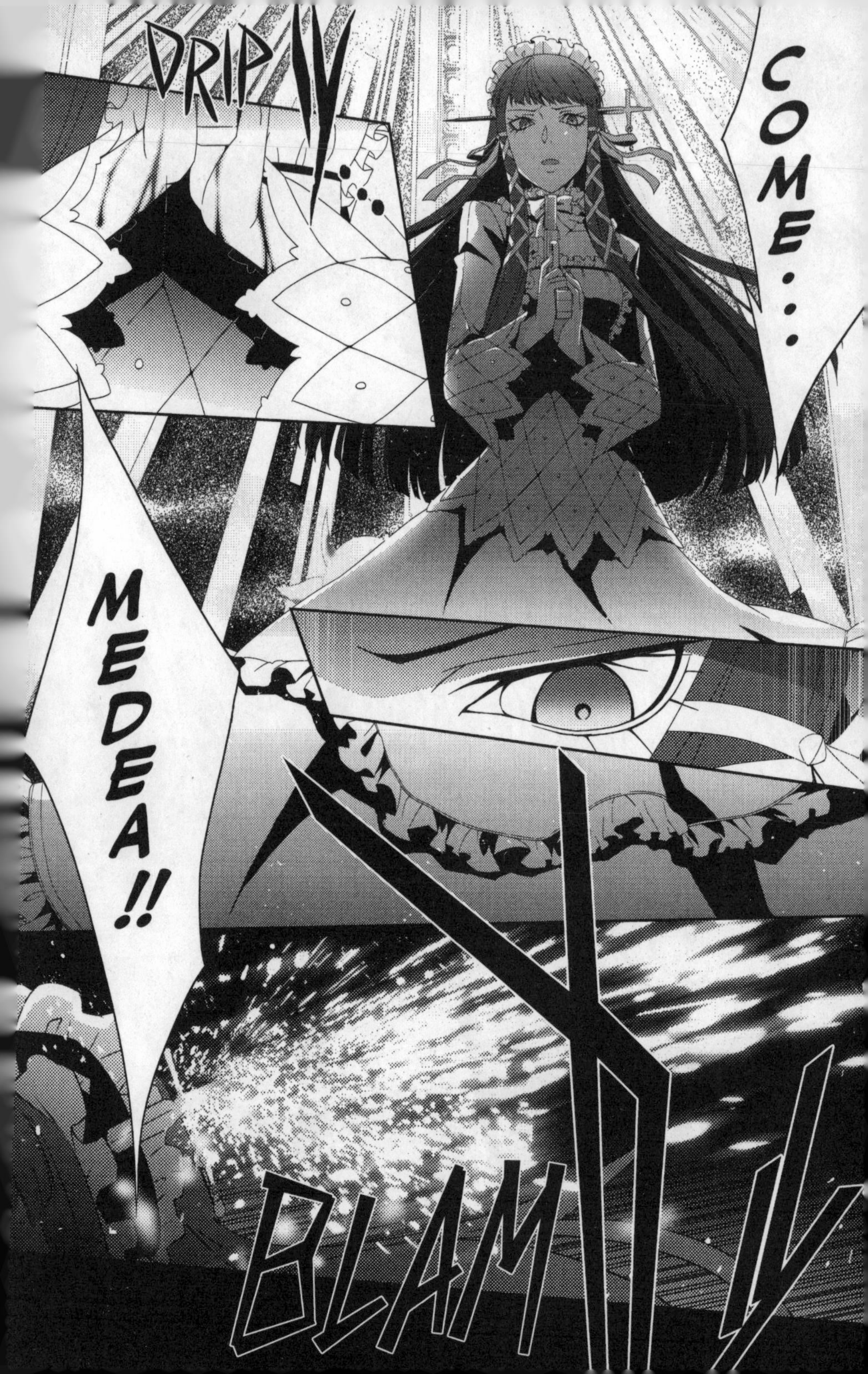
COME...
DRIP
MEDEA!!
BLAM

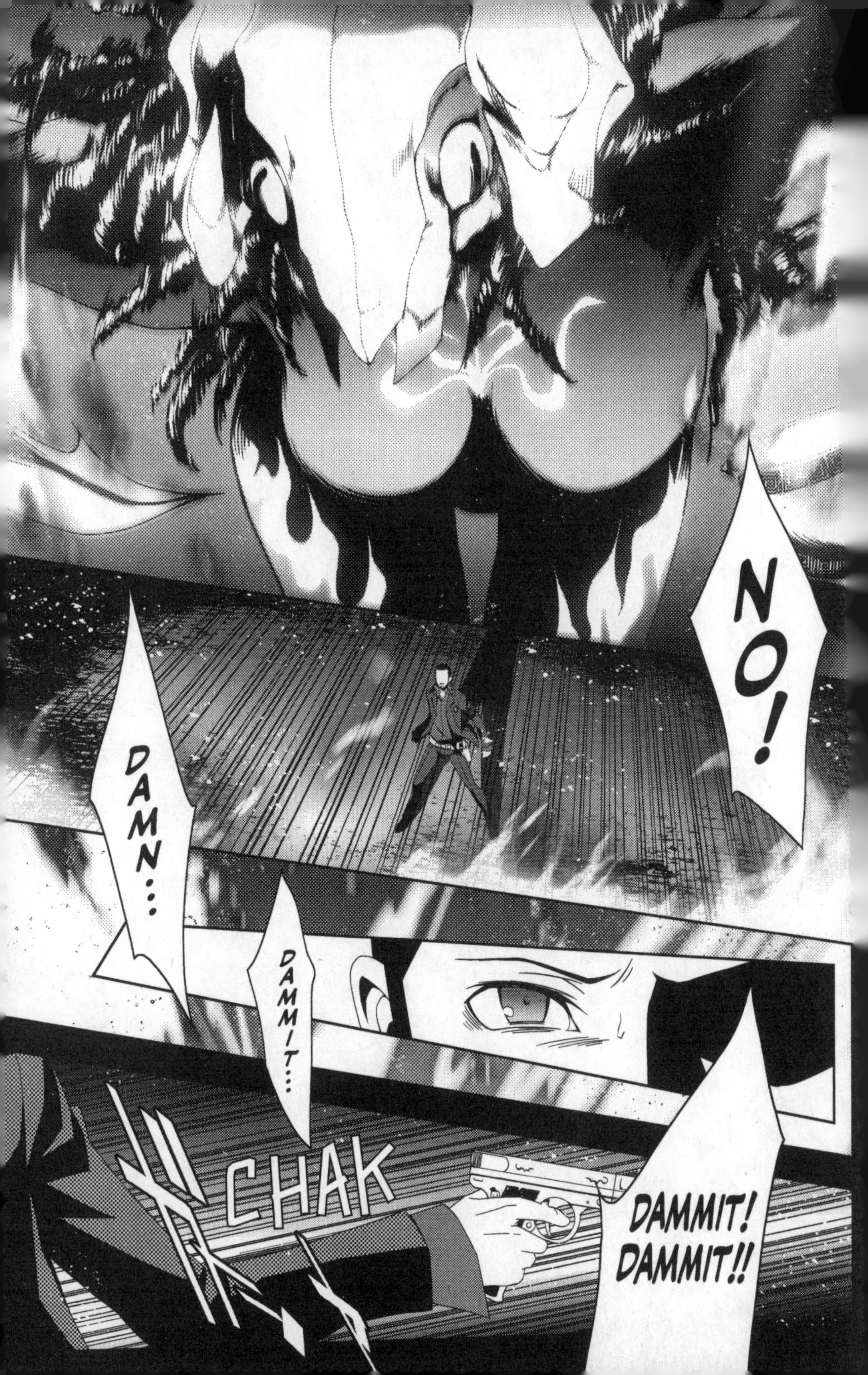
NO!
DAMN...
DAMMIT...
DAMMIT! DAMMIT!!
CHAK

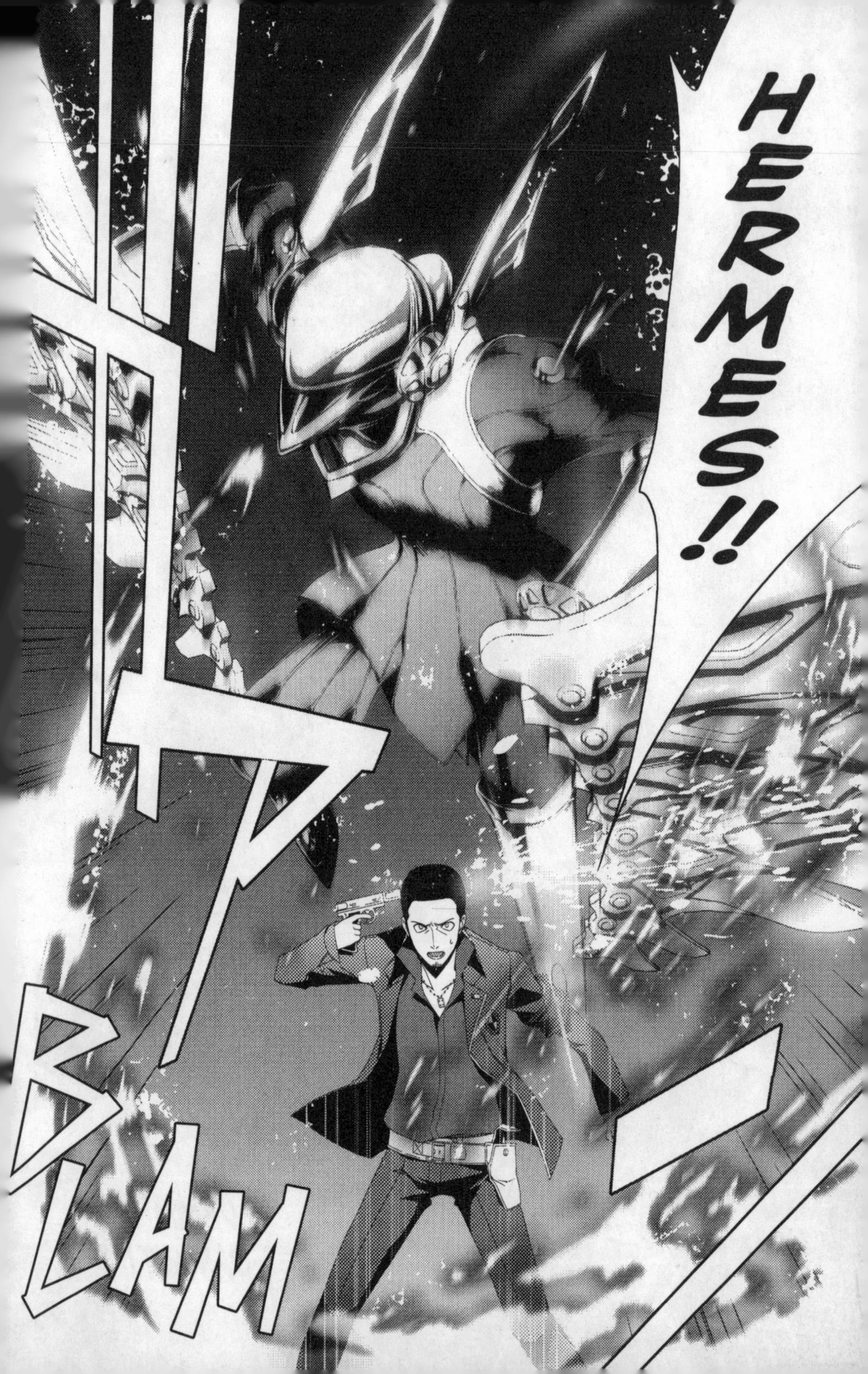
HERMES!!
BLAM

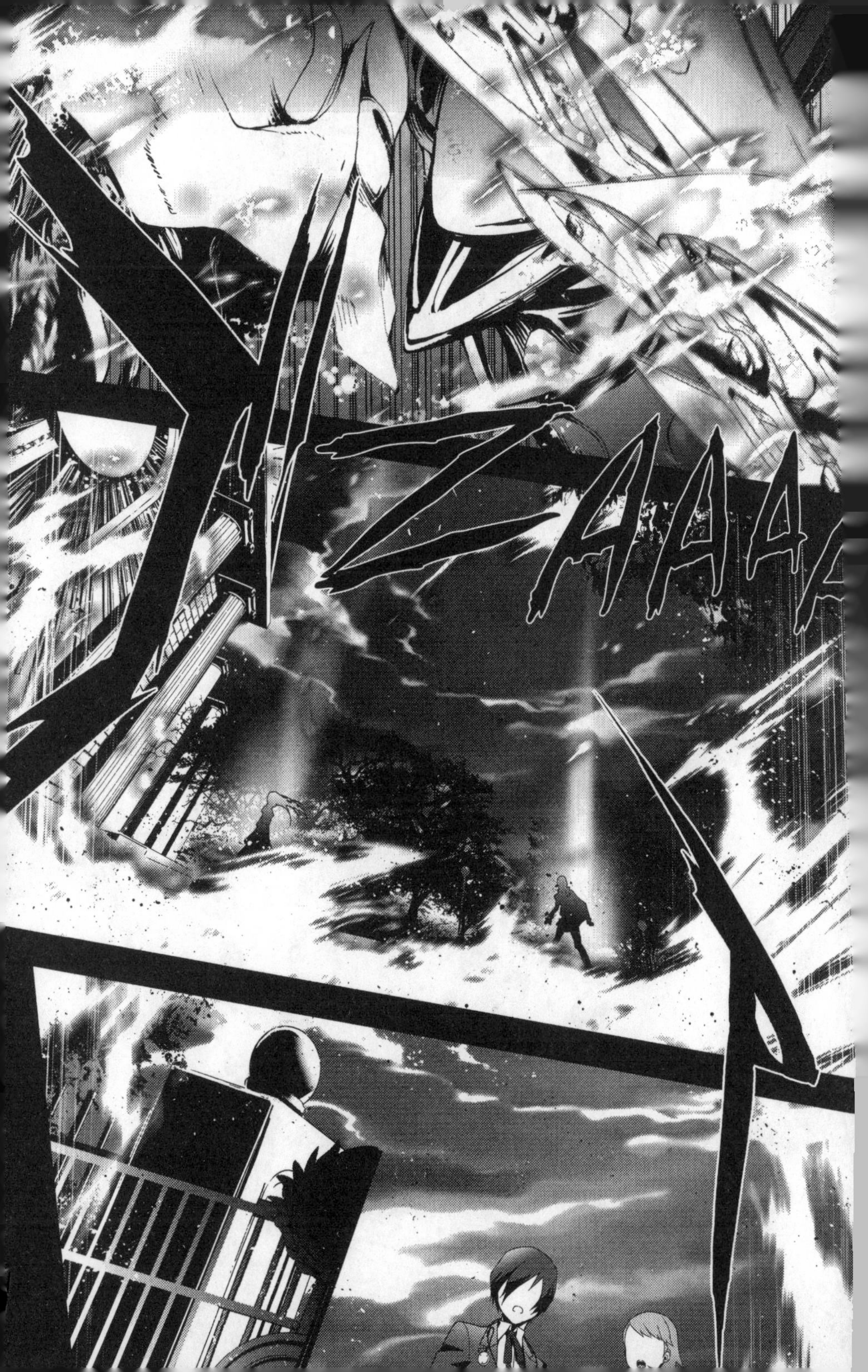
ZAAA

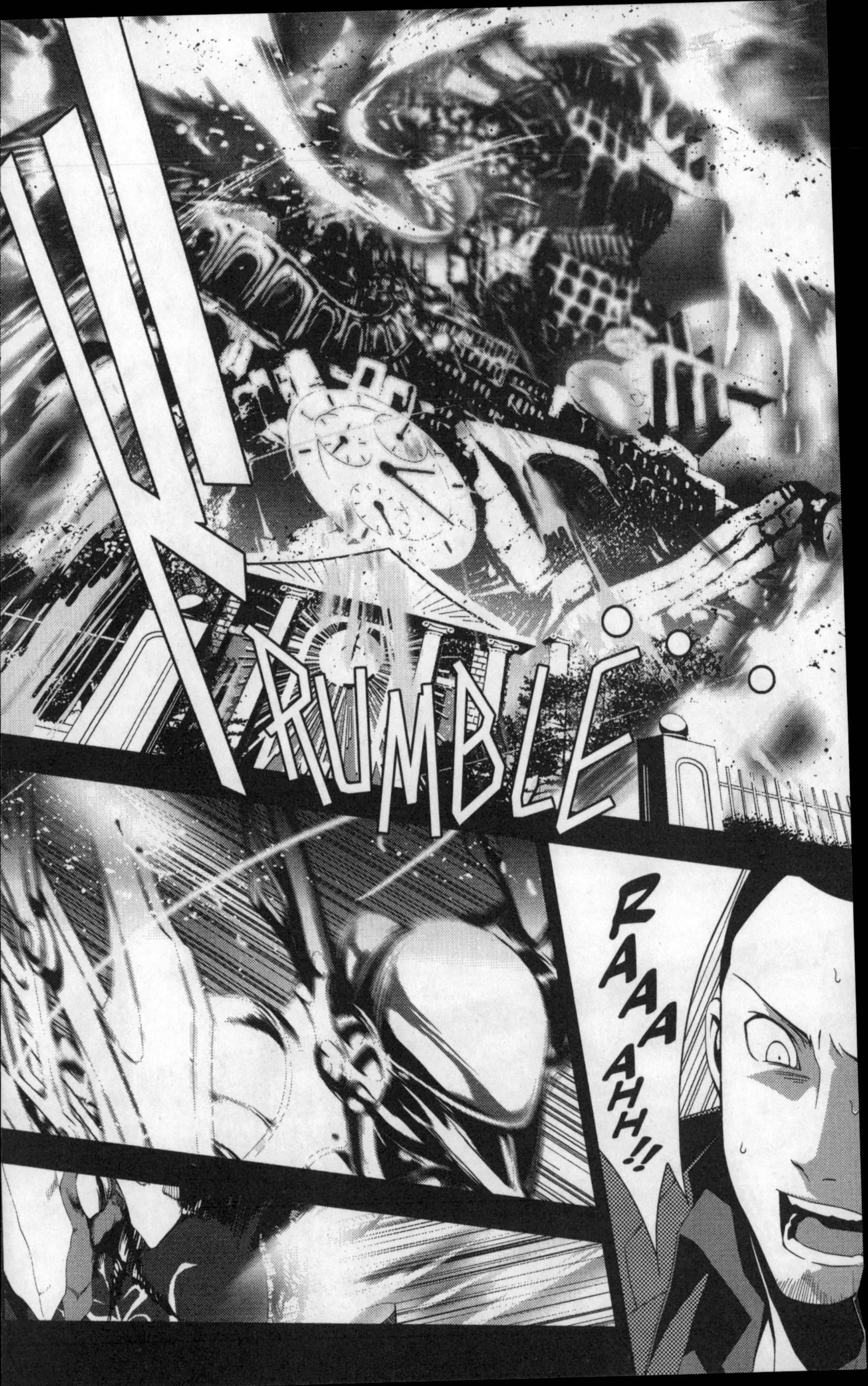
RUMBLE...
RAAAAHH!!

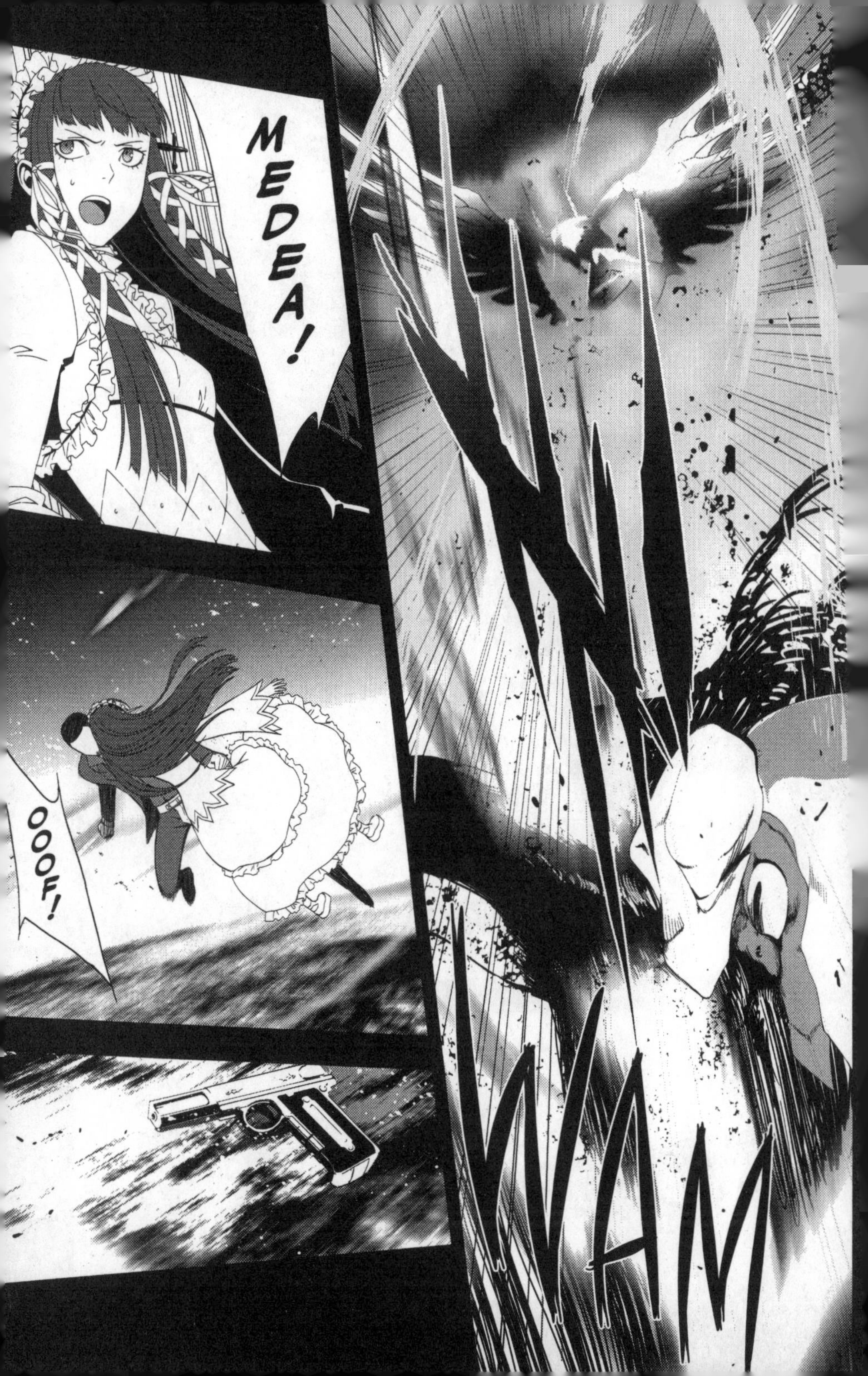
WAM
MEDEA!
OOOF!

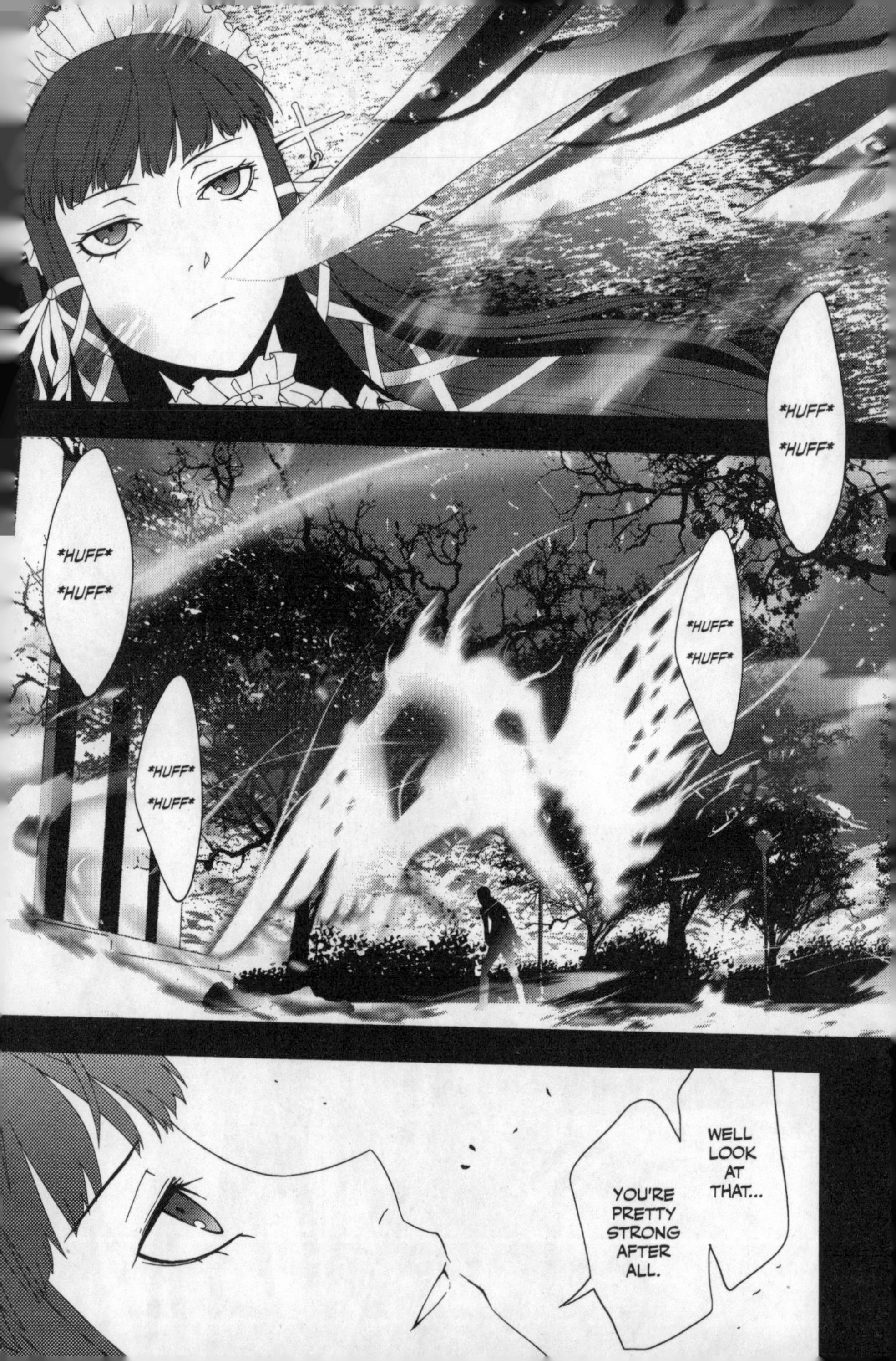
HUFF *HUFF*
HUFF *HUFF*
HUFF *HUFF*
HUFF *HUFF*
WELL LOOK AT THAT...
YOU'RE PRETTY STRONG AFTER ALL.

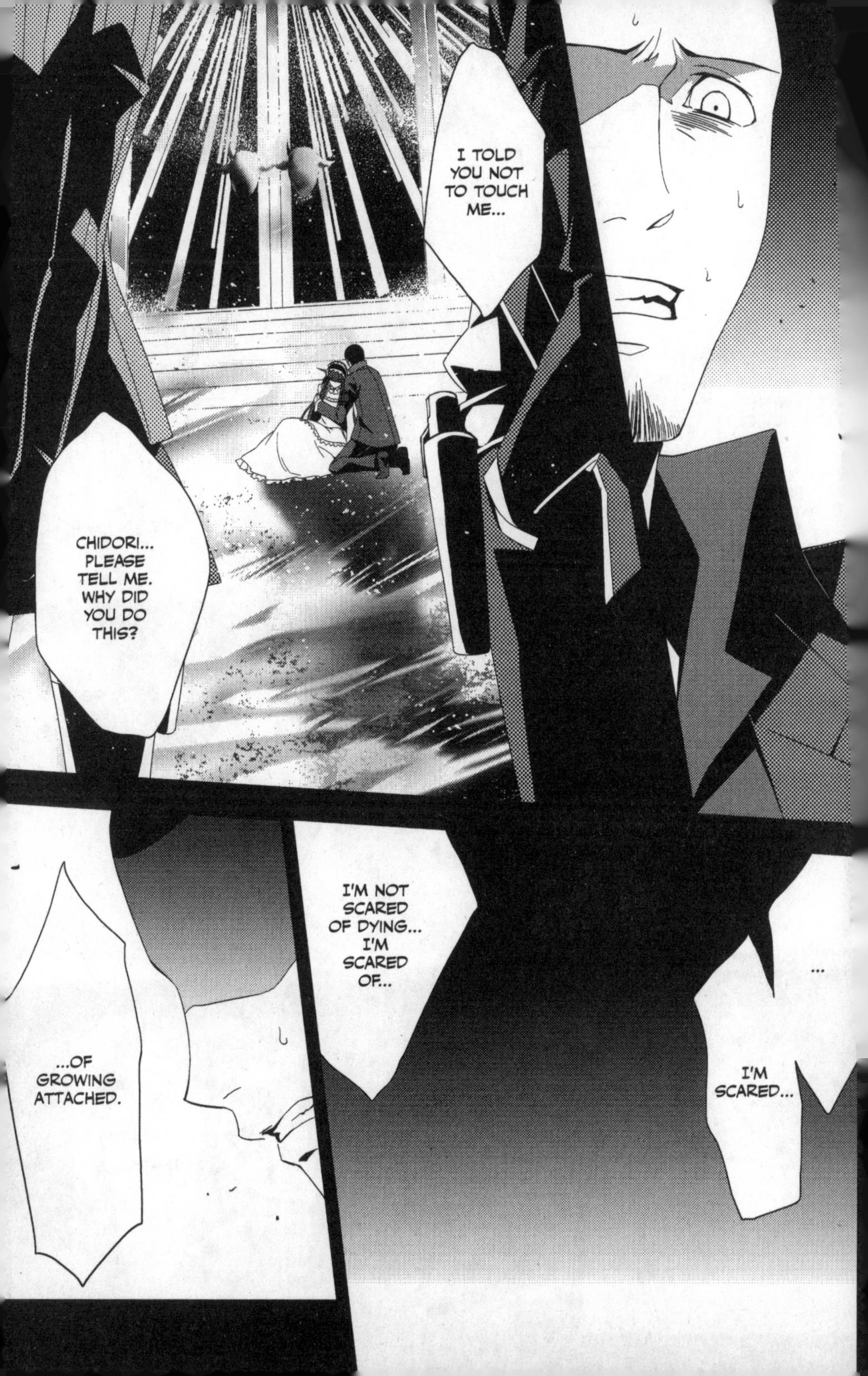
I TOLD YOU NOT TO TOUCH ME...
CHIDORI... PLEASE TELL ME. WHY DID YOU DO THIS?
...
I'M SCARED...
I'M NOT SCARED OF DYING... I'M SCARED OF...
...OF GROWING ATTACHED.

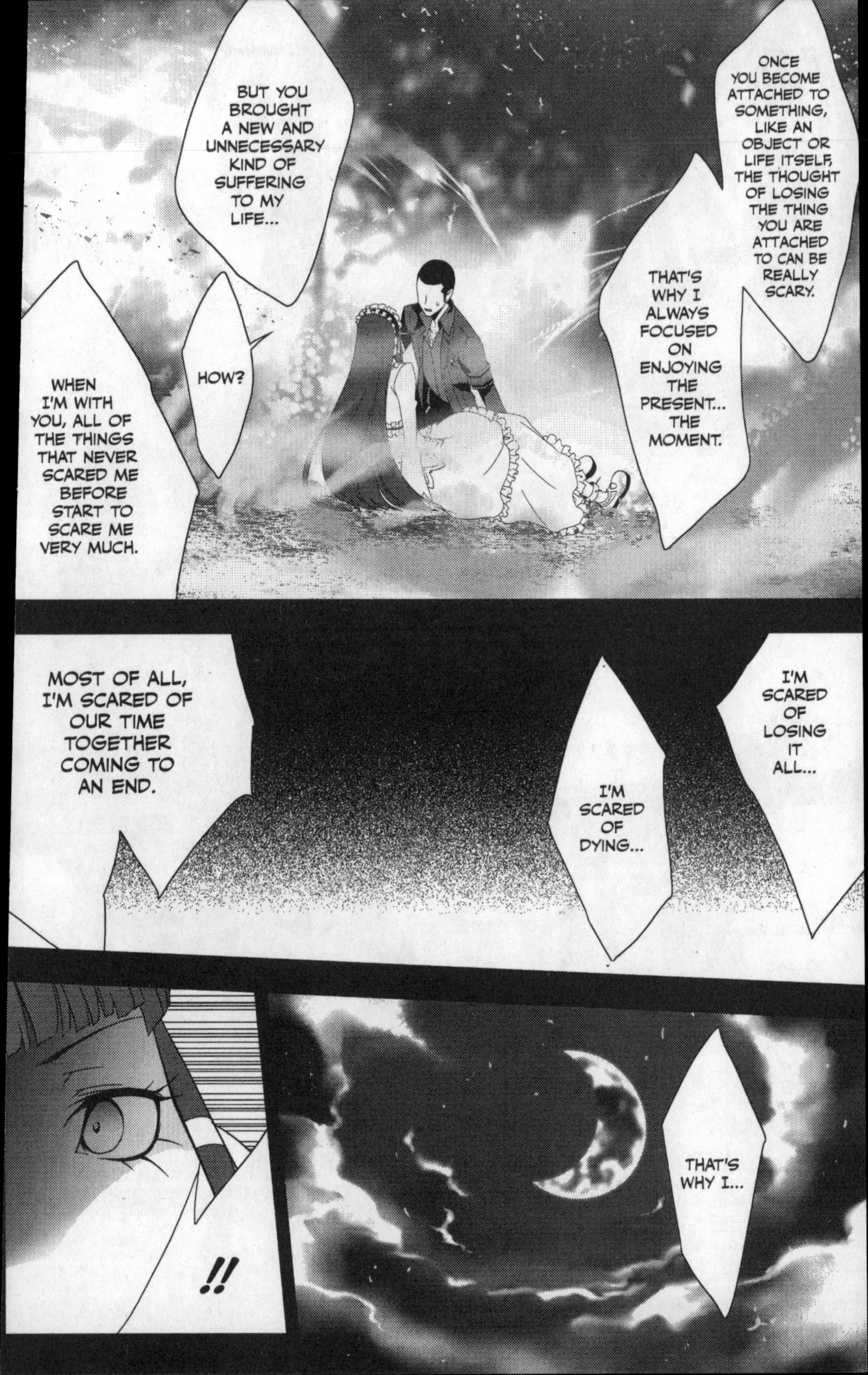
ONCE YOU BECOME ATTACHED TO SOMETHING, LIKE AN OBJECT OR LIFE ITSELF, THE THOUGHT OF LOSING THE THING YOU ARE ATTACHED TO CAN BE REALLY SCARY.
THAT'S WHY I ALWAYS FOCUSED ON ENJOYING THE PRESENT... THE MOMENT.
BUT YOU BROUGHT A NEW AND UNNECESSARY KIND OF SUFFERING TO MY LIFE...
HOW?
WHEN I'M WITH YOU, ALL OF THE THINGS THAT NEVER SCARED ME BEFORE START TO SCARE ME VERY MUCH.
I'M SCARED OF LOSING IT ALL...
I'M SCARED OF DYING...
MOST OF ALL, I'M SCARED OF OUR TIME TOGETHER COMING TO AN END.
THAT'S WHY I...
!!

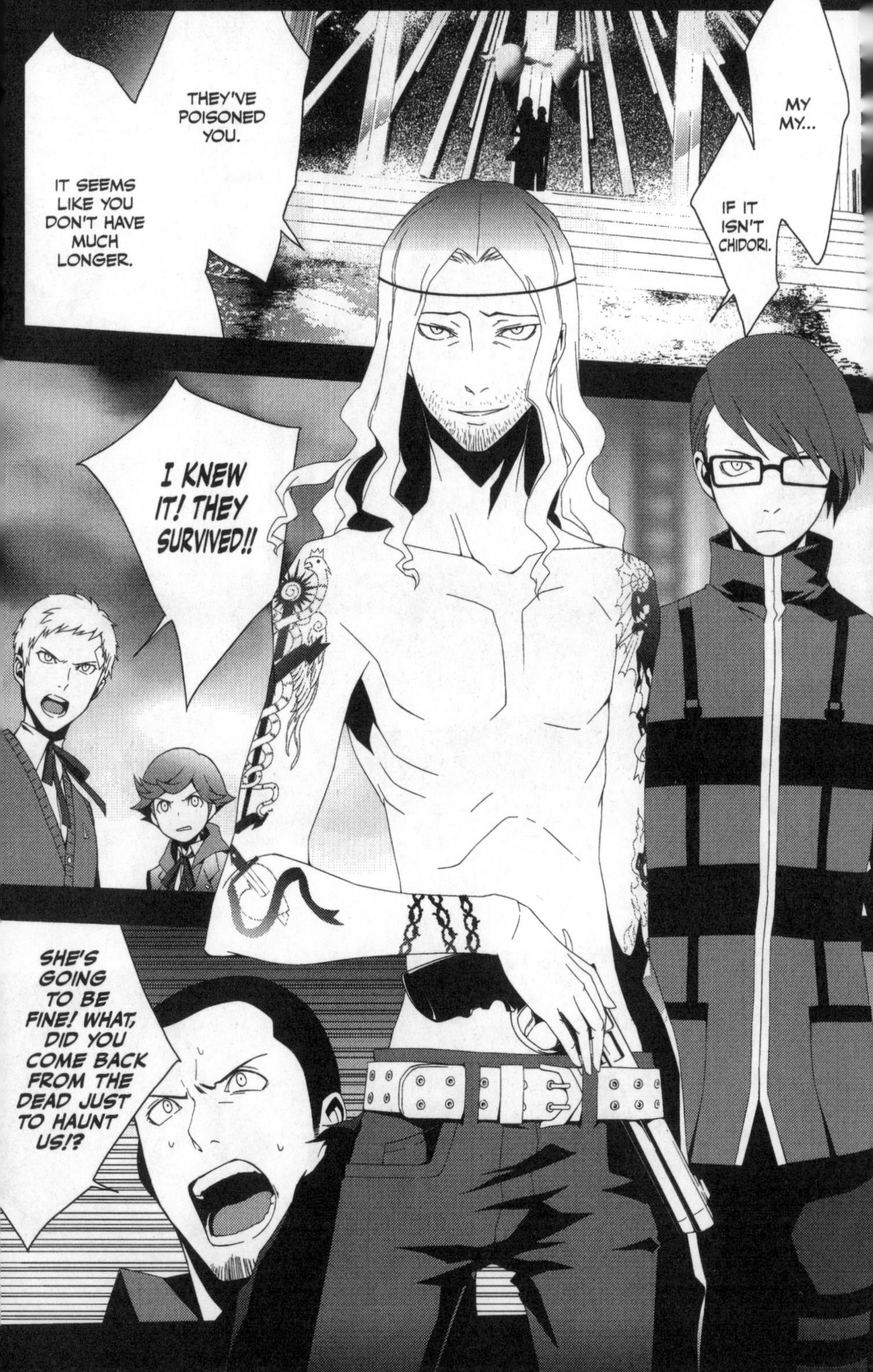
MY MY...
IF IT ISN'T CHIDORI.
THEY'VE POISONED YOU.
IT SEEMS LIKE YOU DON'T HAVE MUCH LONGER.
I KNEW IT! THEY SURVIVED!!
SHE'S GOING TO BE FINE! WHAT, DID YOU COME BACK FROM THE DEAD JUST TO HAUNT US!?

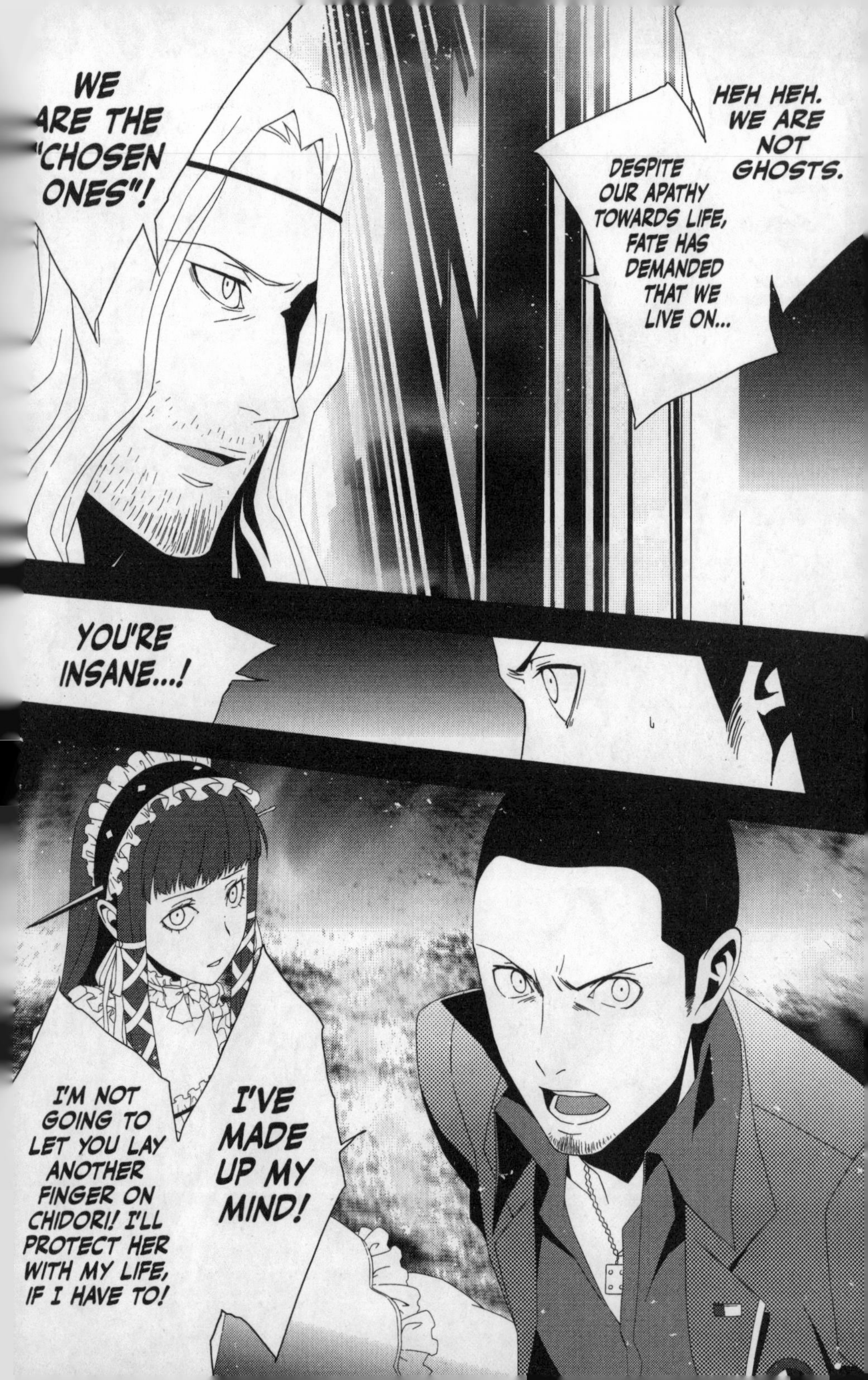
HEH HEH. WE ARE NOT GHOSTS.
DESPITE OUR APATHY TOWARDS LIFE, FATE HAS DEMANDED THAT WE LIVE ON...
WE ARE THE "CHOSEN ONES"!
YOU'RE INSANE...!
I'VE MADE UP MY MIND!
I'M NOT GOING TO LET YOU LAY ANOTHER FINGER ON CHIDORI! I'LL PROTECT HER WITH MY LIFE, IF I HAVE TO!

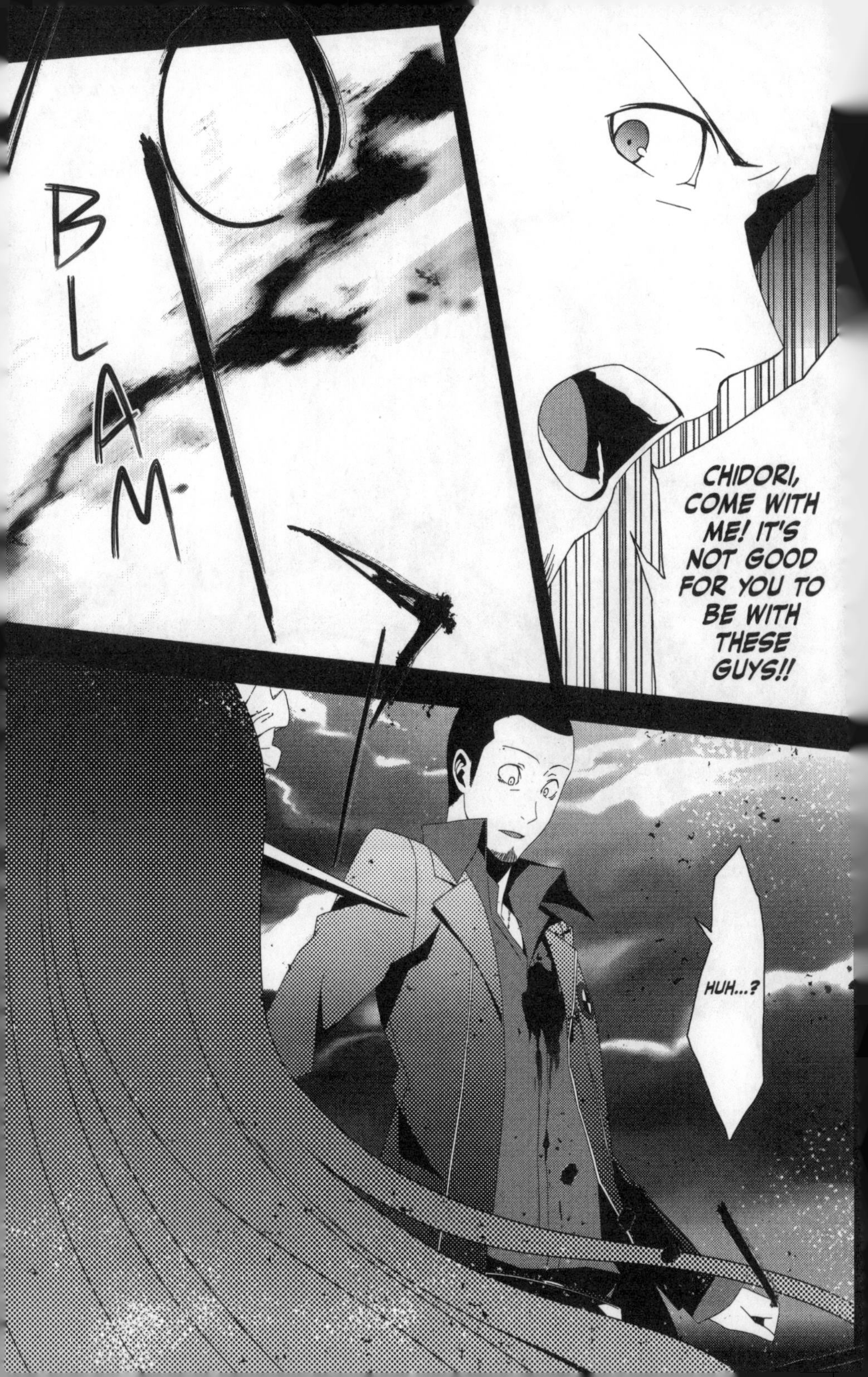
CHIDORI, COME WITH ME! IT'S NOT GOOD FOR YOU TO BE WITH THESE GUYS!!
BLAM
HUH...?

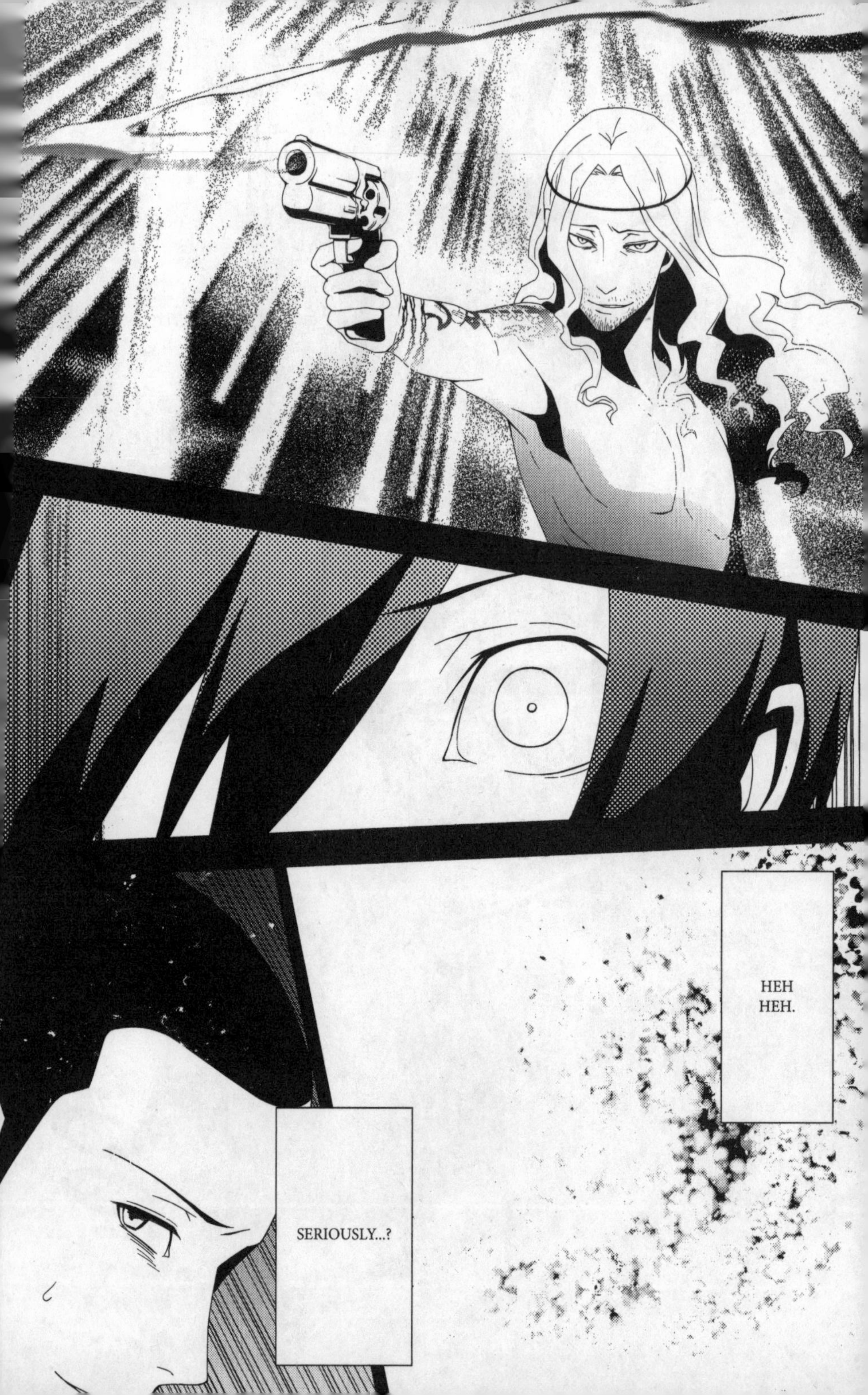
HEH HEH.
SERIOUSLY...?

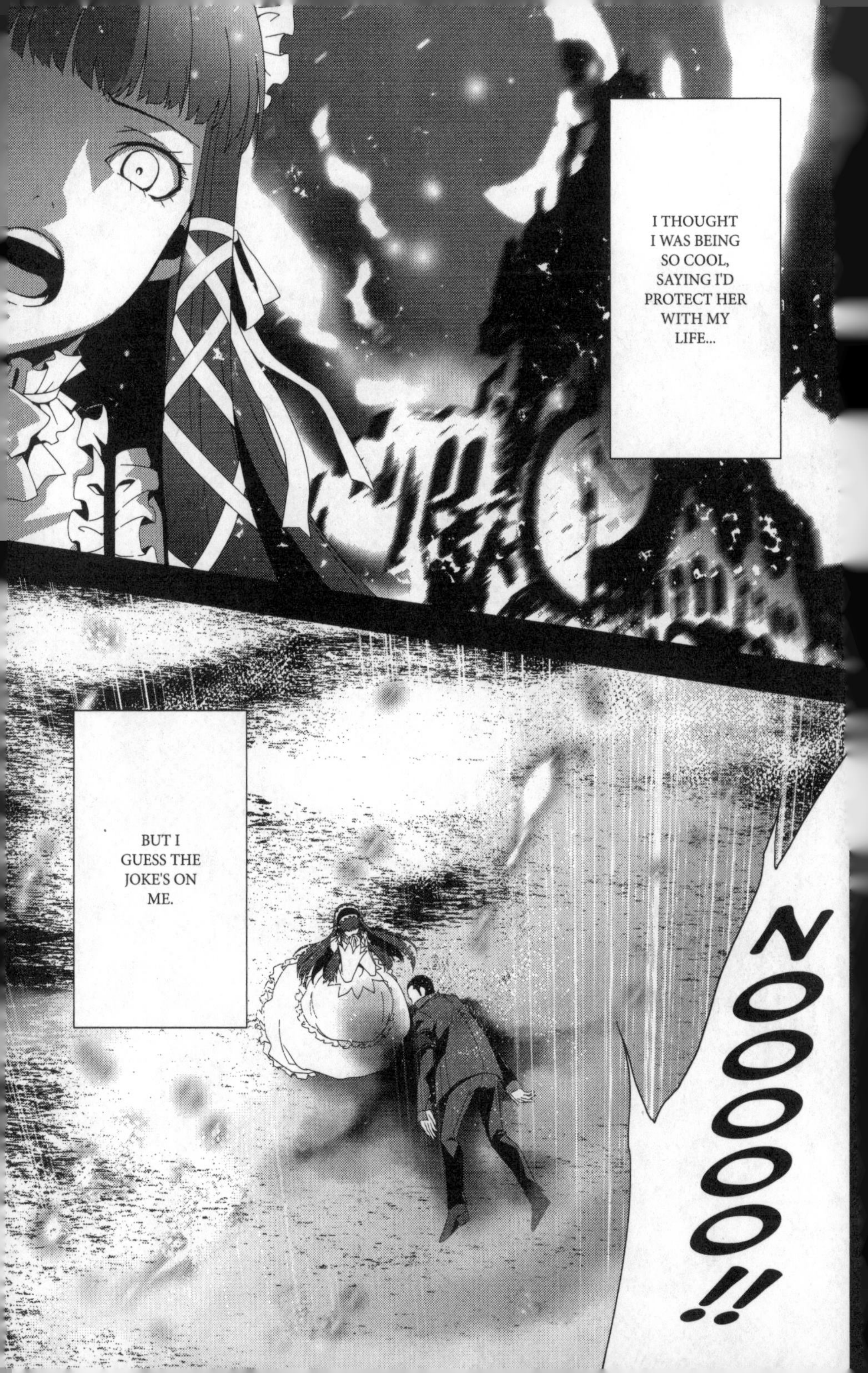
I THOUGHT I WAS BEING SO COOL, SAYING I'D PROTECT HER WITH MY LIFE...
BUT I GUESS THE JOKE'S ON ME.
NOOOOOO!!

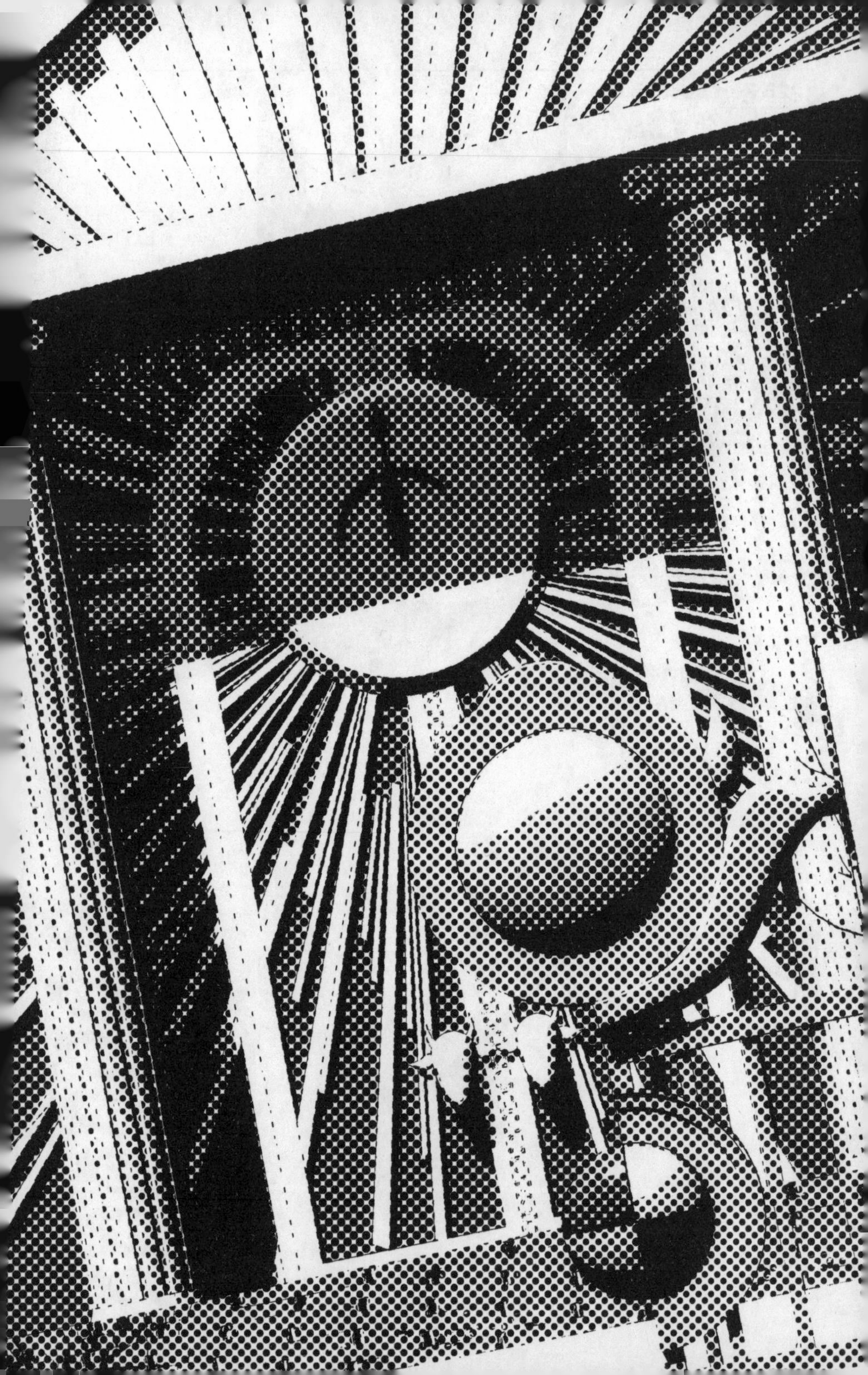

#26 Perspective:06
REBIRTH

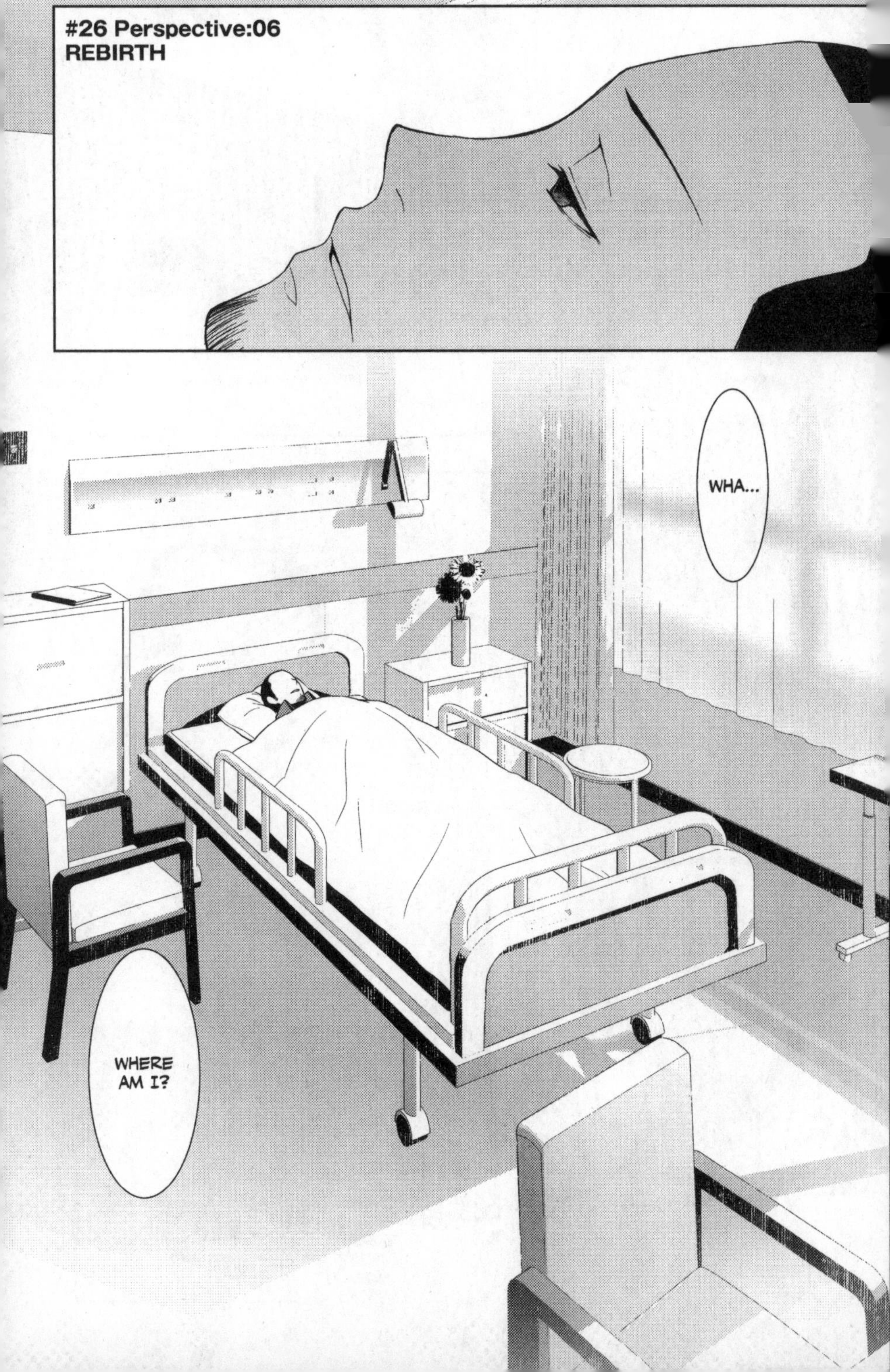
WHA...
WHERE AM I?

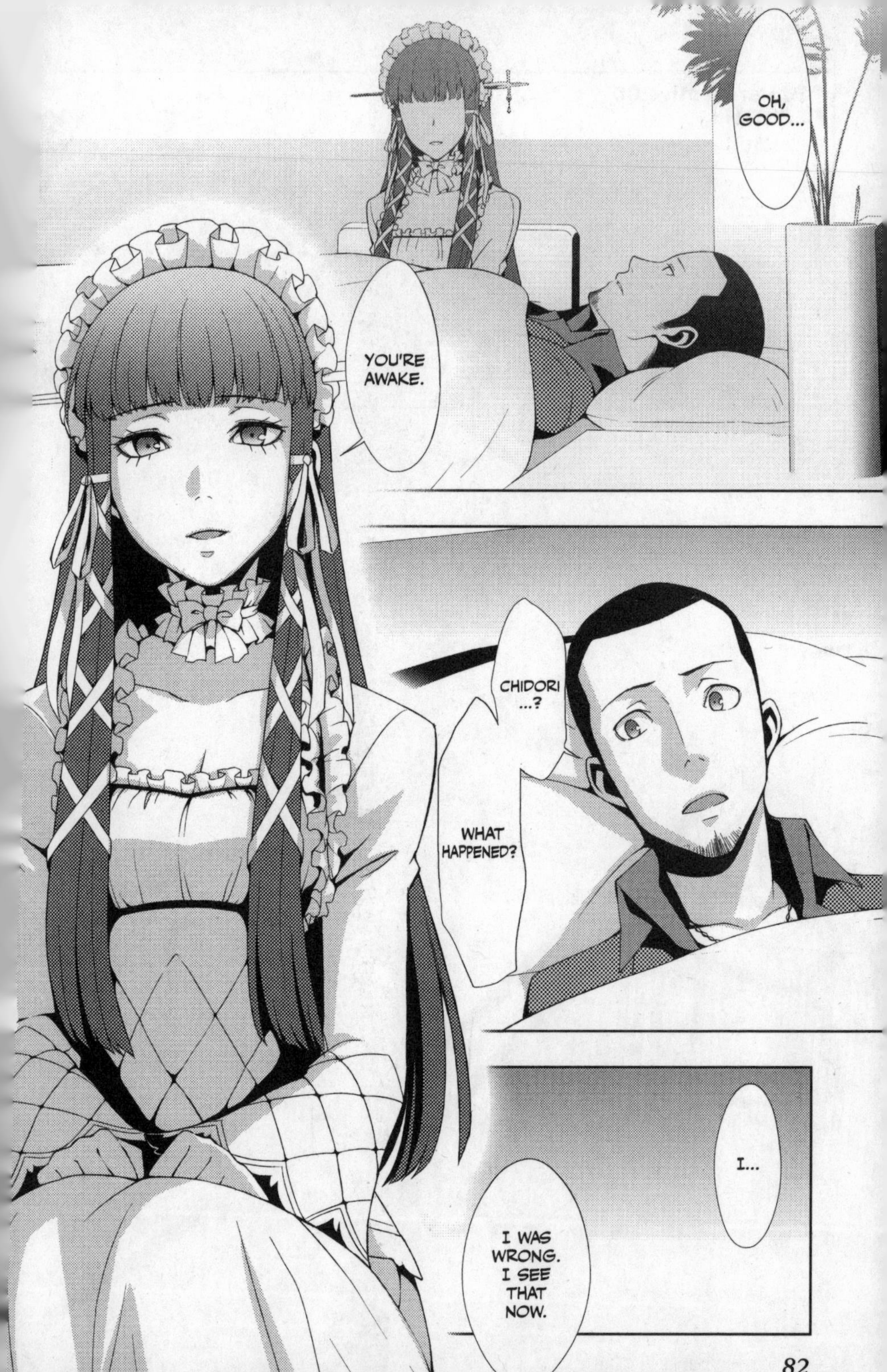
OH, GOOD...
YOU'RE AWAKE.
CHIDORI ...?
WHAT HAPPENED?
I...
I WAS WRONG. I SEE THAT NOW.

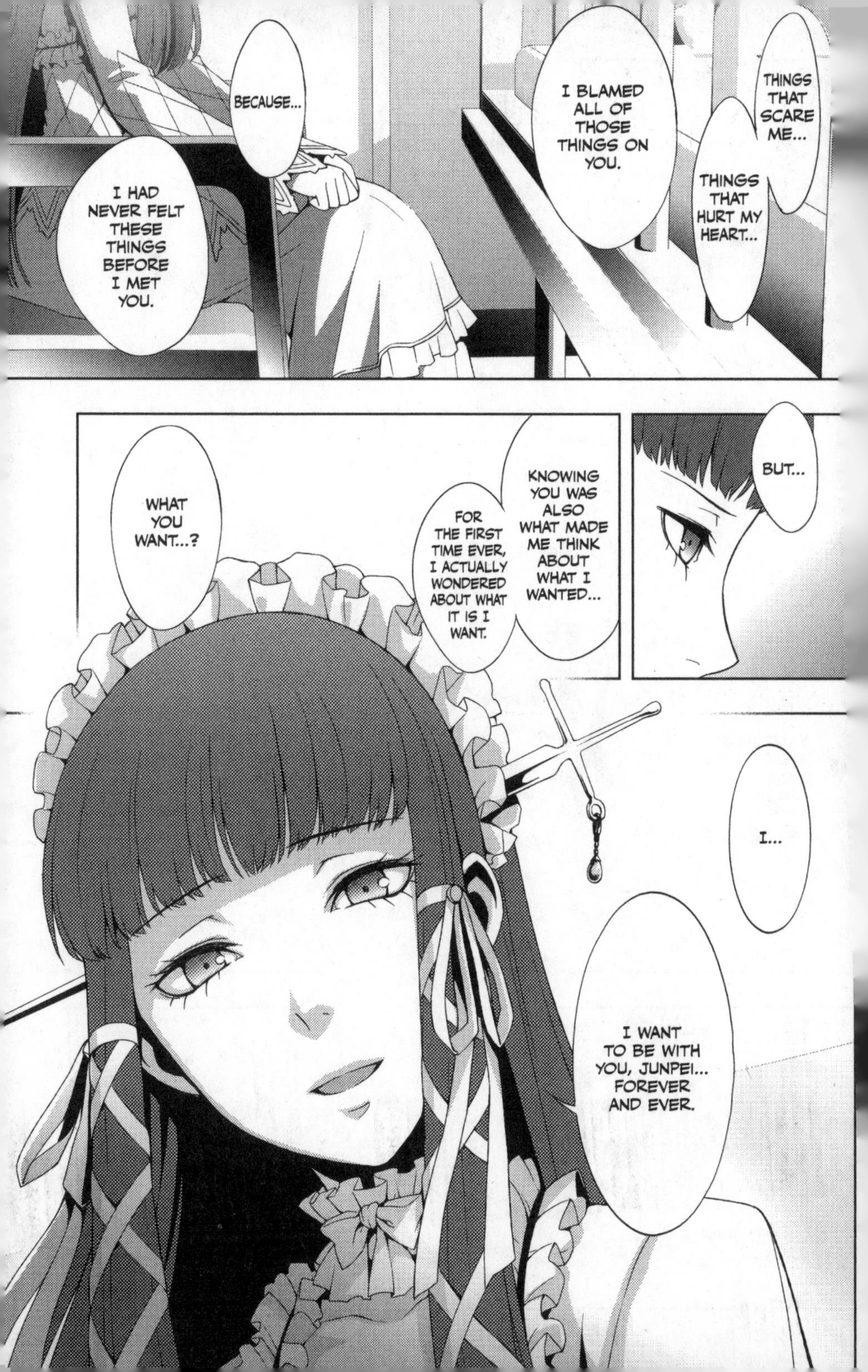
THINGS THAT SCARE ME...
THINGS THAT HURT MY HEART...
I BLAMED ALL OF THOSE THINGS ON YOU.
BECAUSE...
I HAD NEVER FELT THESE THINGS BEFORE I MET YOU.
BUT...
KNOWING YOU WAS ALSO WHAT MADE ME THINK ABOUT WHAT I WANTED...
FOR THE FIRST TIME EVER, I ACTUALLY WONDERED ABOUT WHAT IT IS I WANT.
WHAT YOU WANT...?
I...
I WANT TO BE WITH YOU, JUNPEI... FOREVER AND EVER.

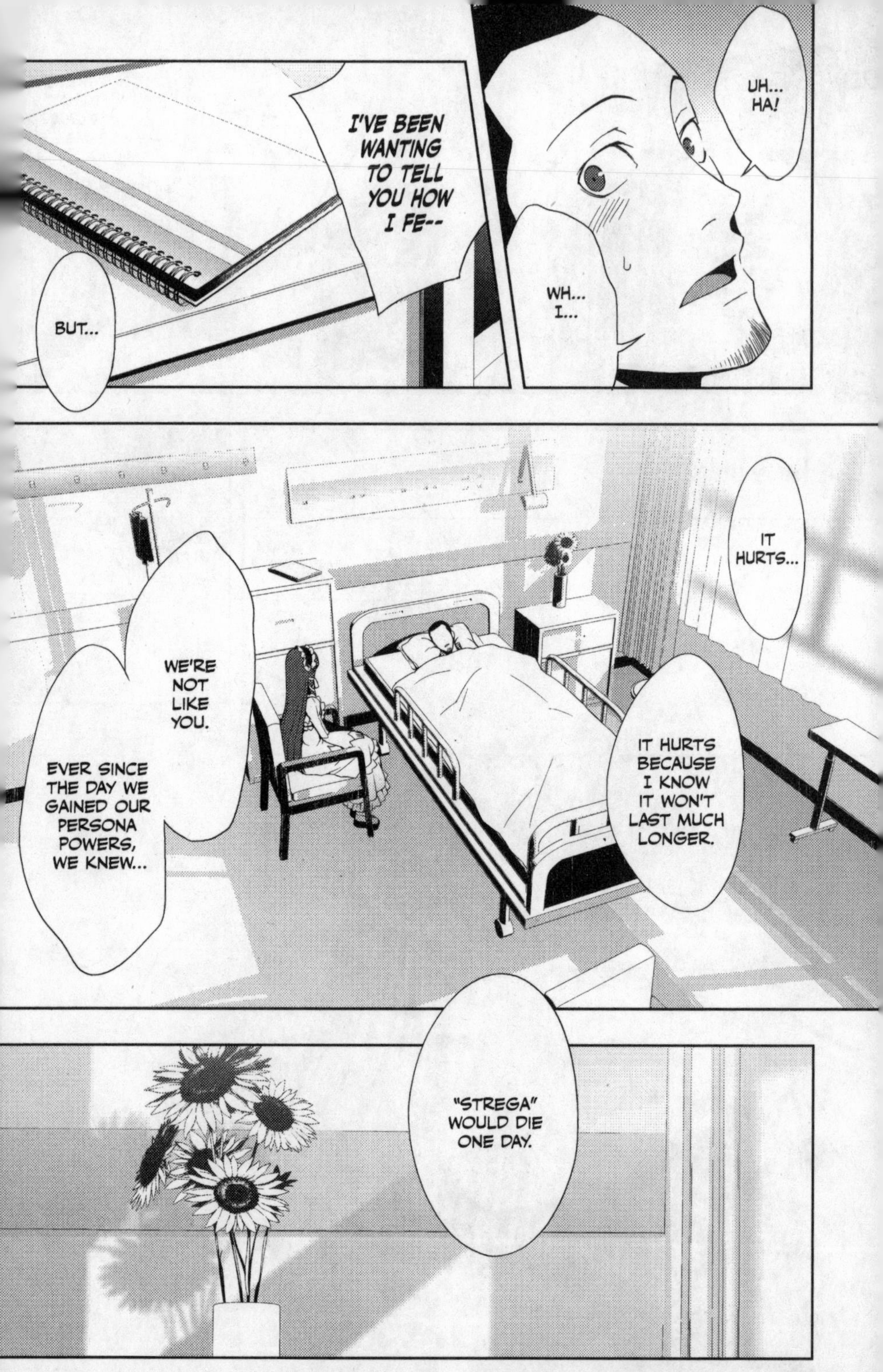
UH... HA!
WH... I...
I'VE BEEN WANTING TO TELL YOU HOW I FE--
BUT...
IT HURTS...
IT HURTS BECAUSE I KNOW IT WON'T LAST MUCH LONGER.
WE'RE NOT LIKE YOU.
EVER SINCE THE DAY WE GAINED OUR PERSONA POWERS, WE KNEW...
"STREGA" WOULD DIE ONE DAY.

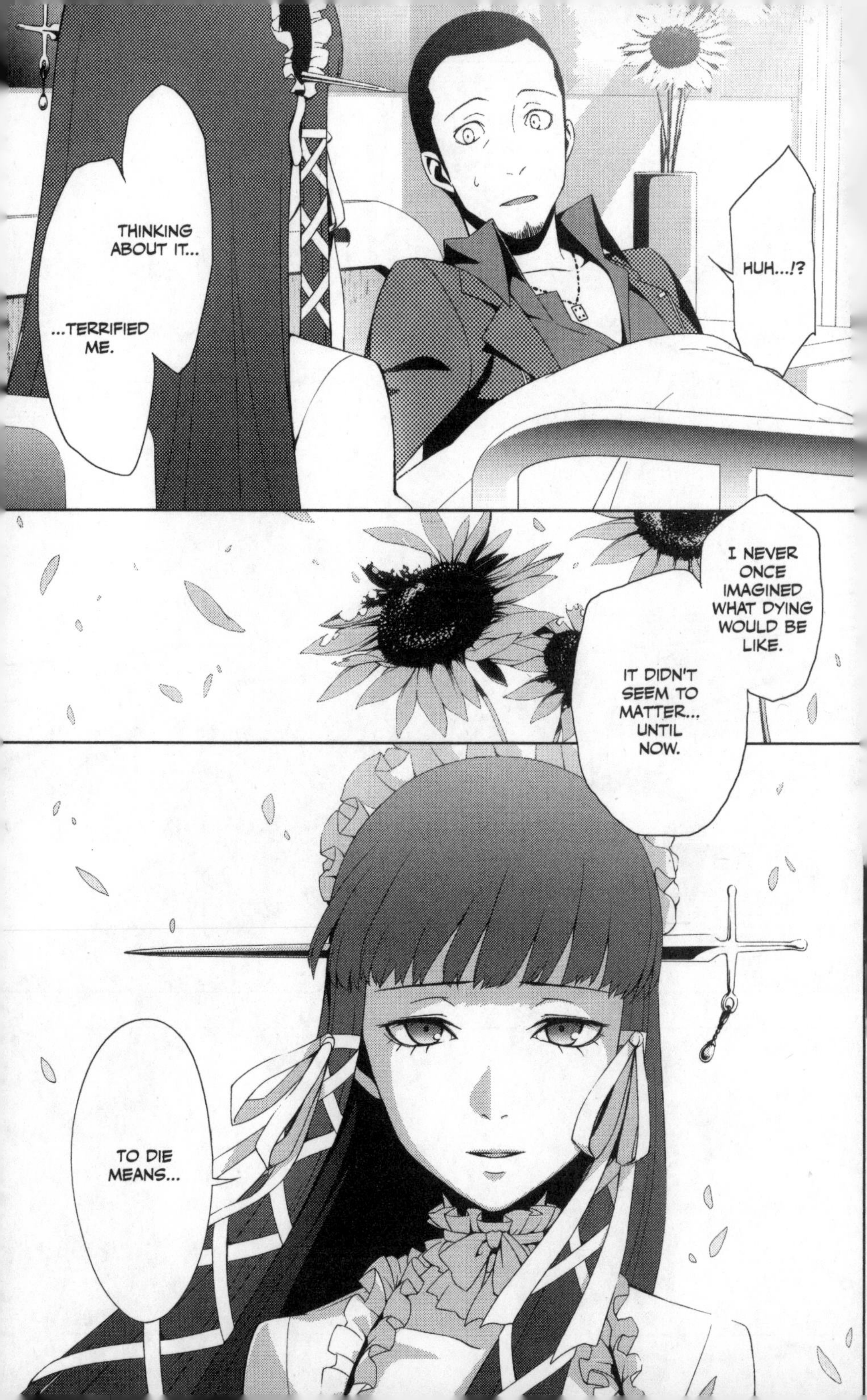
THINKING ABOUT IT...
...TERRIFIED ME.
HUH...!?
I NEVER ONCE IMAGINED WHAT DYING WOULD BE LIKE.
IT DIDN'T SEEM TO MATTER... UNTIL NOW.
TO DIE MEANS...

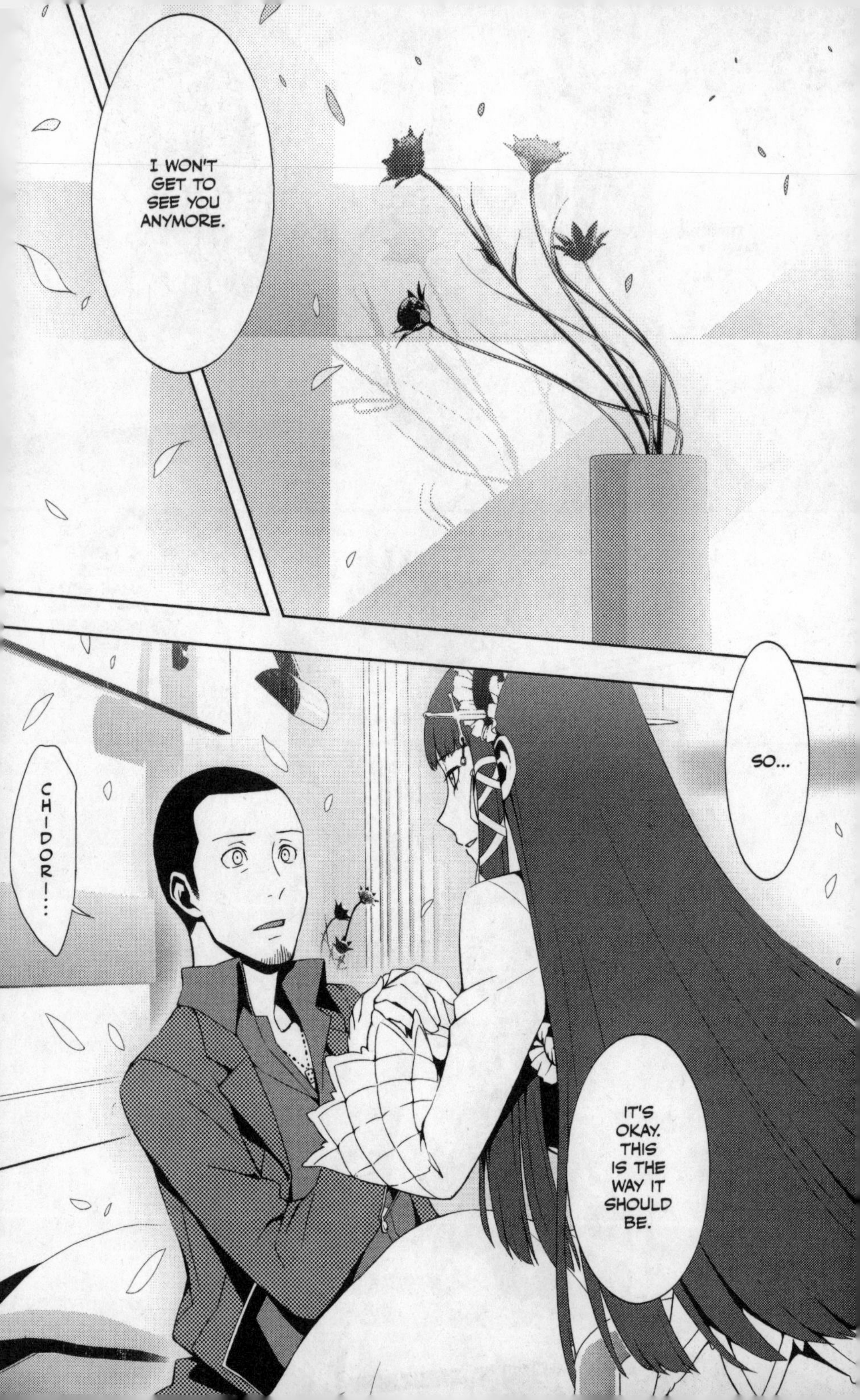
I WON'T GET TO SEE YOU ANYMORE.
SO...
CHIDORI!...
IT'S OKAY. THIS IS THE WAY IT SHOULD BE.

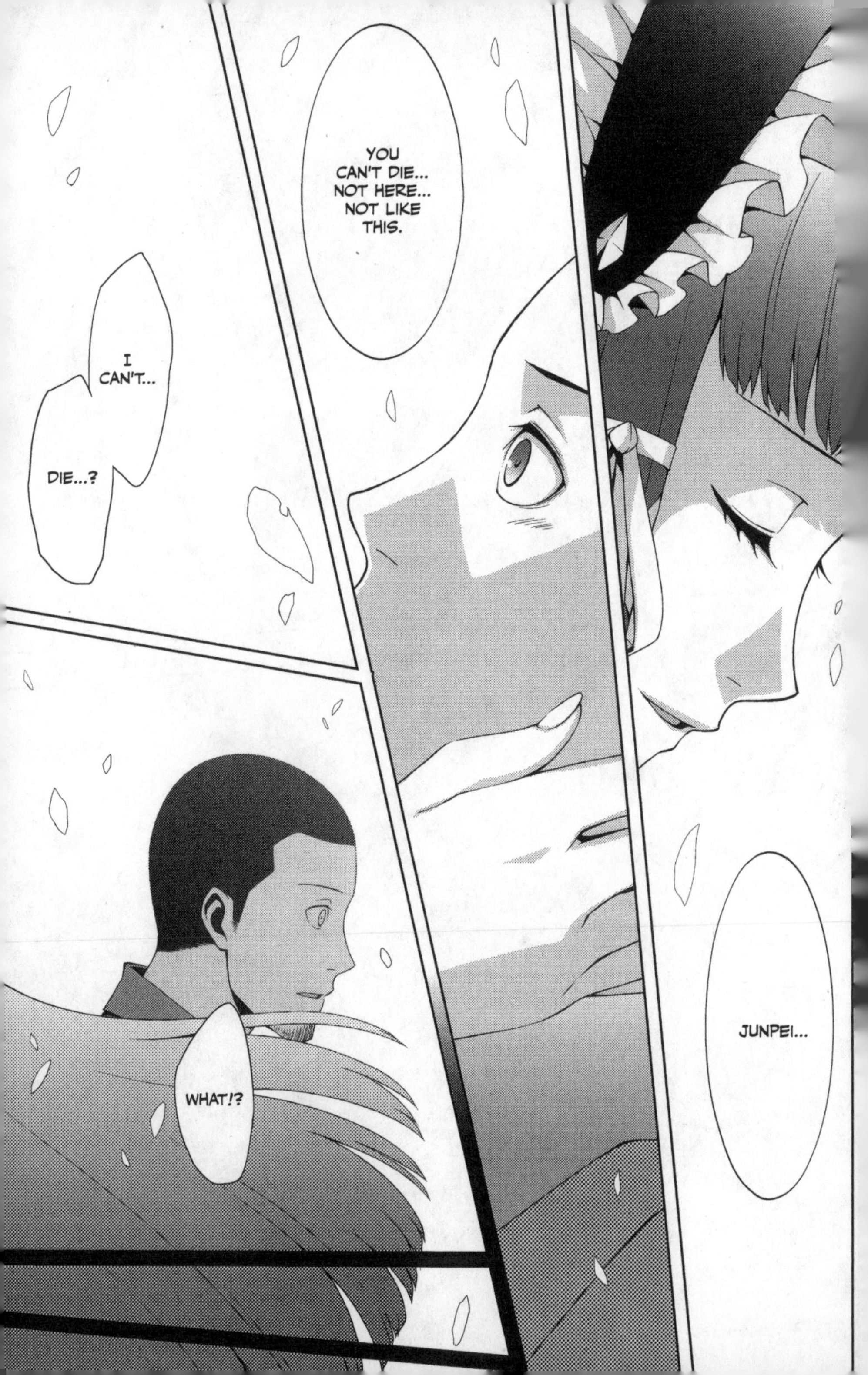
JUNPEI...
YOU CAN'T DIE... NOT HERE... NOT LIKE THIS.
I CAN'T...
DIE...?
WHAT!?

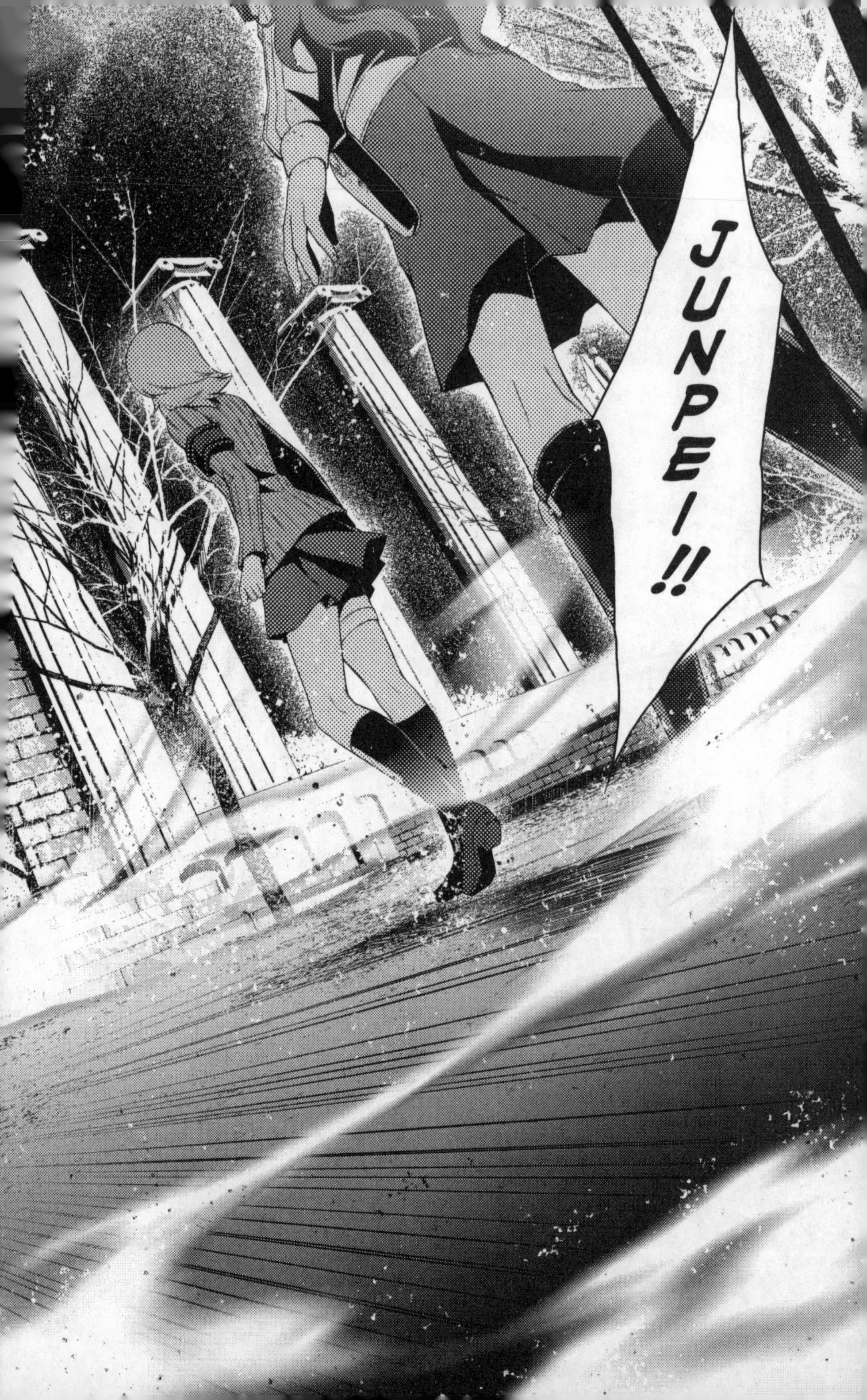
JUNPEI!!

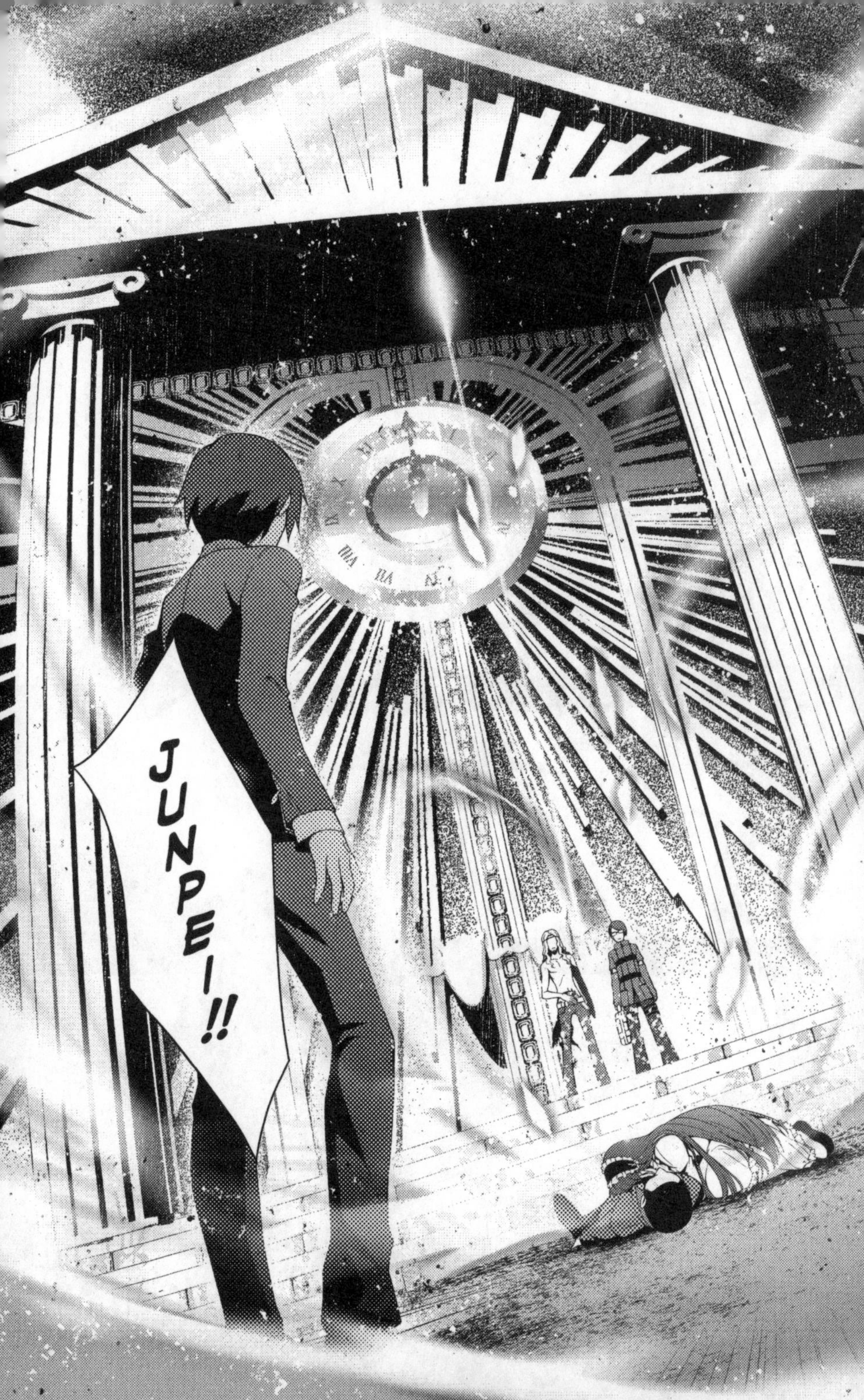
JUNPEI!!

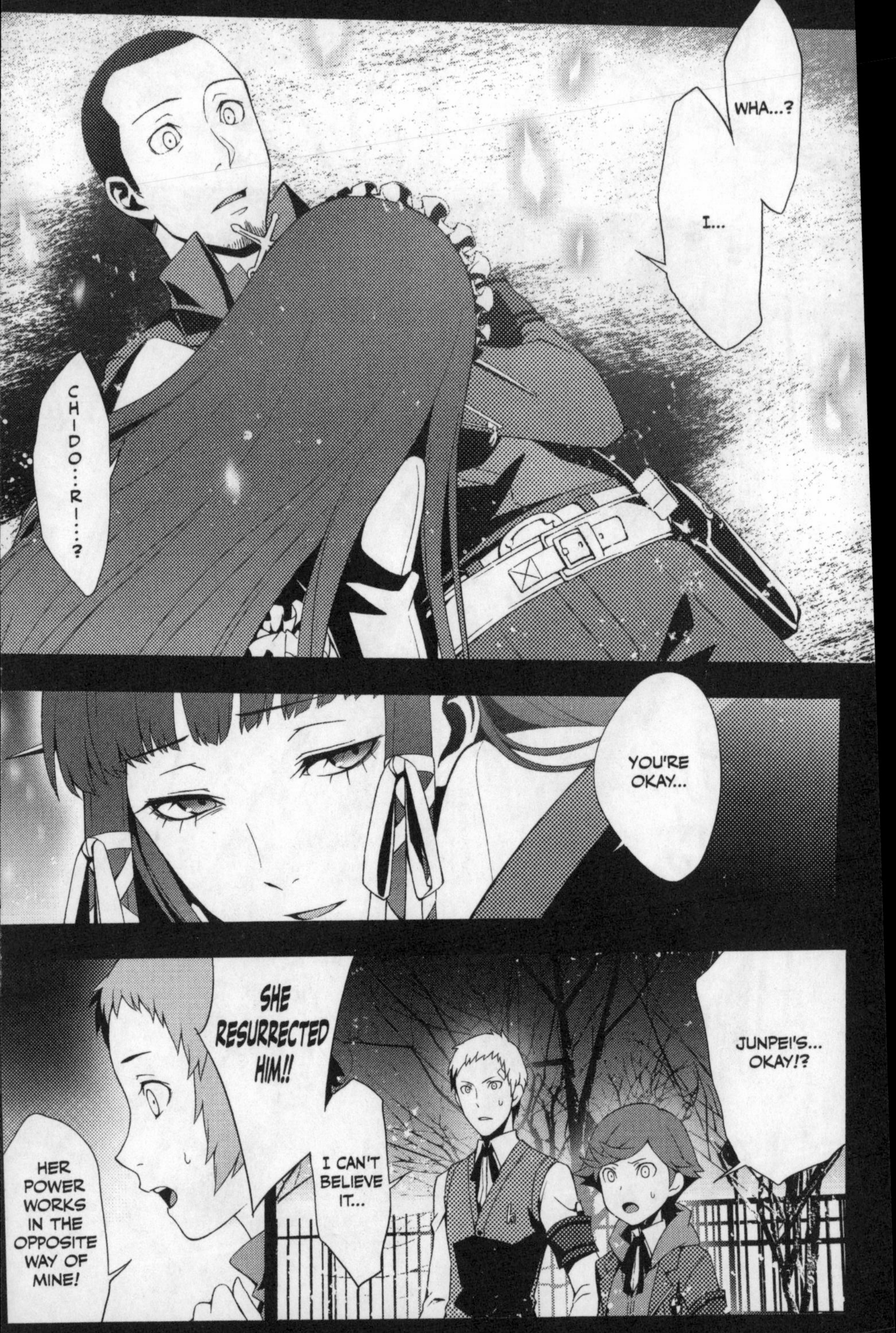
WHA...? I...
CHIDO...RI...?
YOU'RE OKAY...
JUNPEI'S... OKAY!?
SHE RESURRECTED HIM!!
I CAN'T BELIEVE IT...
HER POWER WORKS IN THE OPPOSITE WAY OF MINE!

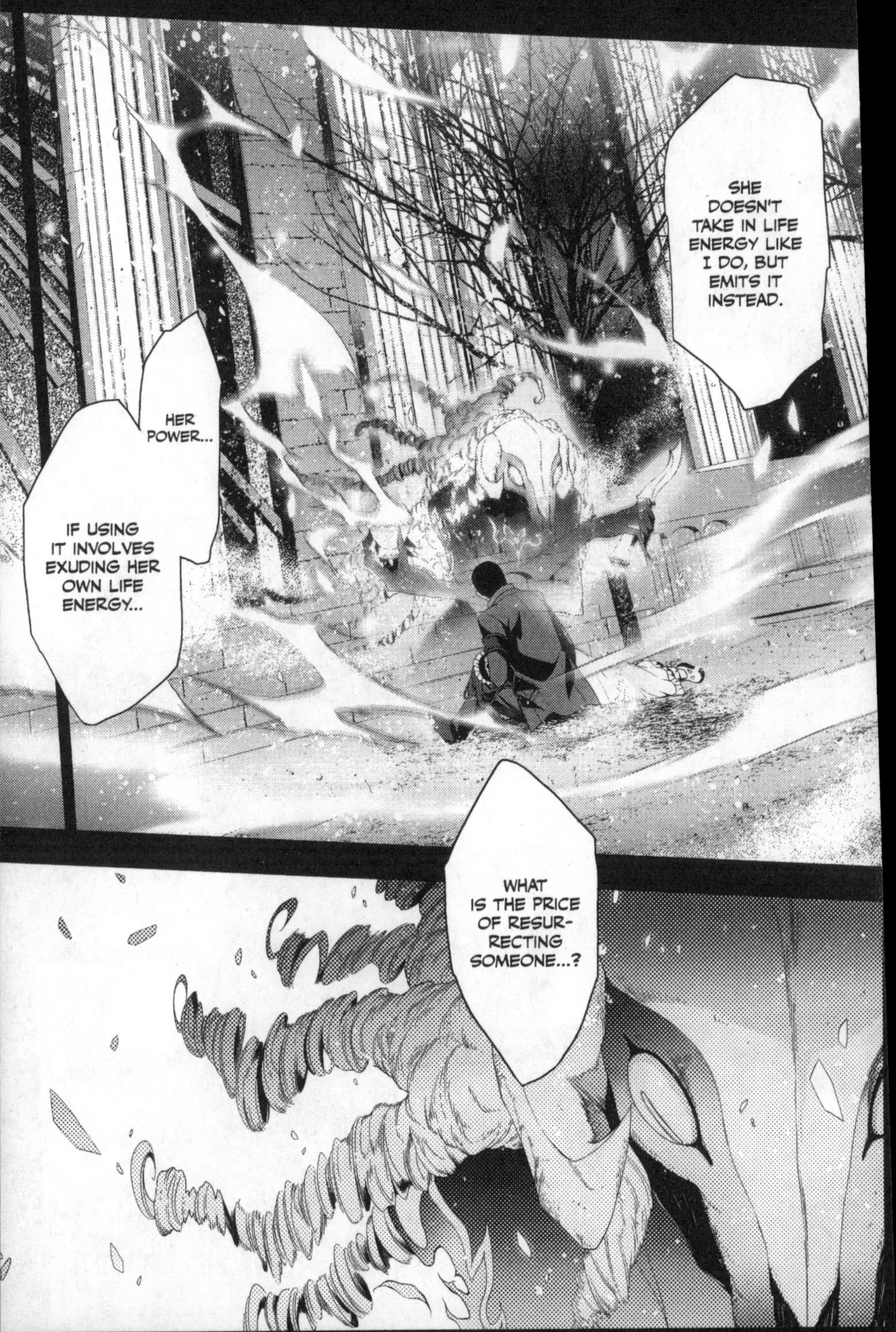
SHE DOESN'T TAKE IN LIFE ENERGY LIKE I DO, BUT EMITS IT INSTEAD.
HER POWER...
IF USING IT INVOLVES EXUDING HER OWN LIFE ENERGY...
WHAT IS THE PRICE OF RESUR-RECTING SOMEONE...?

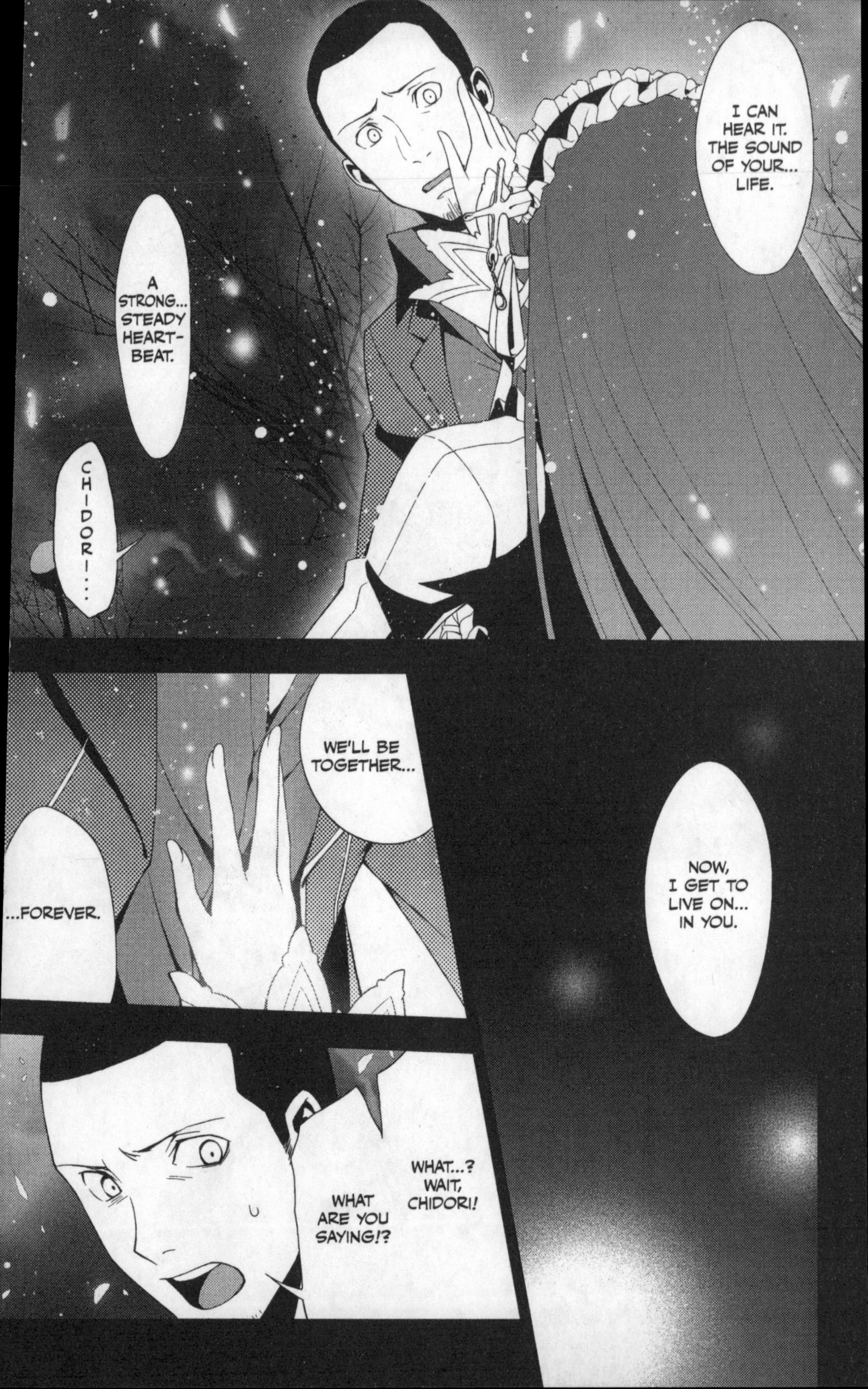
I CAN HEAR IT. THE SOUND OF YOUR... LIFE.
A STRONG... STEADY HEART-BEAT.
CHIDORI...
NOW, I GET TO LIVE ON... IN YOU.
WE'LL BE TOGETHER...
...FOREVER.
WHAT...? WAIT, CHIDORI!
WHAT ARE YOU SAYING!?

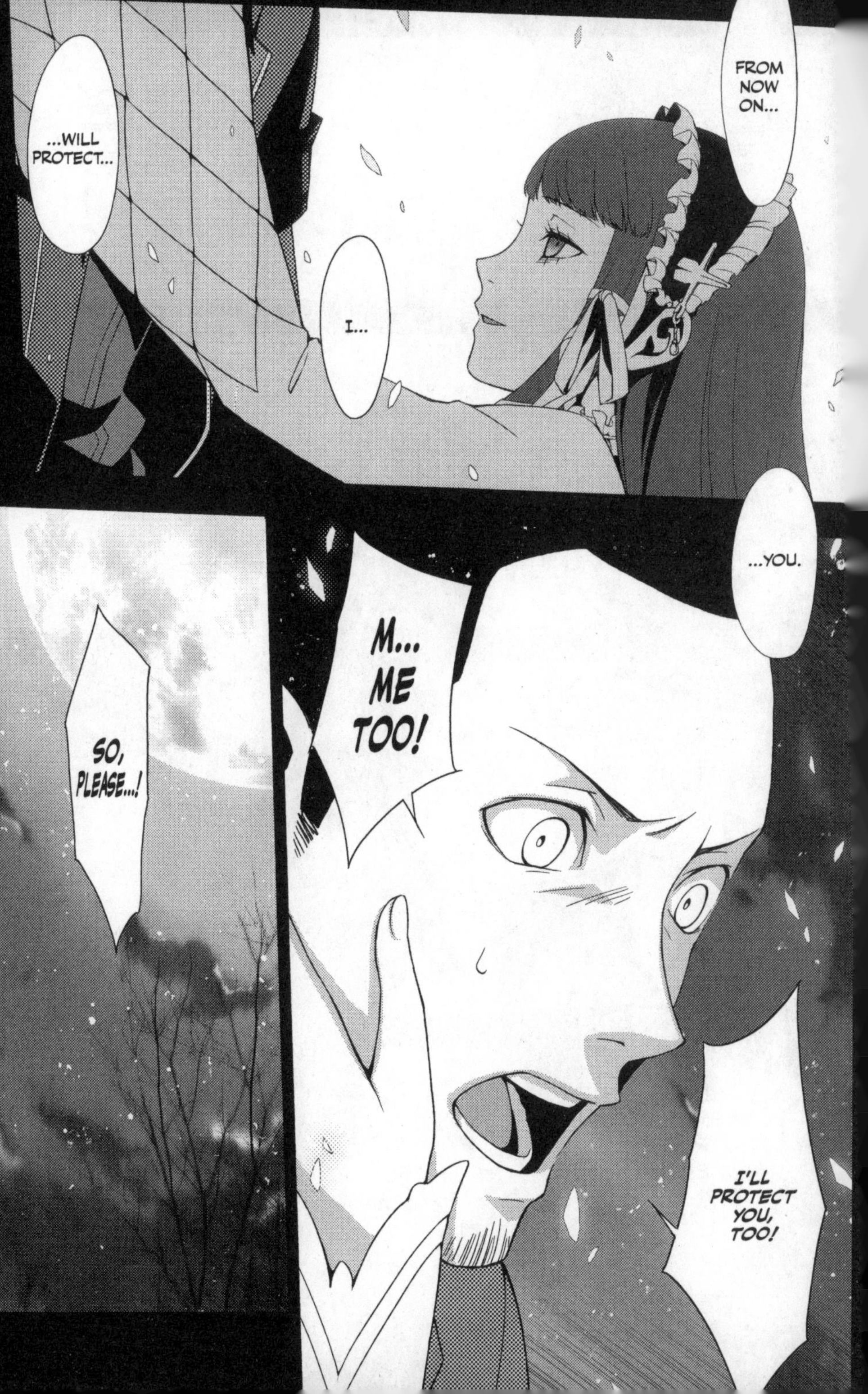
FROM NOW ON...
I...
...WILL PROTECT...
...YOU.
M... ME TOO!
I'LL PROTECT YOU, TOO!
SO, PLEASE...!

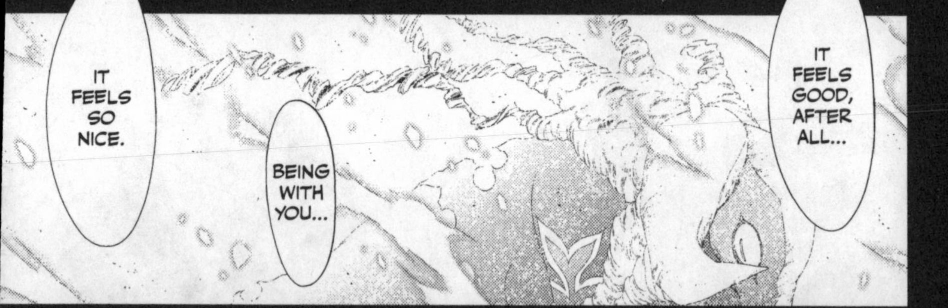
IT FEELS GOOD, AFTER ALL...
BEING WITH YOU...
IT FEELS SO NICE.

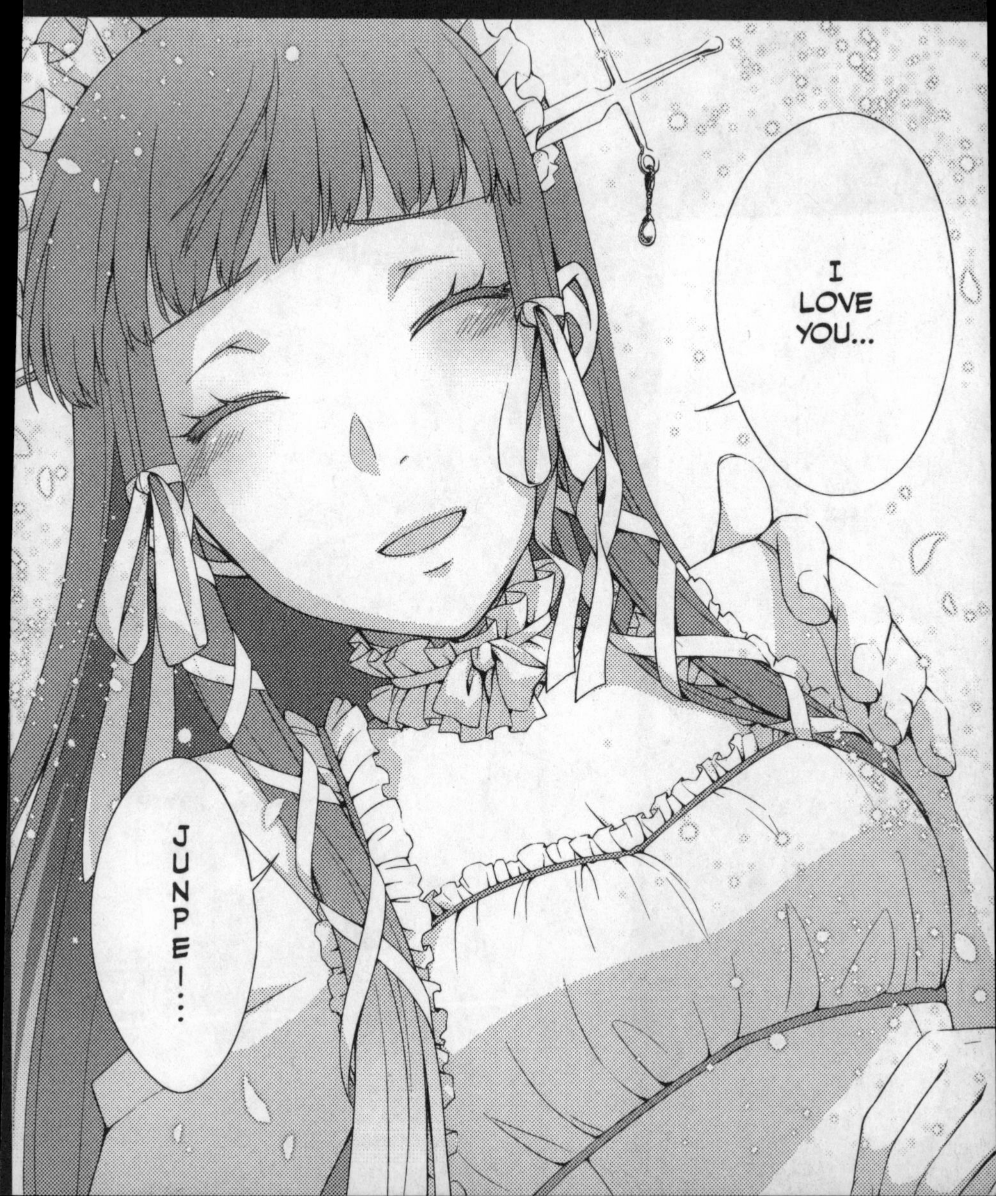
I LOVE YOU...
JUNPEI...

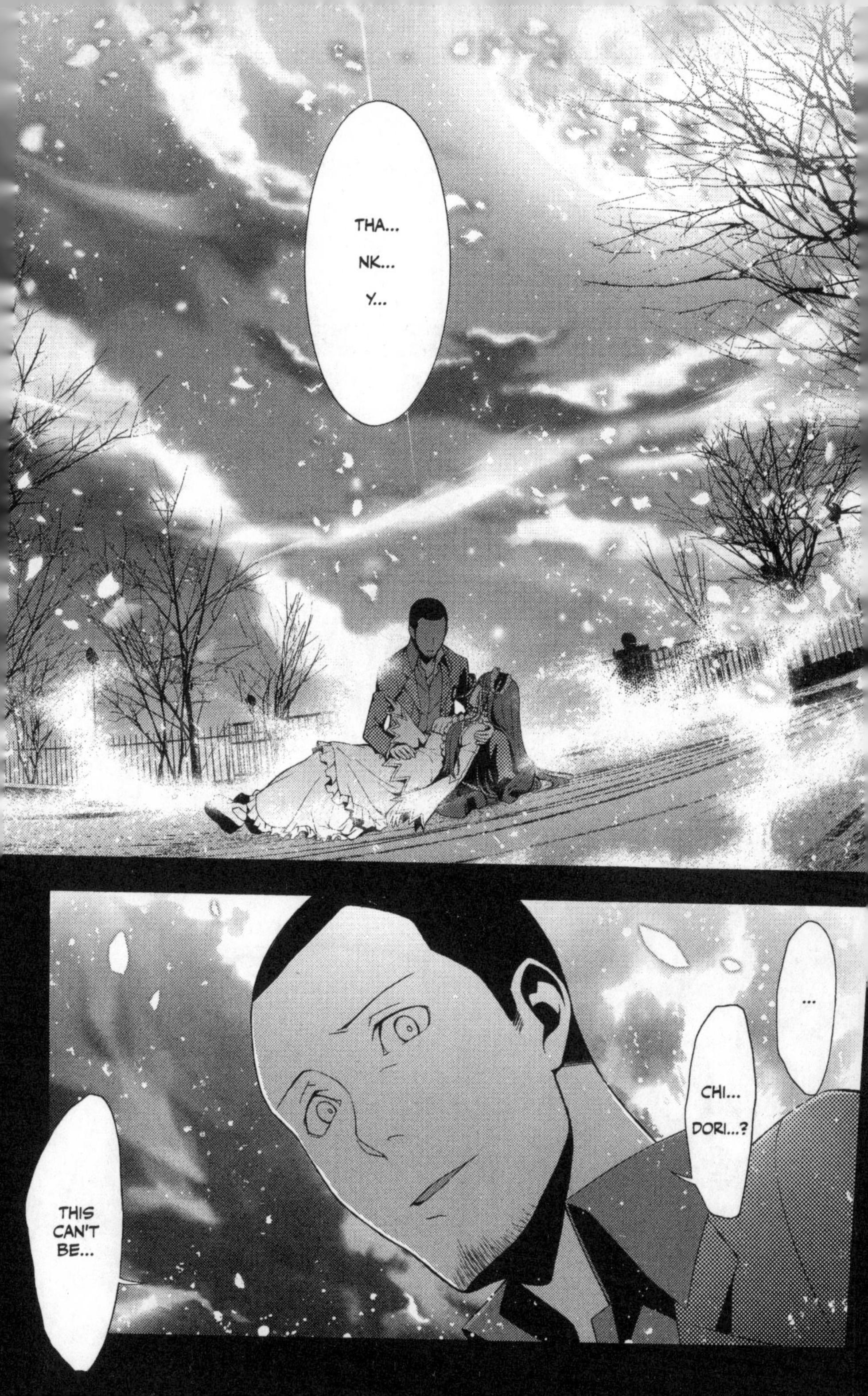
THA... NK... Y...
...
CHI... DORI...?
THIS CAN'T BE...

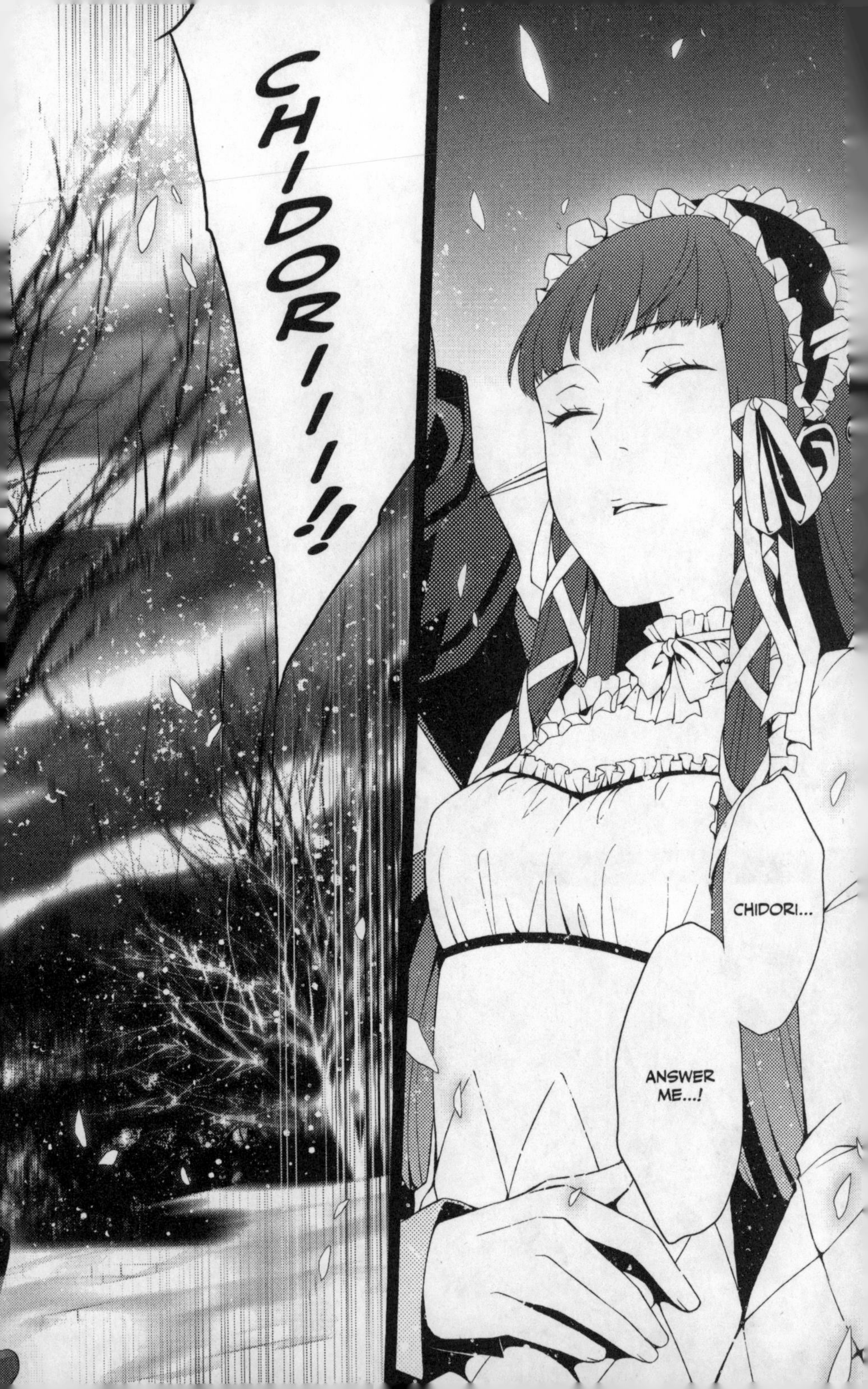
CHIDORIIII!!
CHIDORI...
ANSWER ME...!

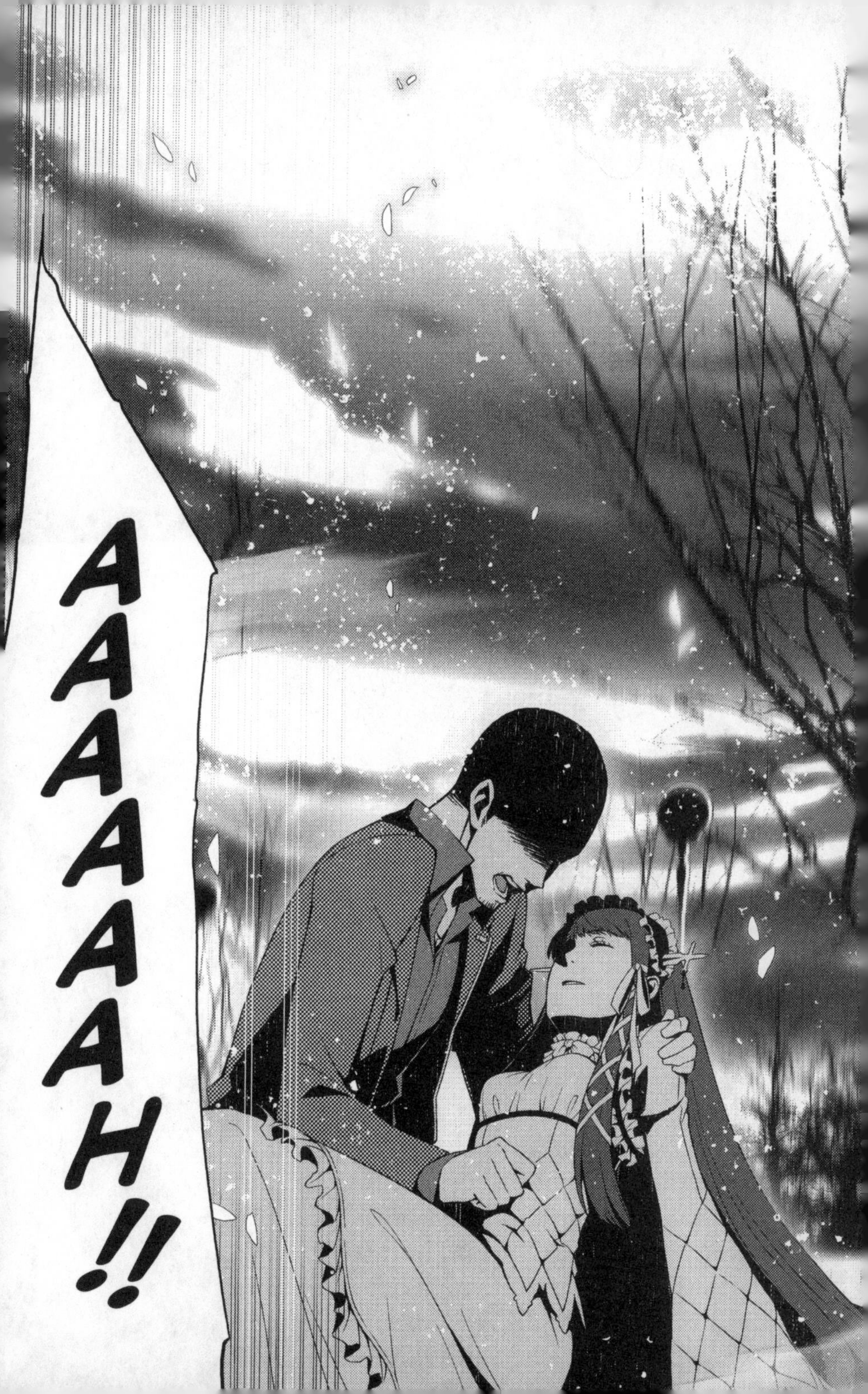
AAAAAAAH!!

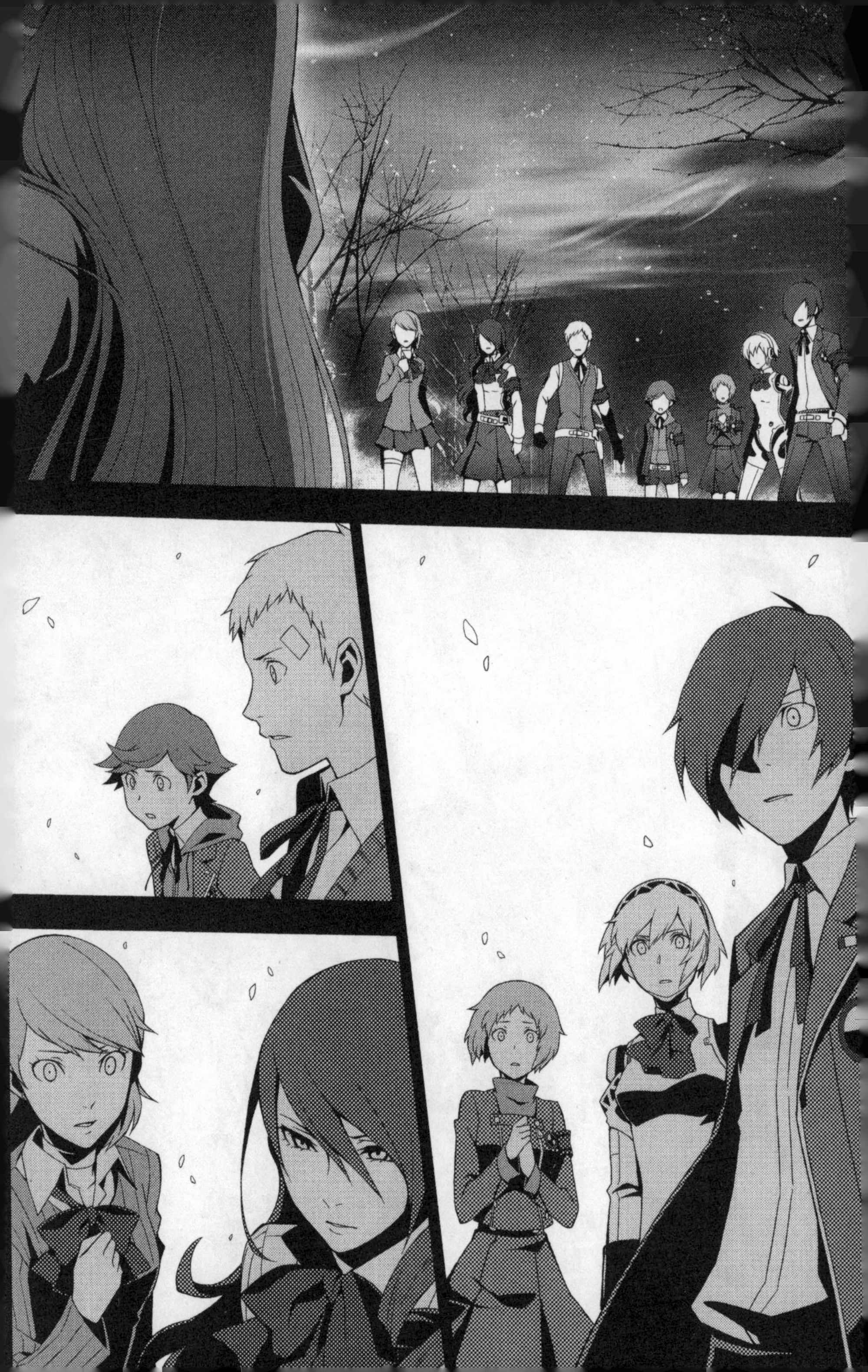

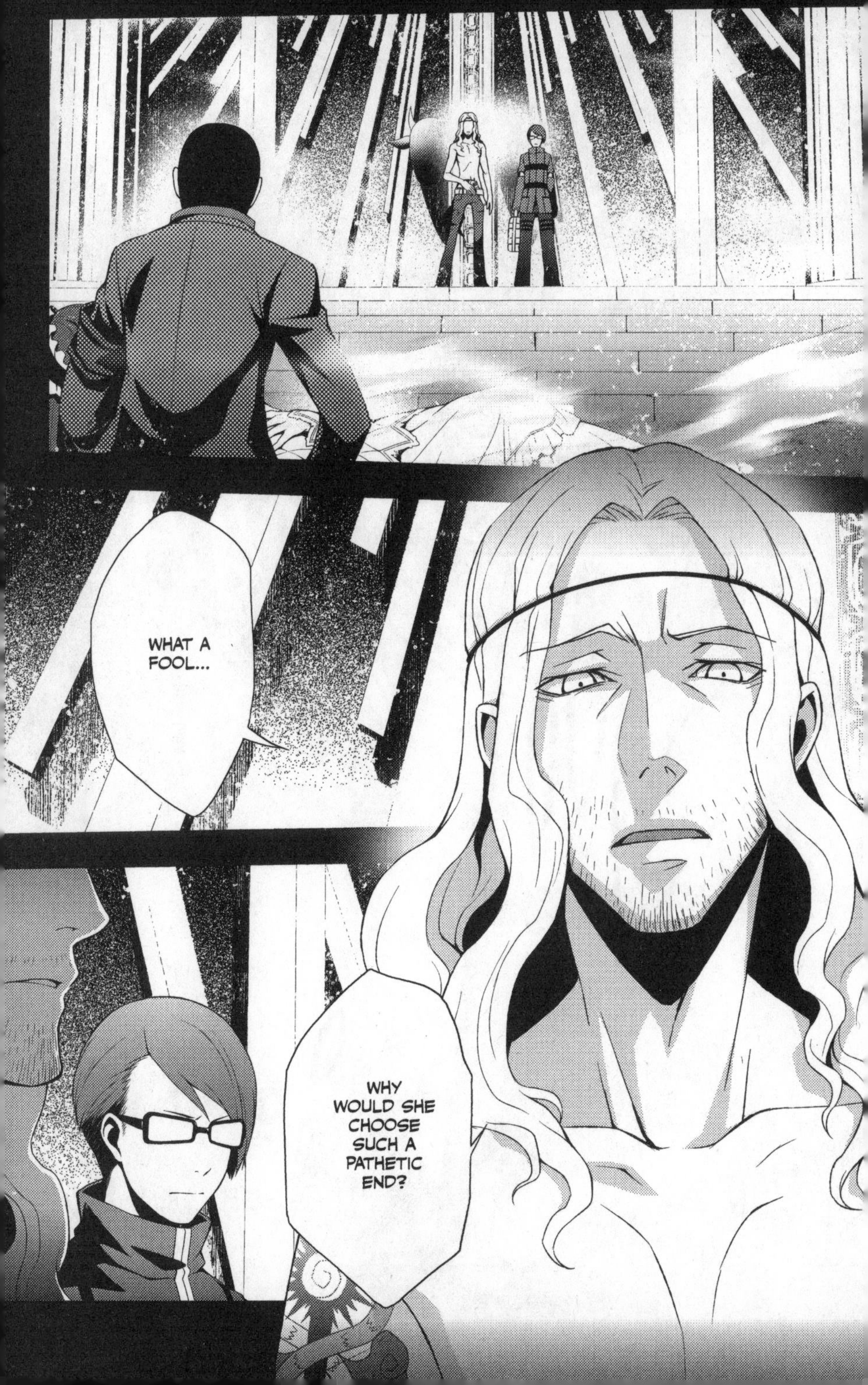
WHAT A FOOL...
WHY WOULD SHE CHOOSE SUCH A PATHETIC END?

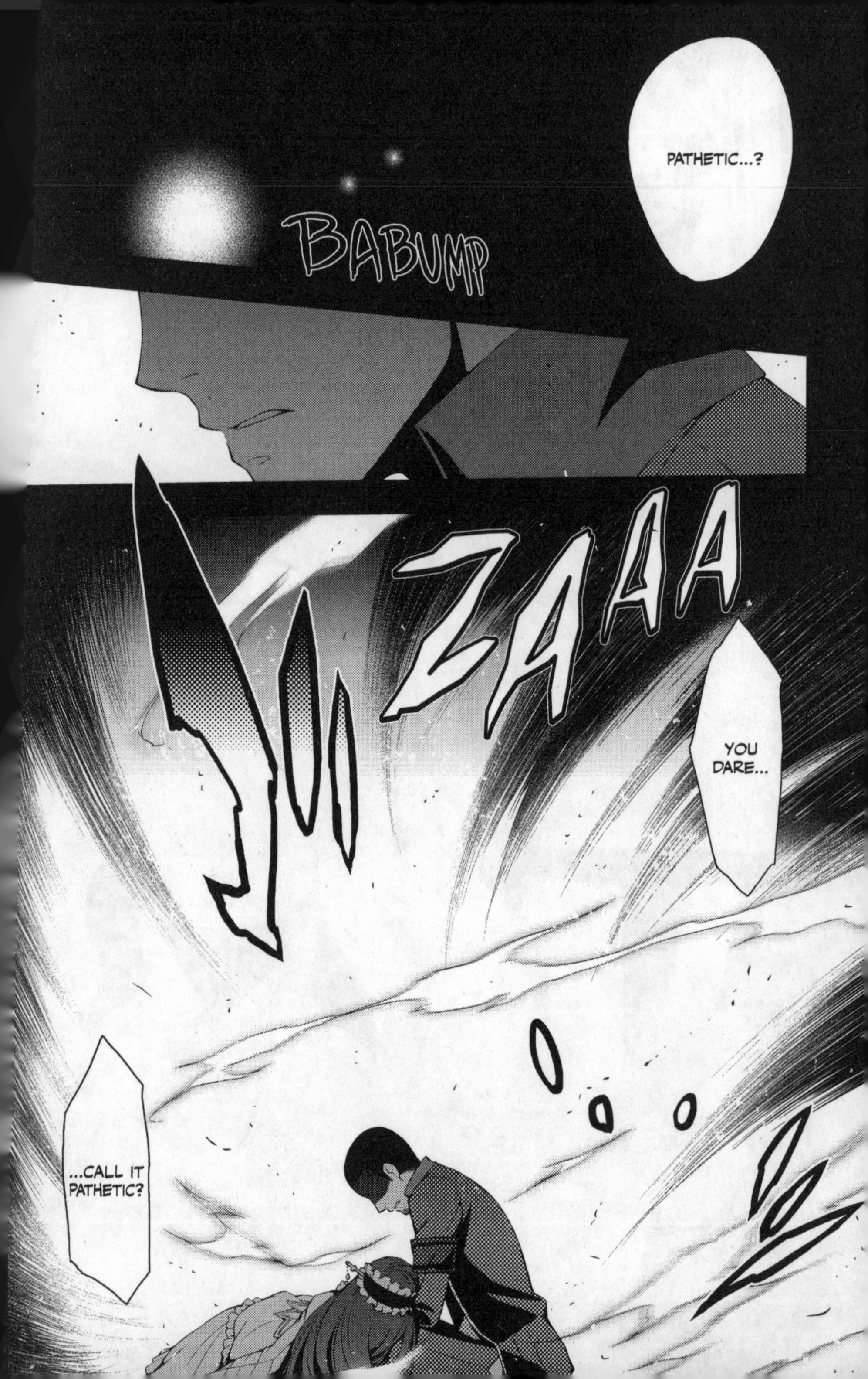
PATHETIC...?
BABUMP
ZAAA
YOU DARE...
...CALL IT PATHETIC?

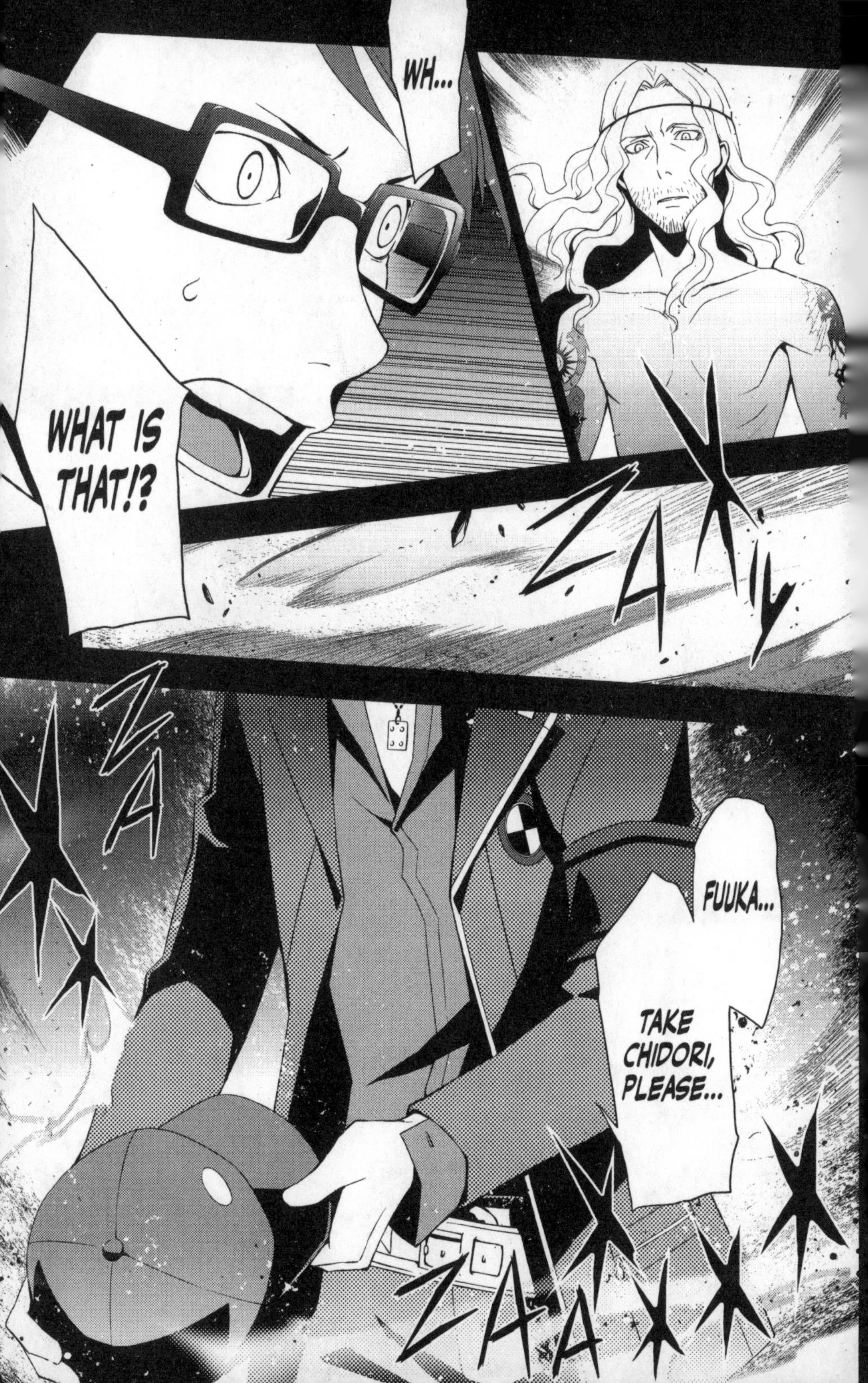
WH...
WHAT IS THAT!?
ZA
FUUKA...
TAKE CHIDORI, PLEASE...
ZA
ZA

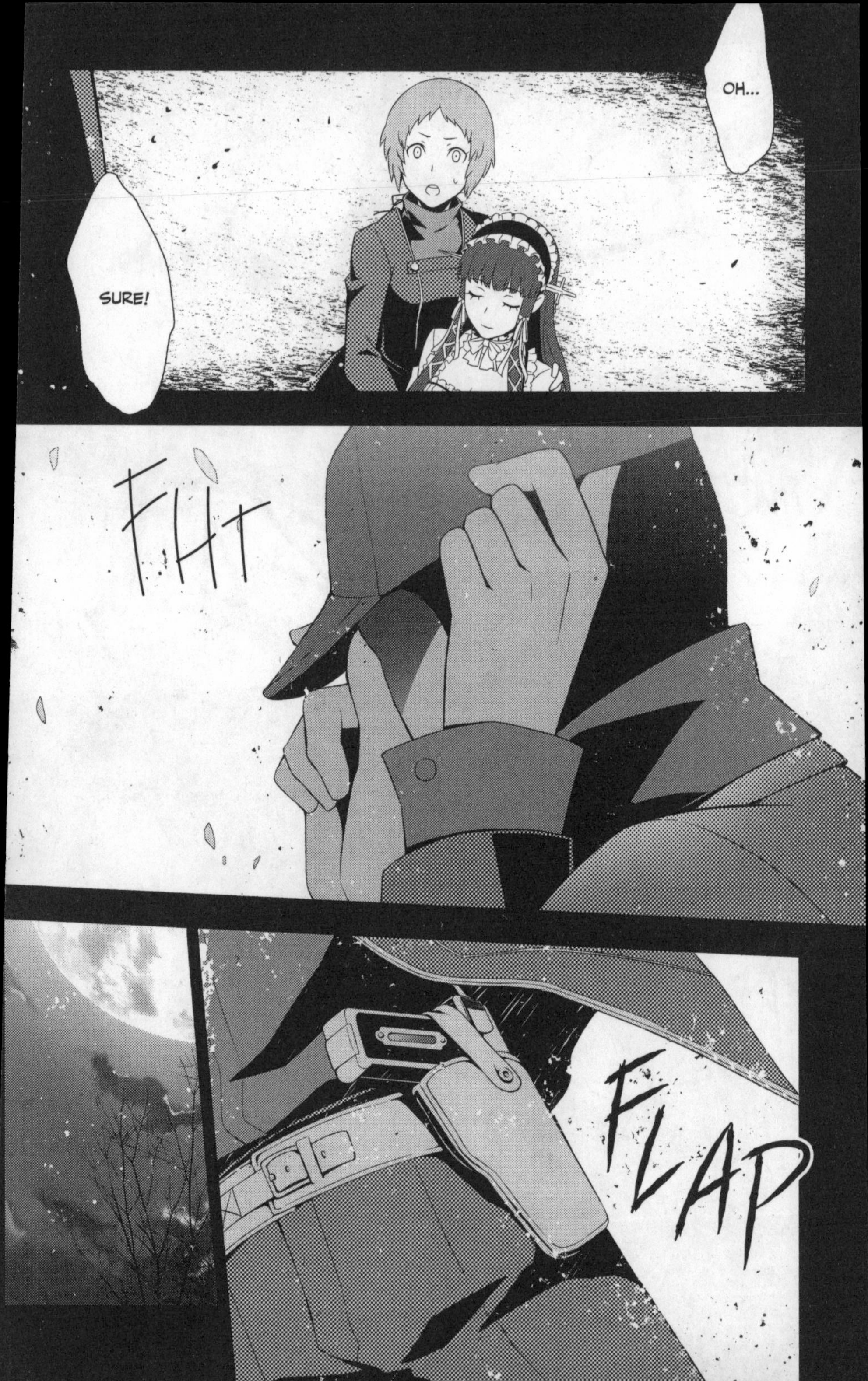
OH...
SURE!
FHT
FLAP

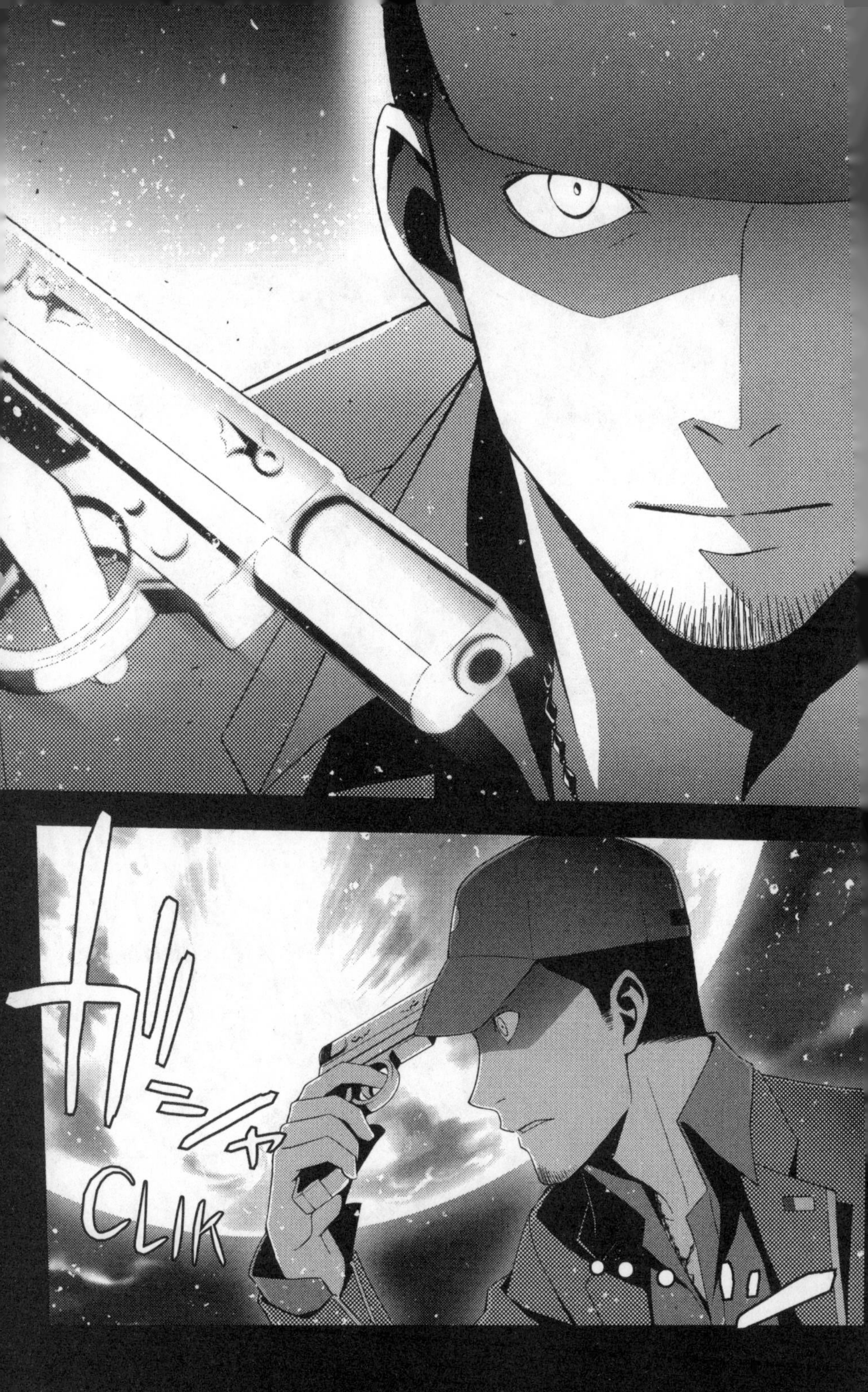
CLIK
....

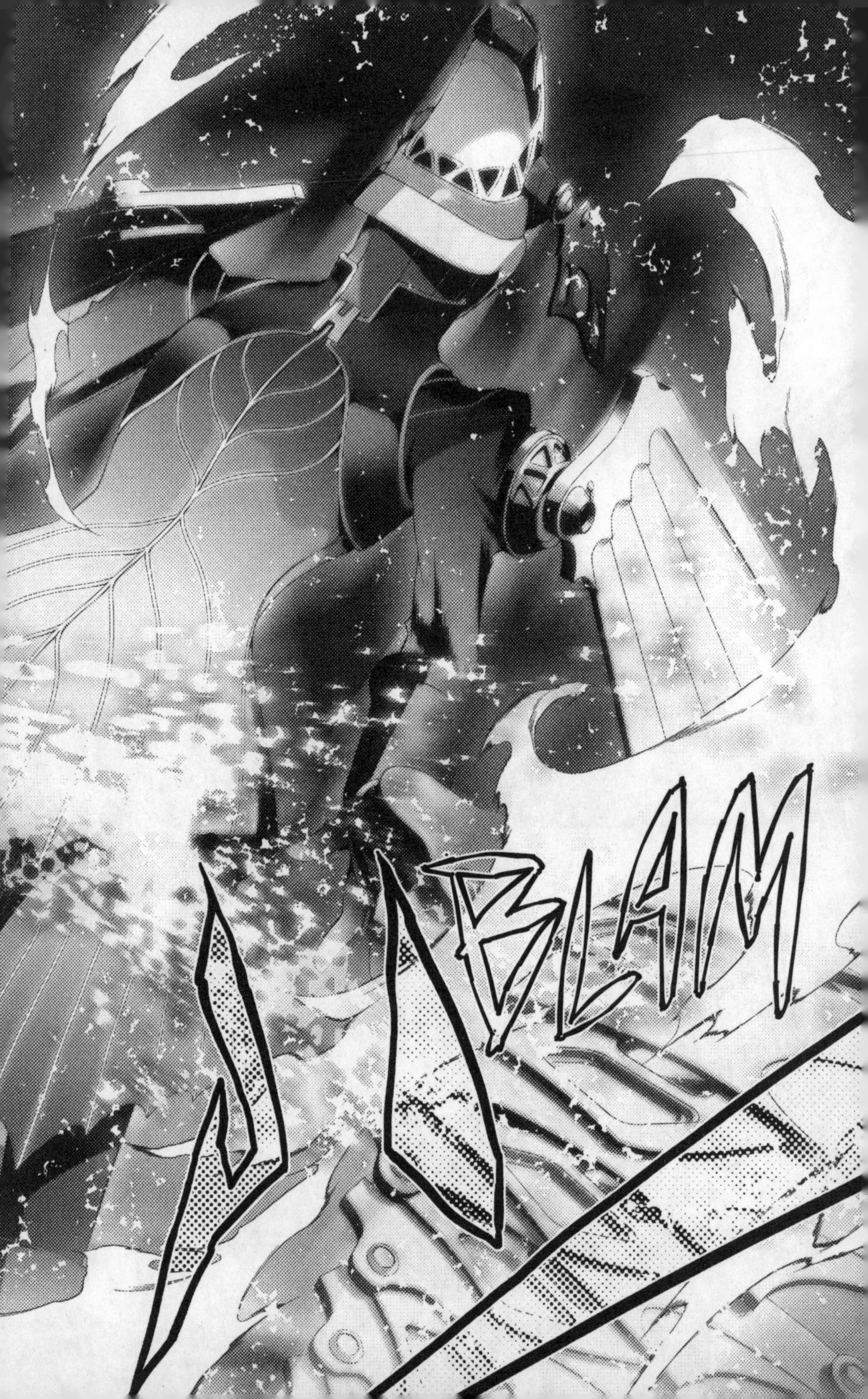
BLAM

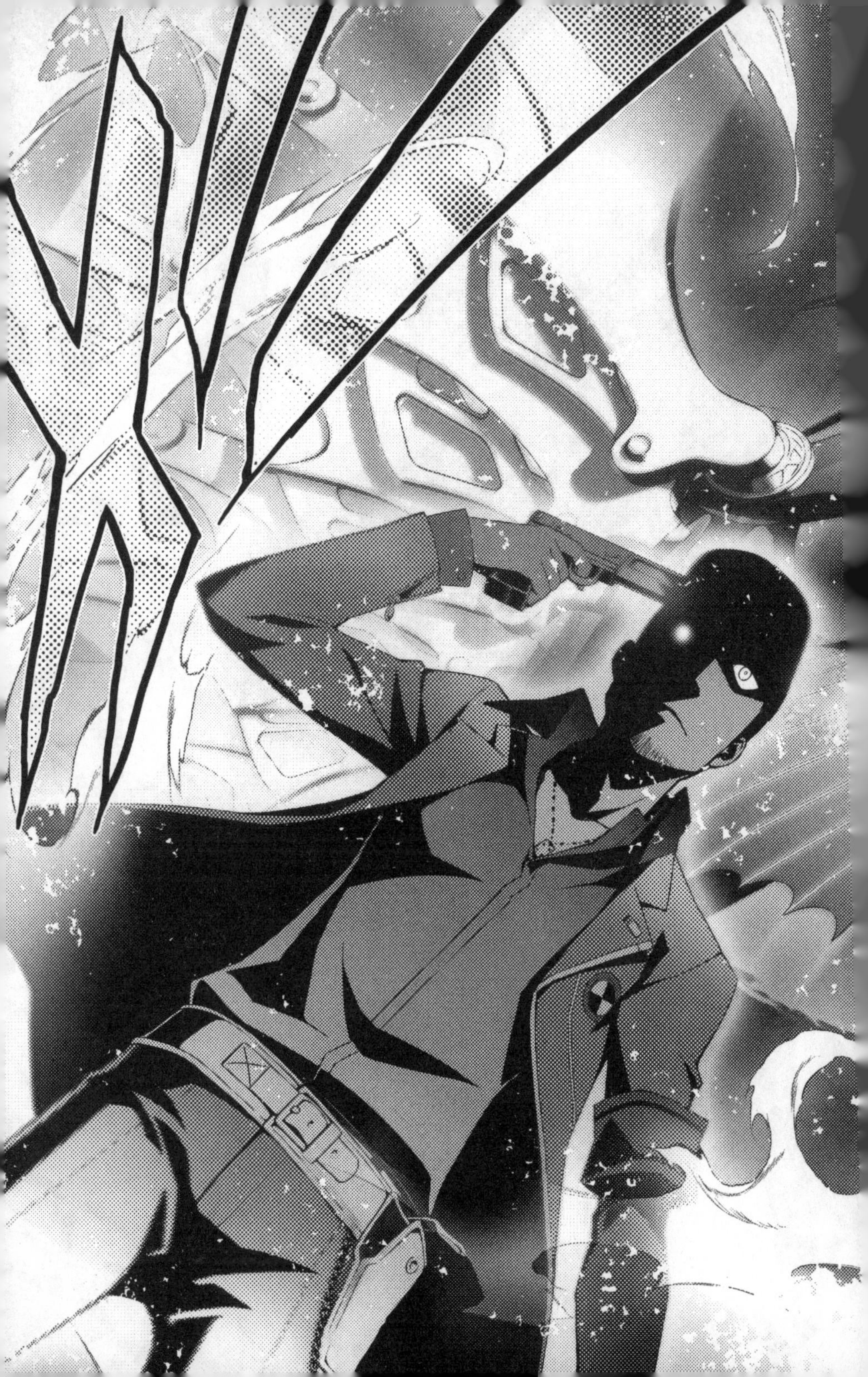

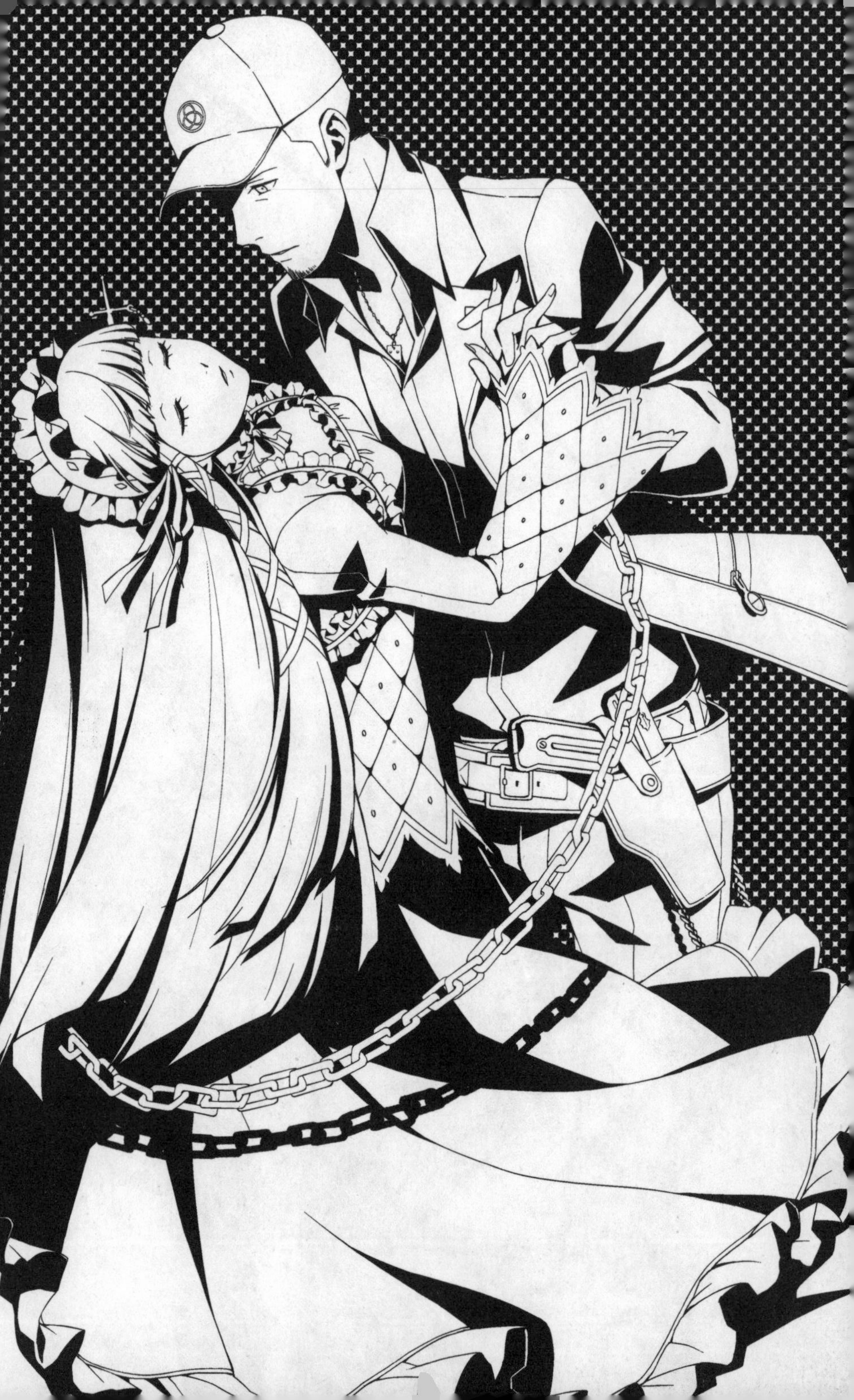

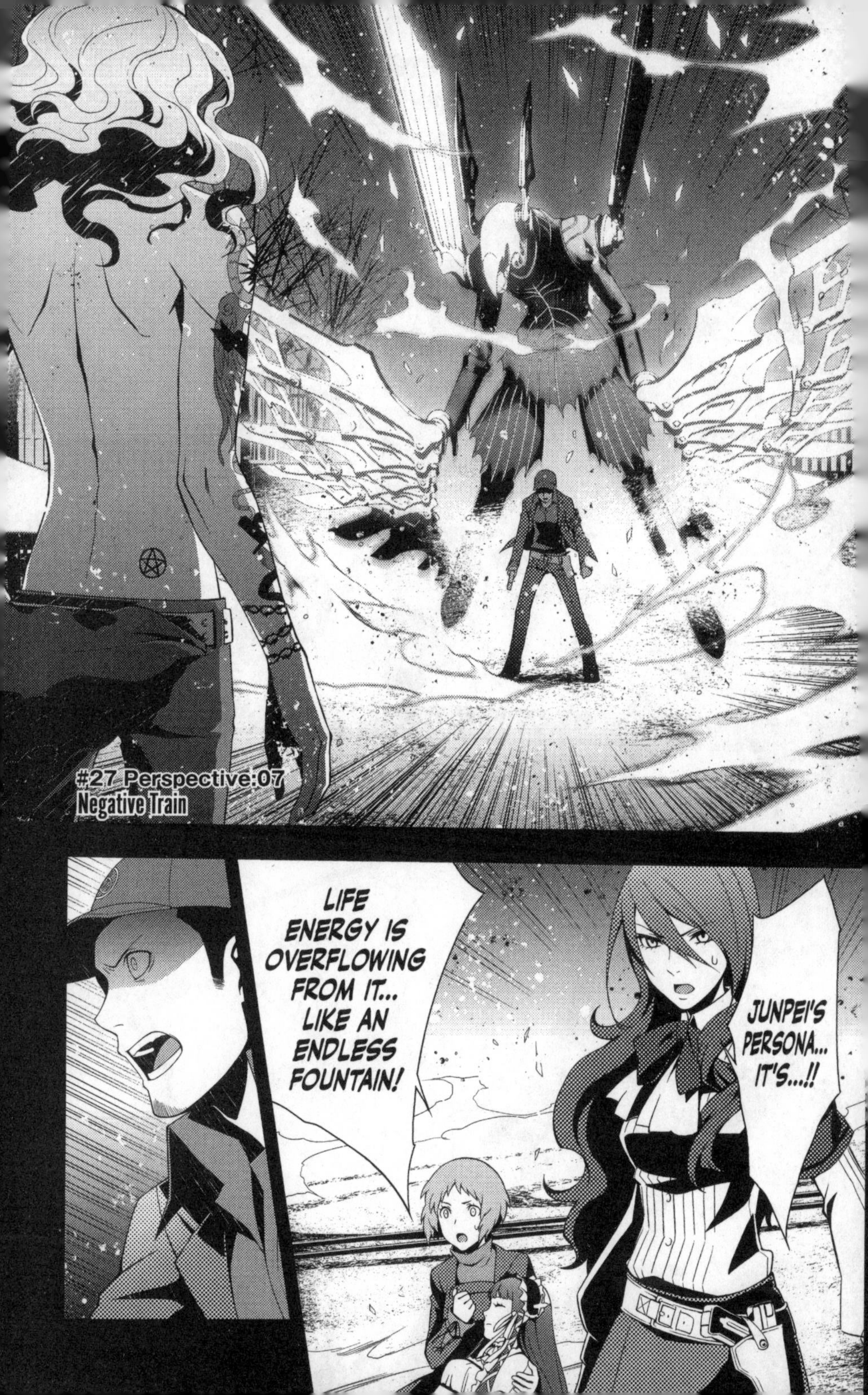
#27 Perspective:07
Negative Train
JUNPEI'S PERSONA... IT'S...!!
LIFE ENERGY IS OVERFLOWING FROM IT... LIKE AN ENDLESS FOUNTAIN!

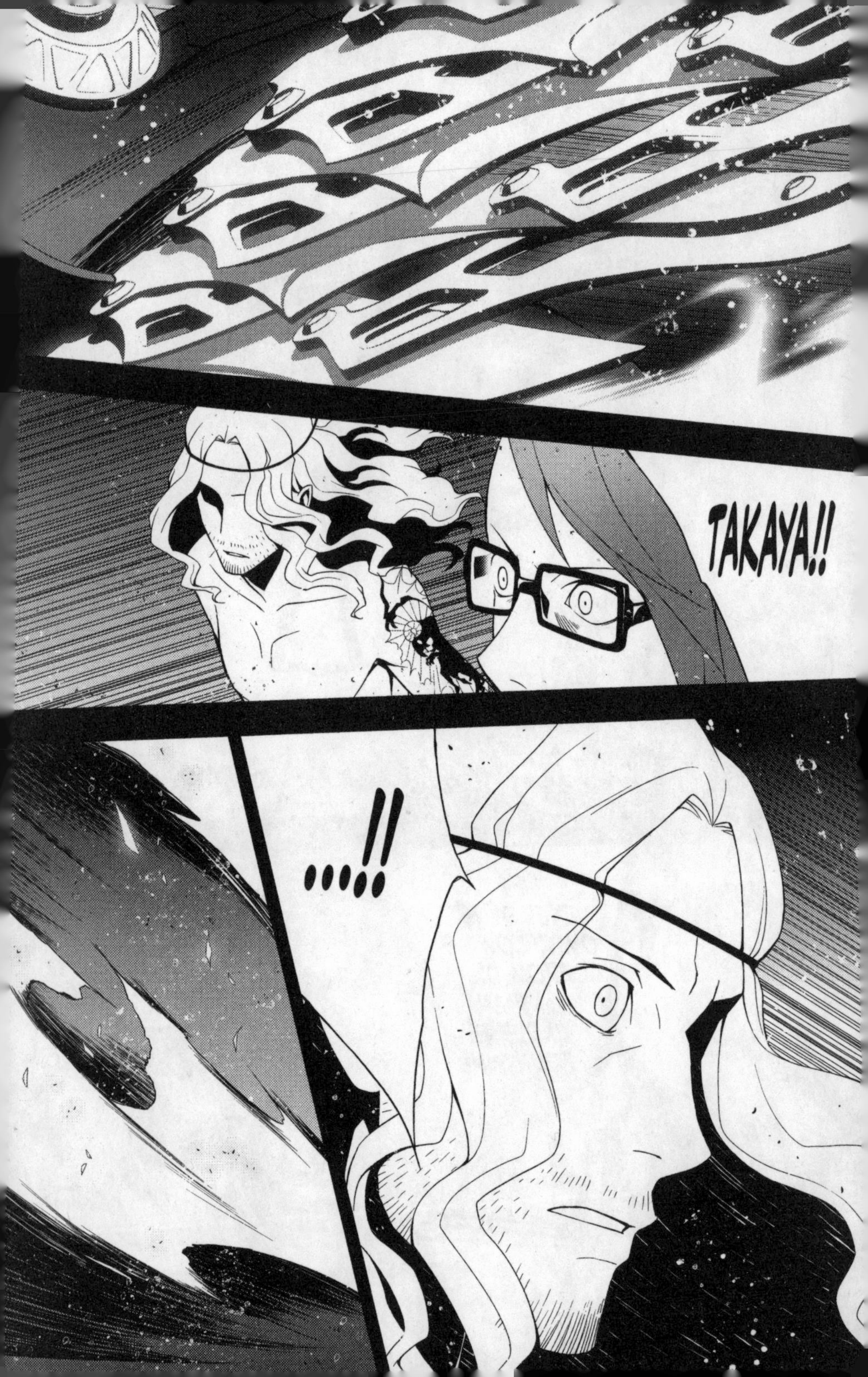
TAKAYA!!
....!!

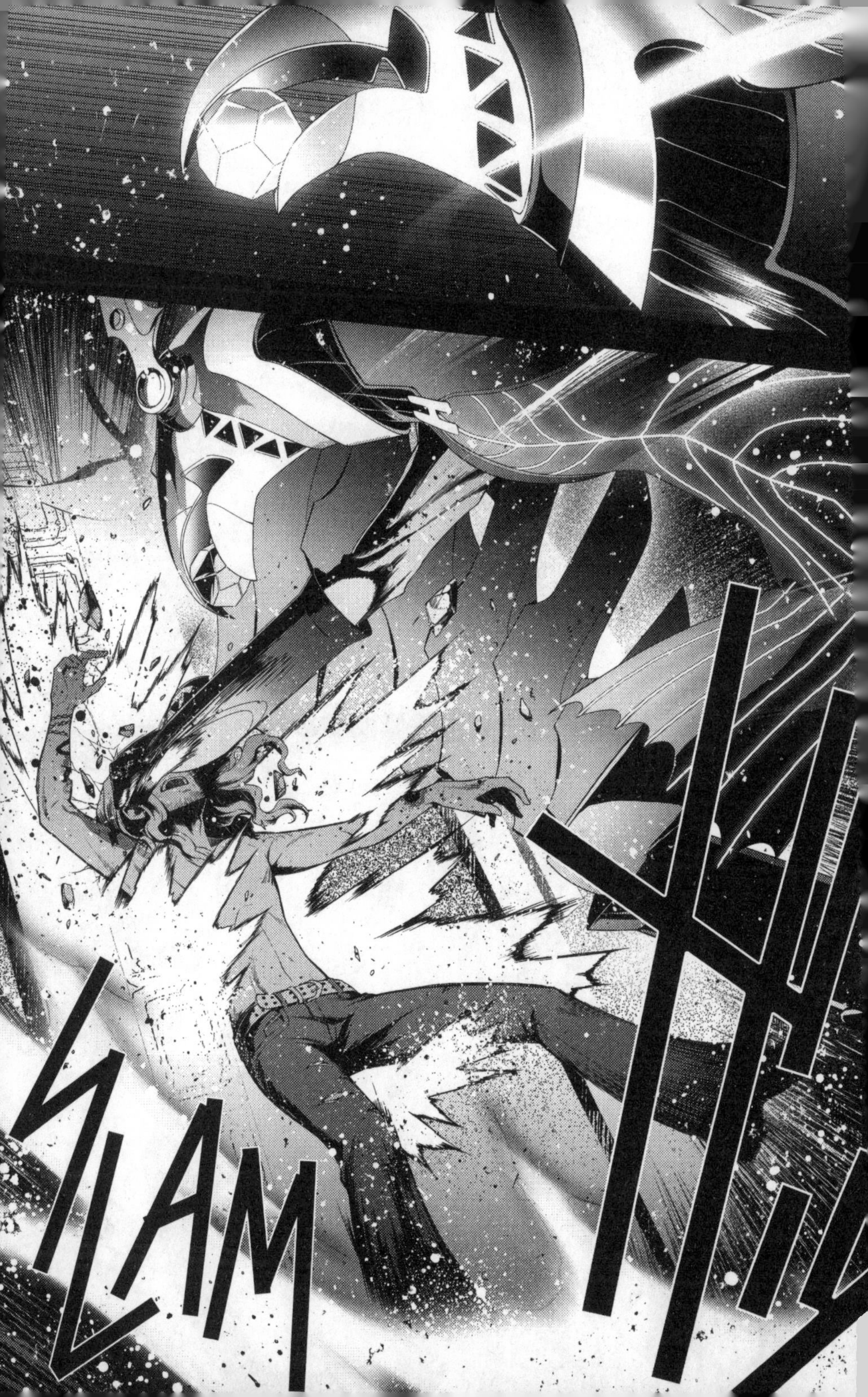
SLAM

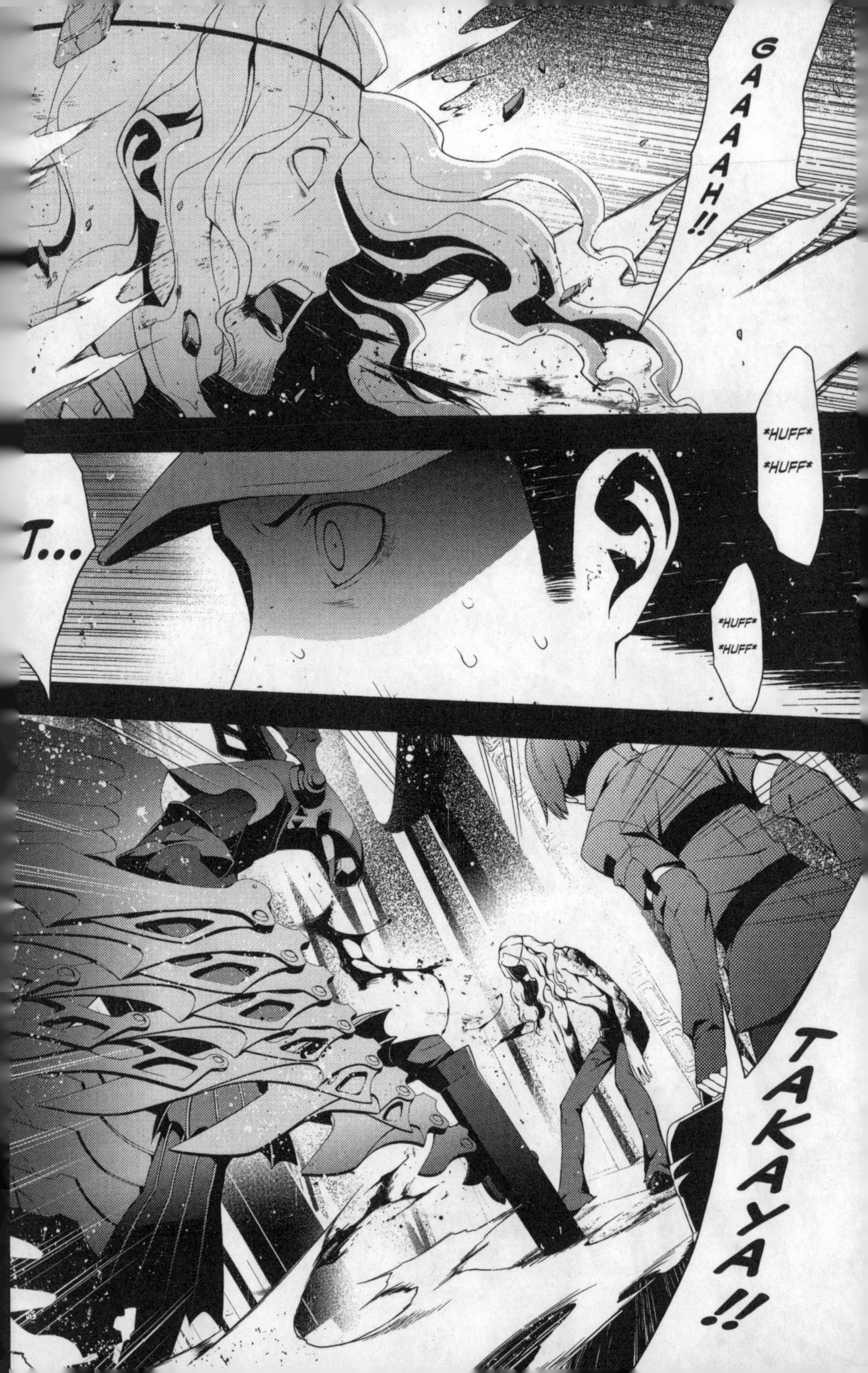
GAAAAH!!
HUFF *HUFF*
HUFF *HUFF*
T...
TAKAYA!!

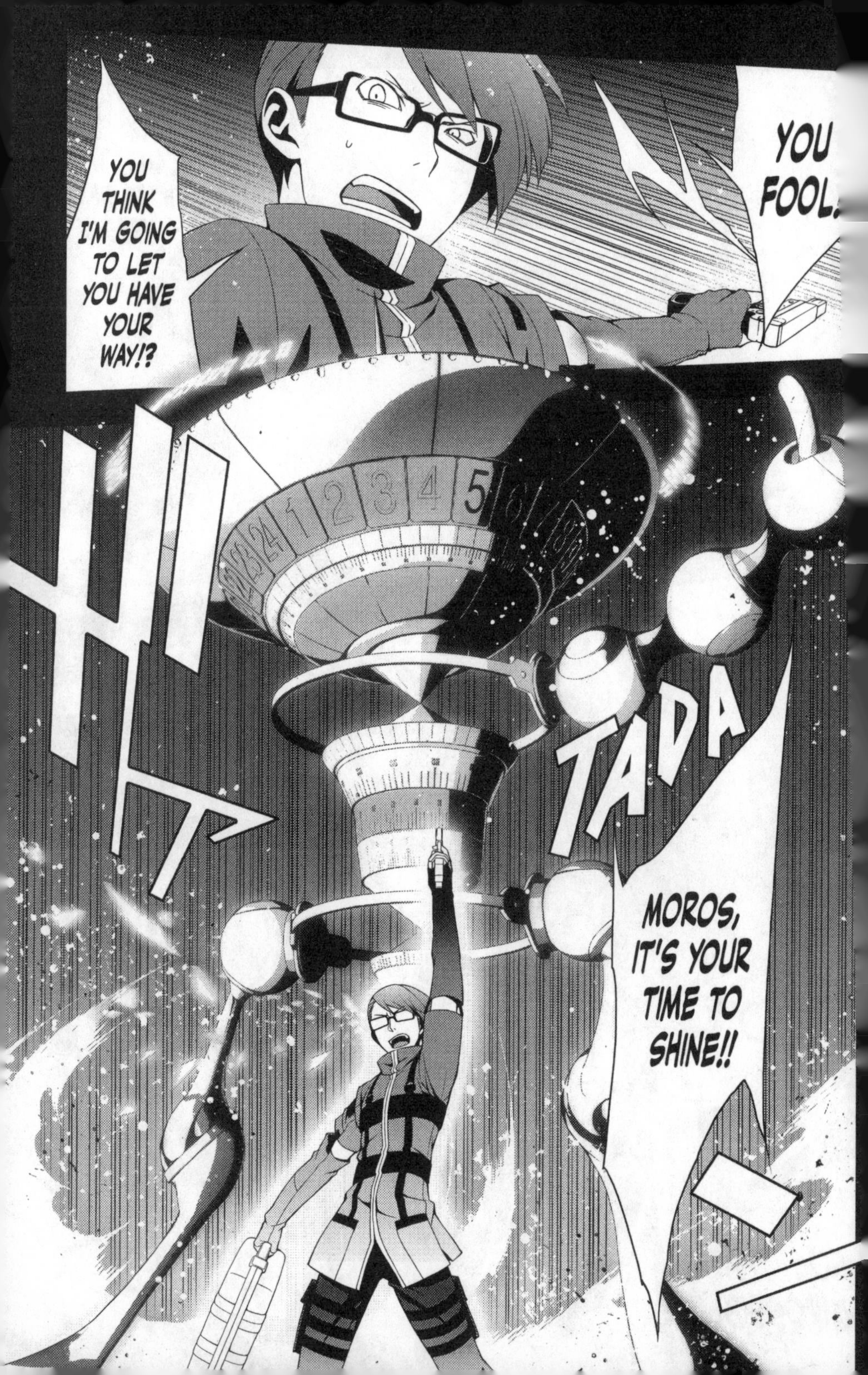
YOU FOOL.
YOU THINK I'M GOING TO LET YOU HAVE YOUR WAY!?
TADA
HIT
MOROS, IT'S YOUR TIME TO SHINE!!

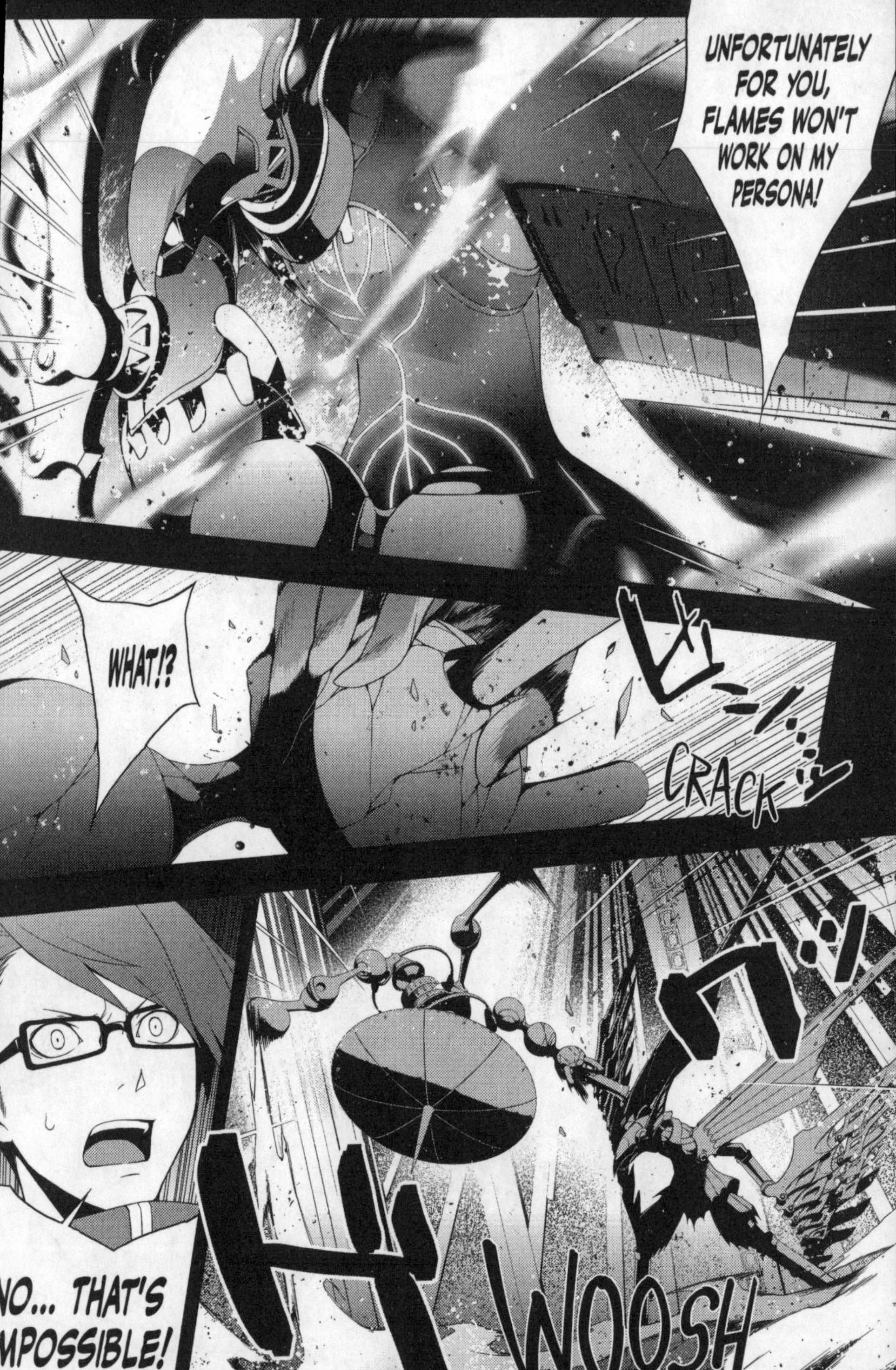
UNFORTUNATELY FOR YOU, FLAMES WON'T WORK ON MY PERSONA!
CRACK
WHAT!?
WOOSH
NO... THAT'S IMPOSSIBLE!

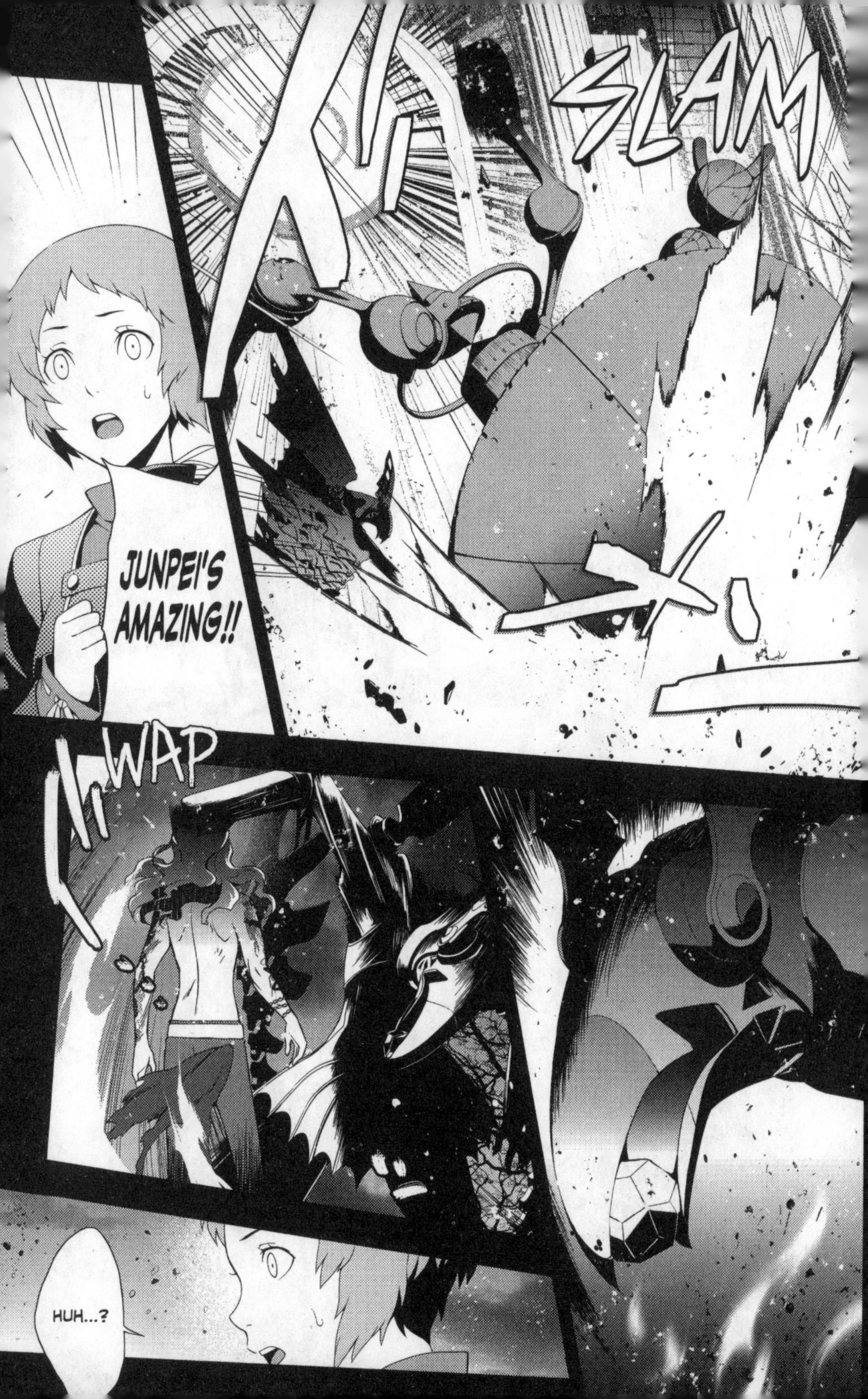
SLAM
JUNPEI'S AMAZING!!
WAP
HUH...?

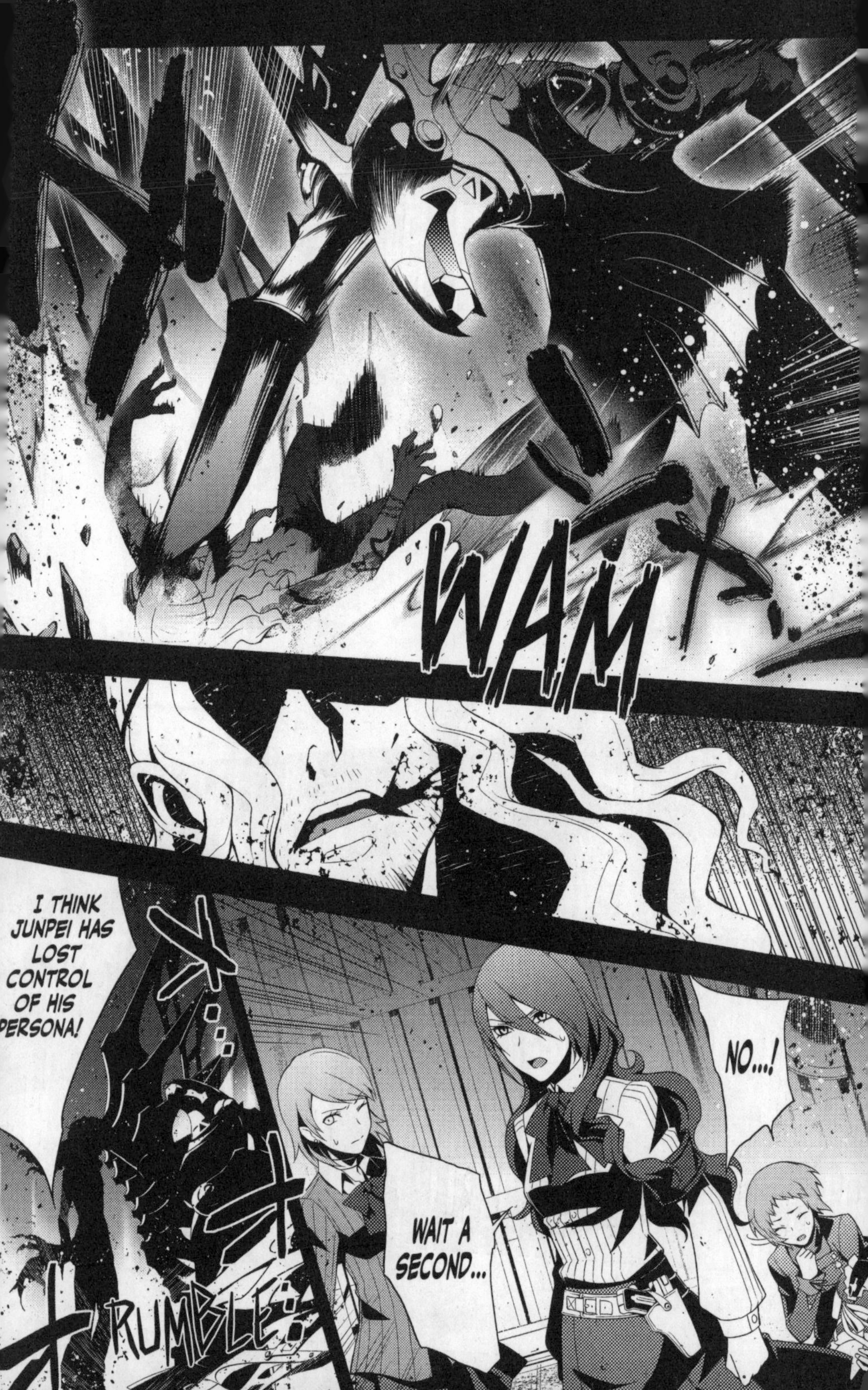
WAM
NO...!
I THINK JUNPEI HAS LOST CONTROL OF HIS PERSONA!
...
WAIT A SECOND...
RUMBLE

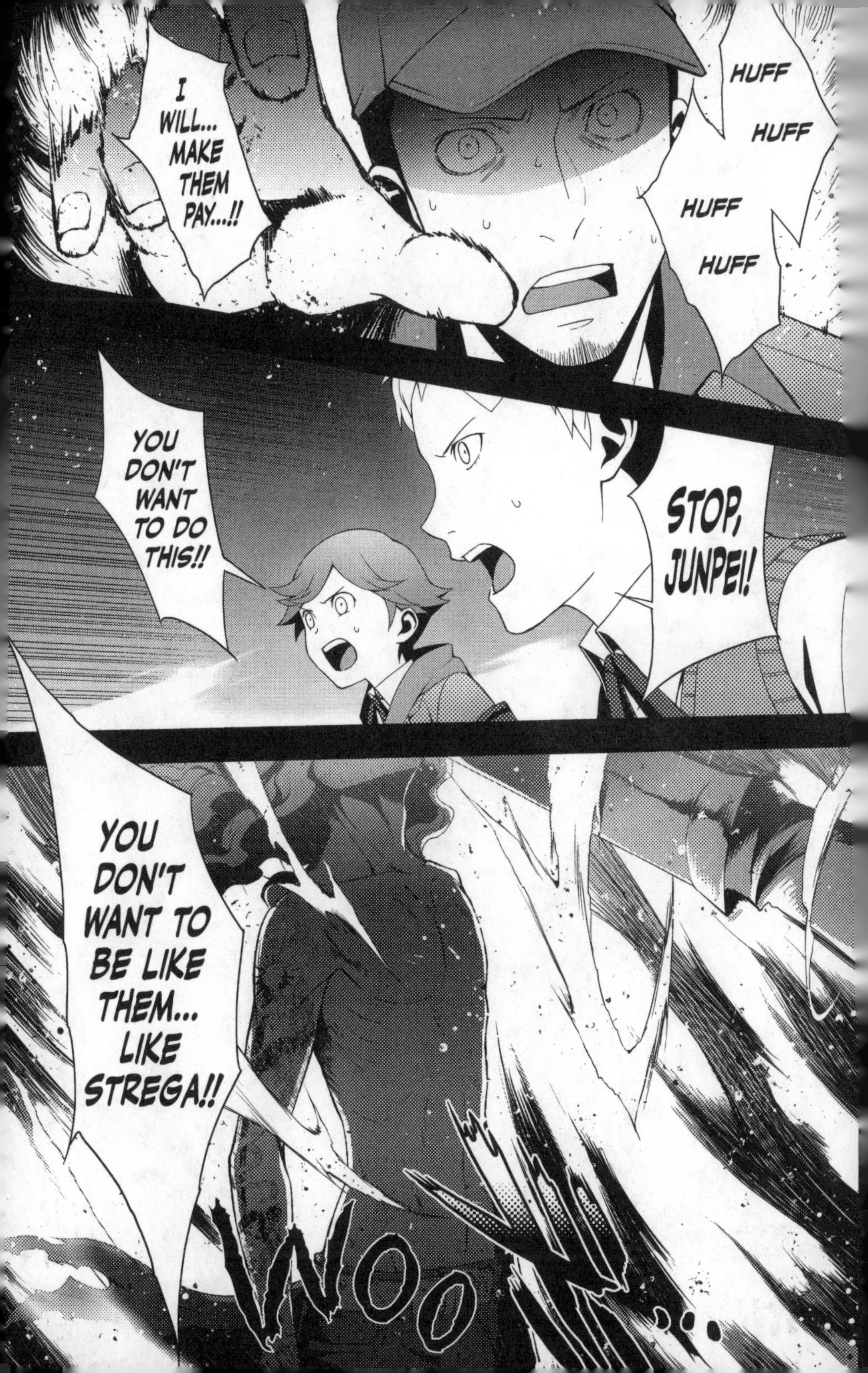
HUFF
HUFF
HUFF
HUFF
I WILL... MAKE THEM PAY...!!
STOP, JUNPEI!
YOU DON'T WANT TO DO THIS!!
YOU DON'T WANT TO BE LIKE THEM... LIKE STREGA!!
WOO...

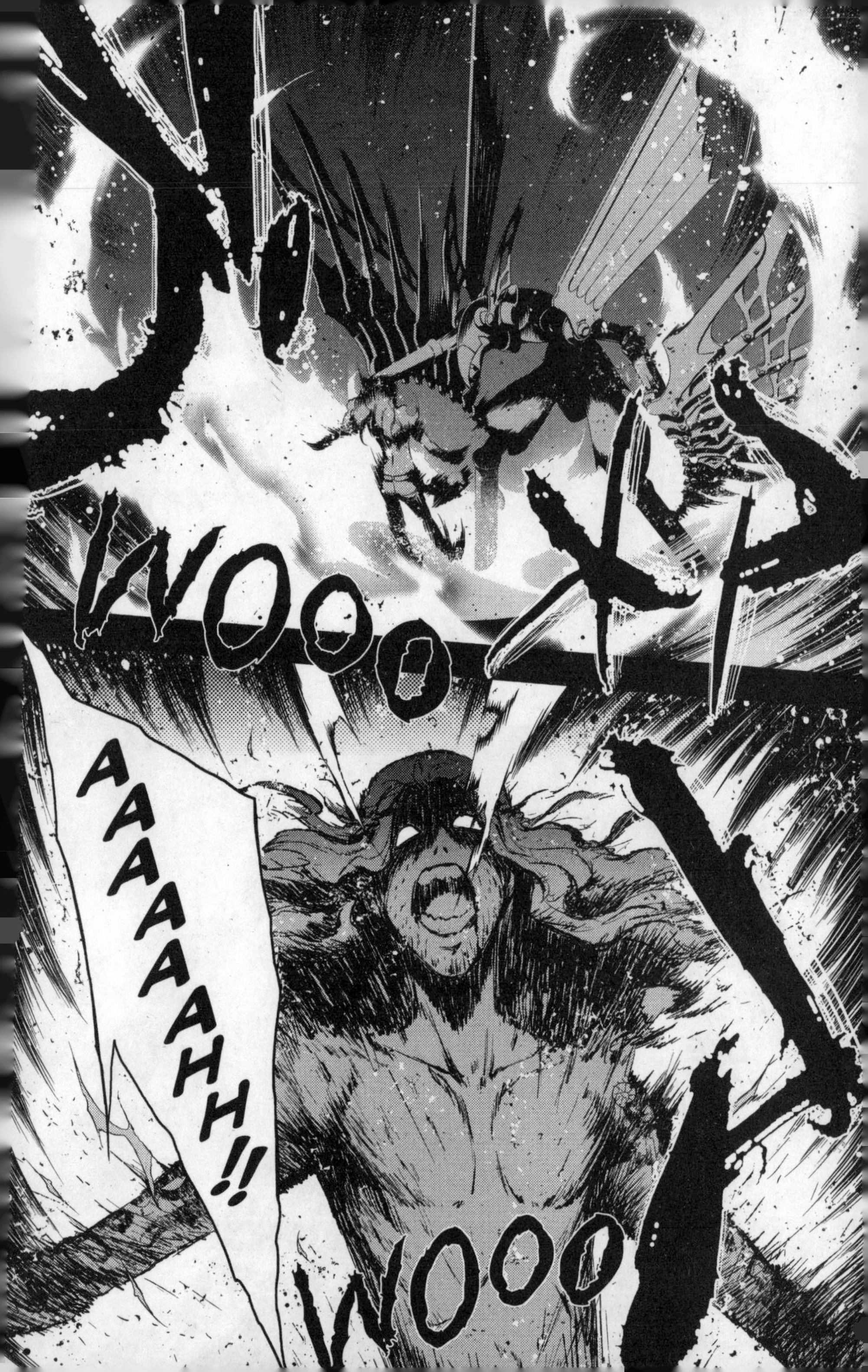
WOOO
AAAAAAHH!!
WOOO

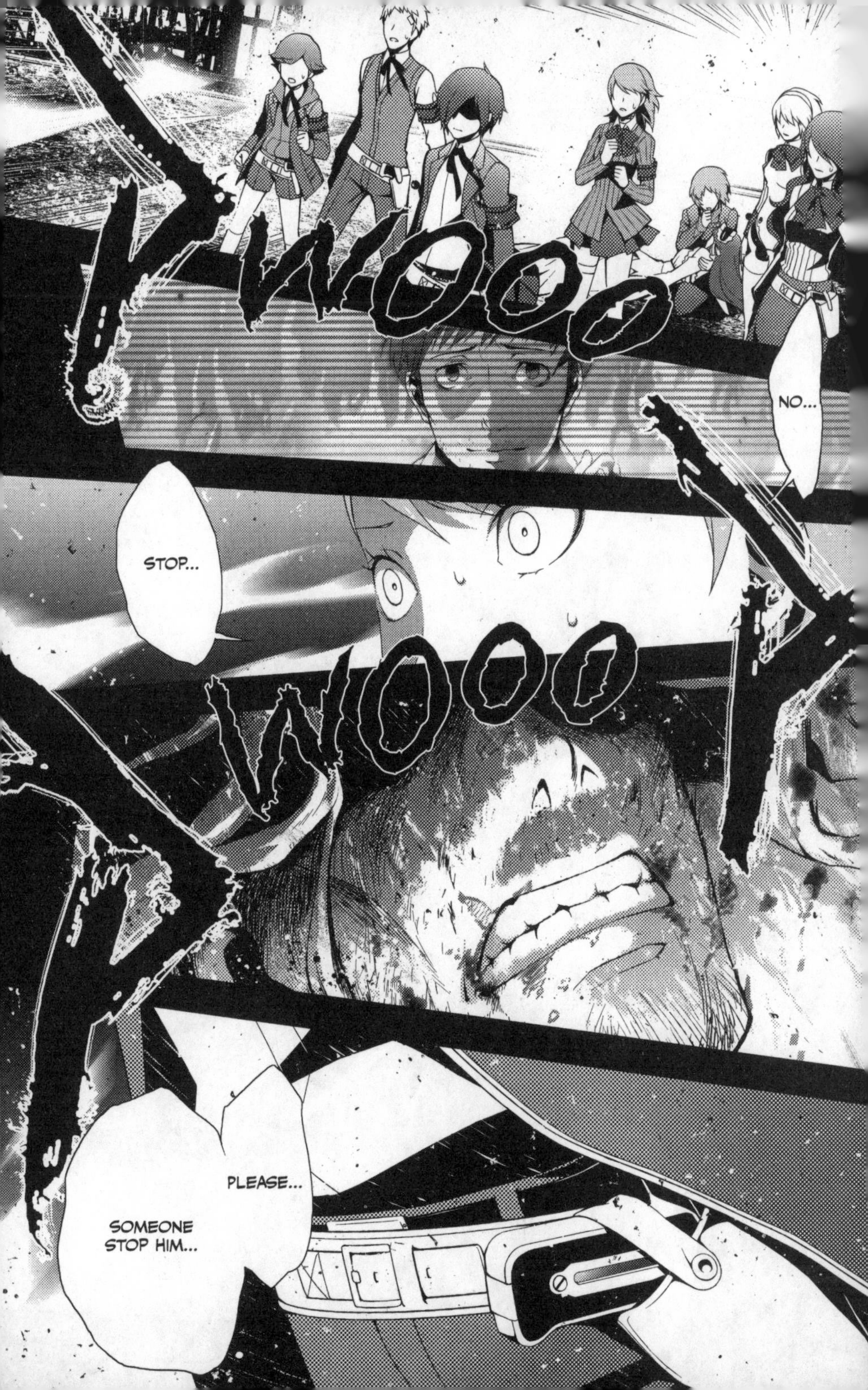
WOOOO
NO...
STOP...
WOOO
PLEASE...
SOMEONE STOP HIM...

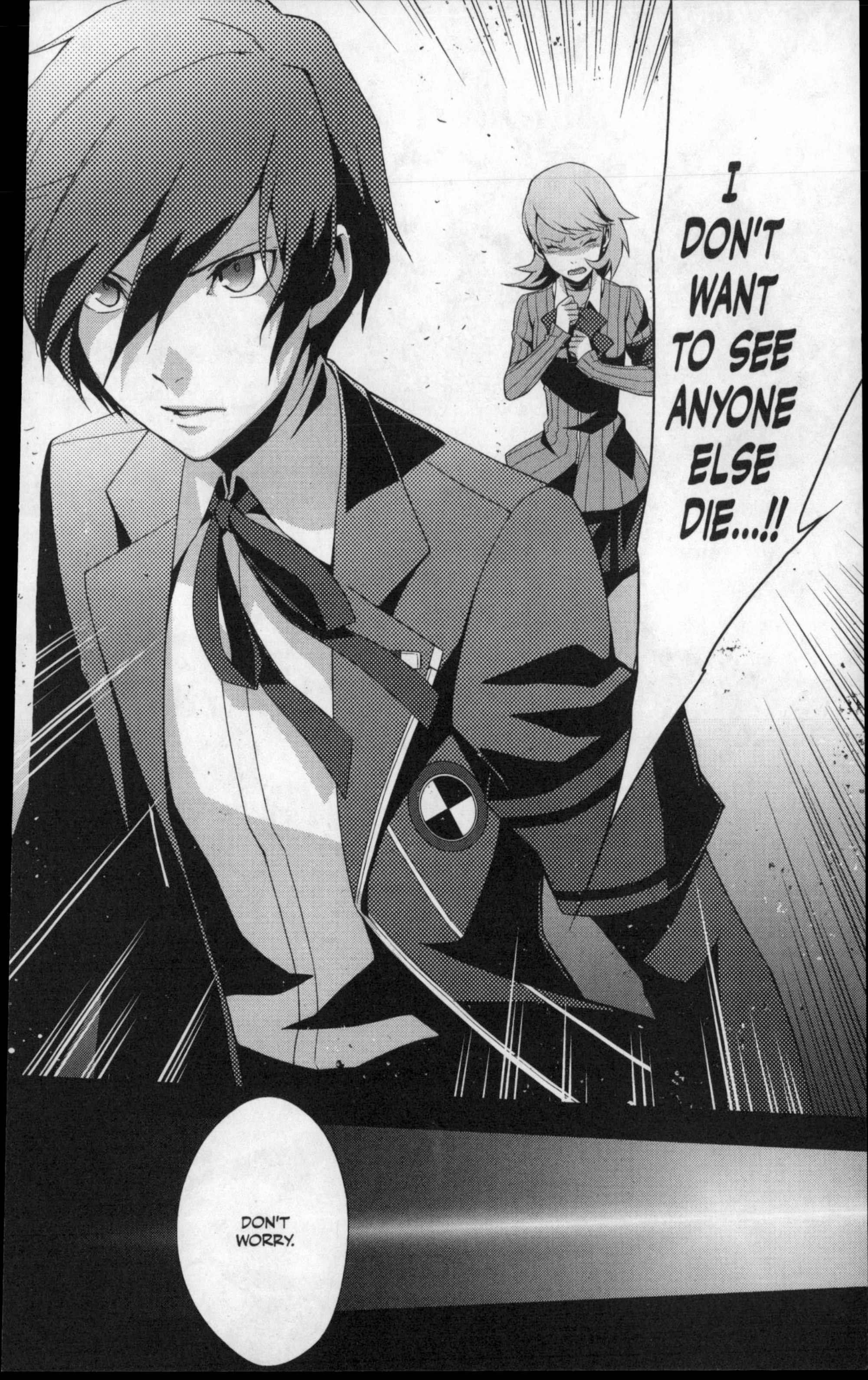
I DON'T WANT TO SEE ANYONE ELSE DIE...!!
DON'T WORRY.

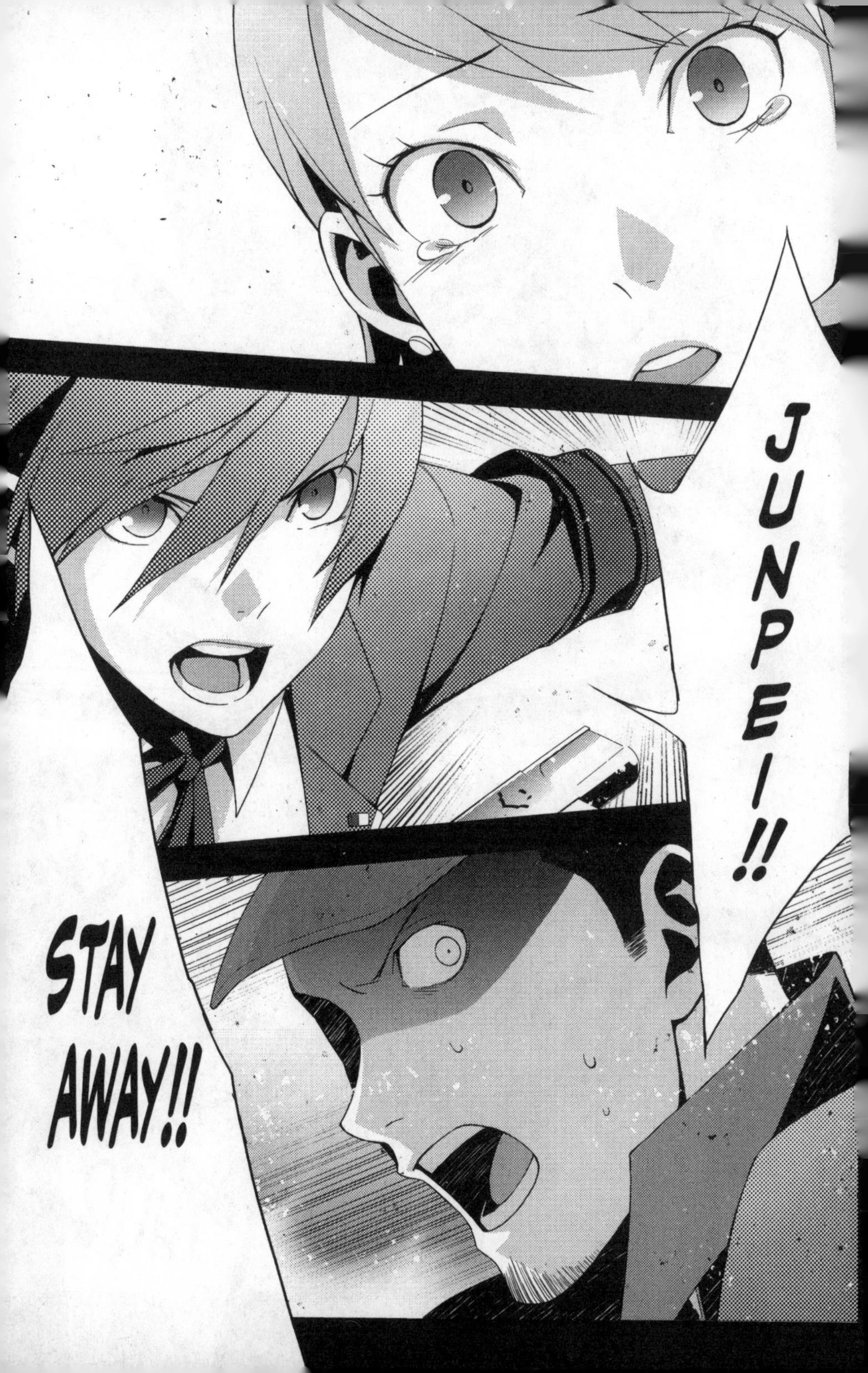
JUNPEI!!
STAY AWAY!!

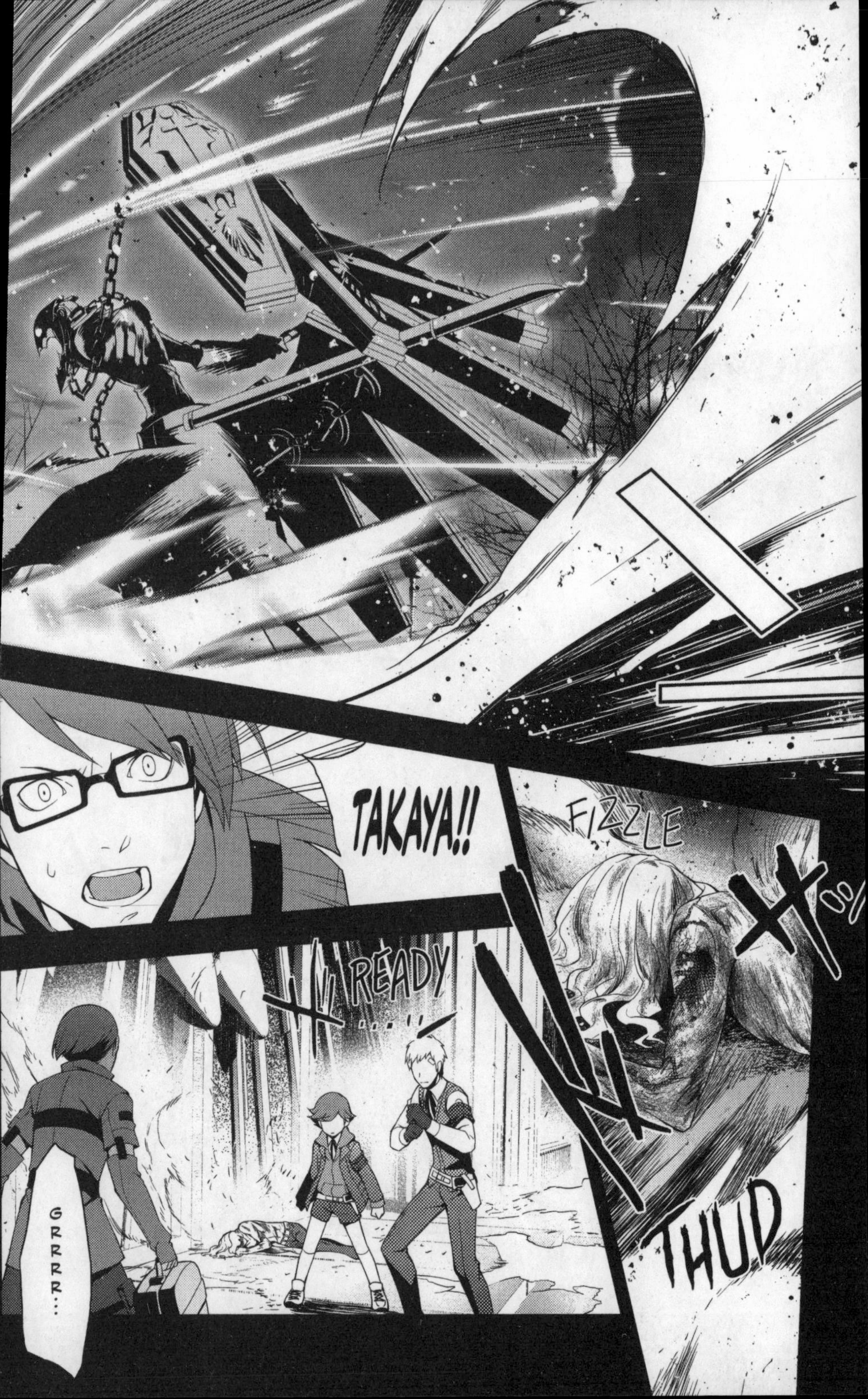
FIZZLE
THUD
TAKAYA!!
READY
GRRRR...

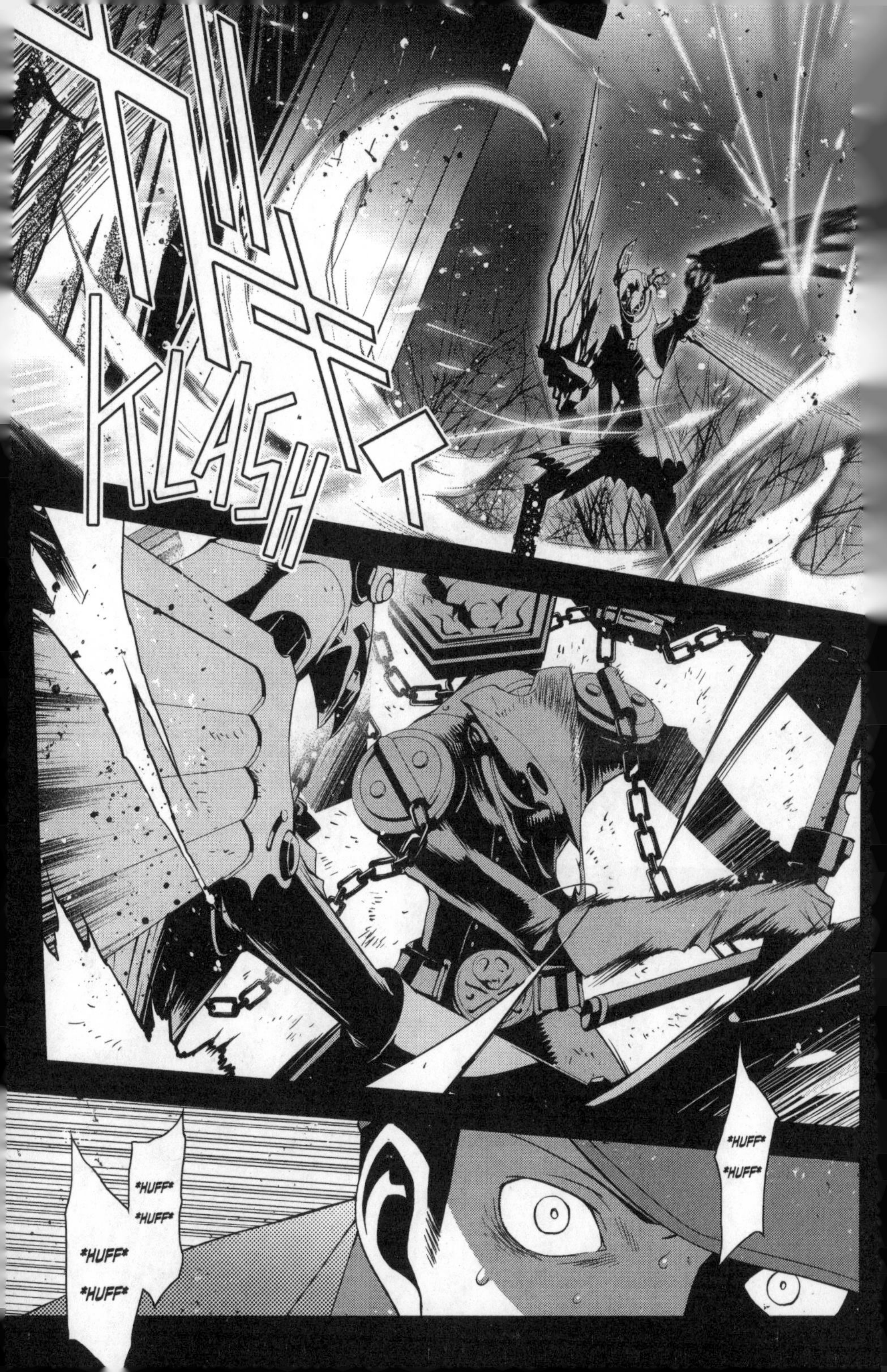
KLASH
HUFF
HUFF
HUFF
HUFF
HUFF
HUFF

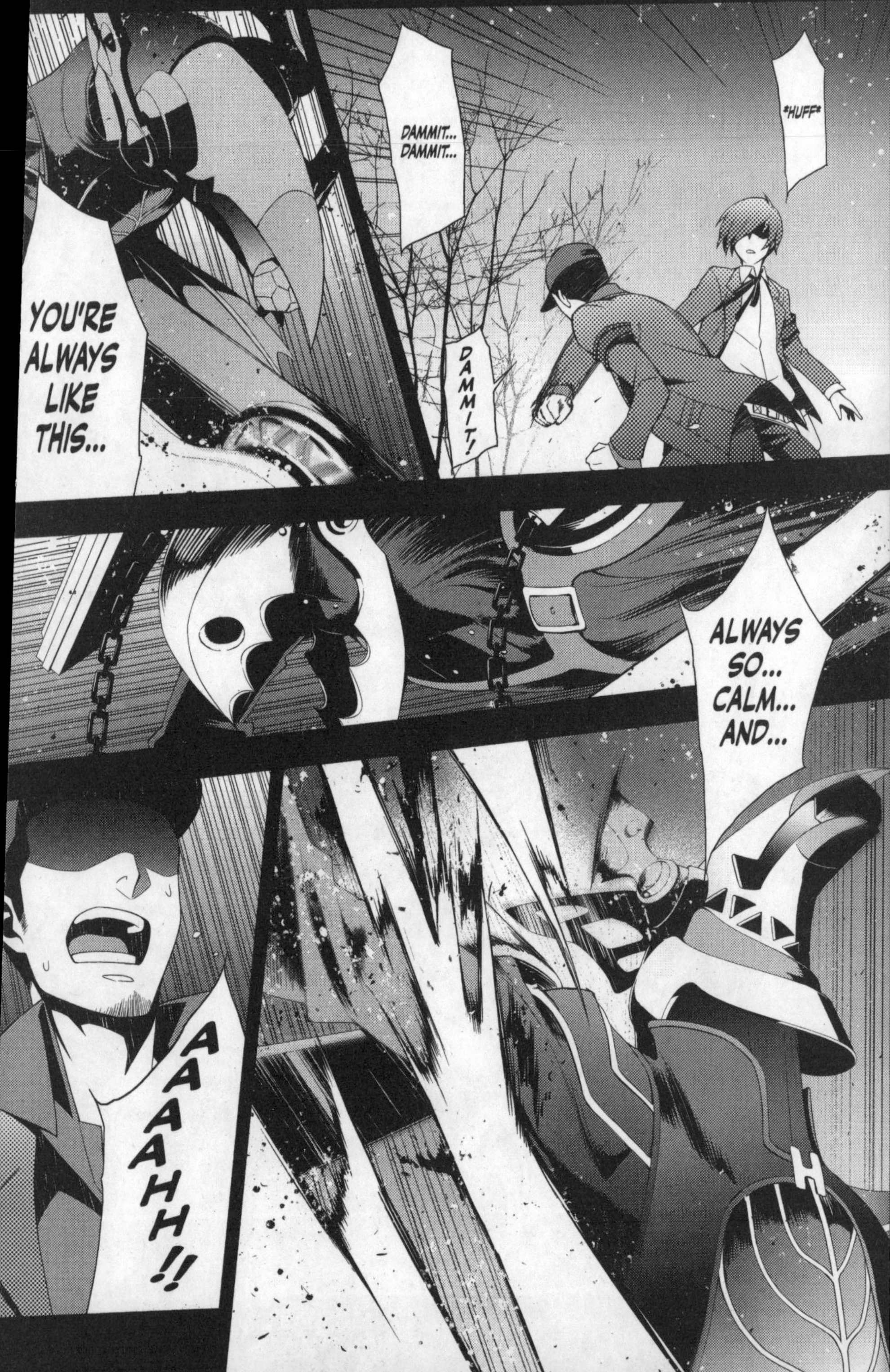
HUFF
DAMMIT... DAMMIT...
DAMMIT!
YOU'RE ALWAYS LIKE THIS...
ALWAYS SO... CALM... AND...
AAAAAHH!!

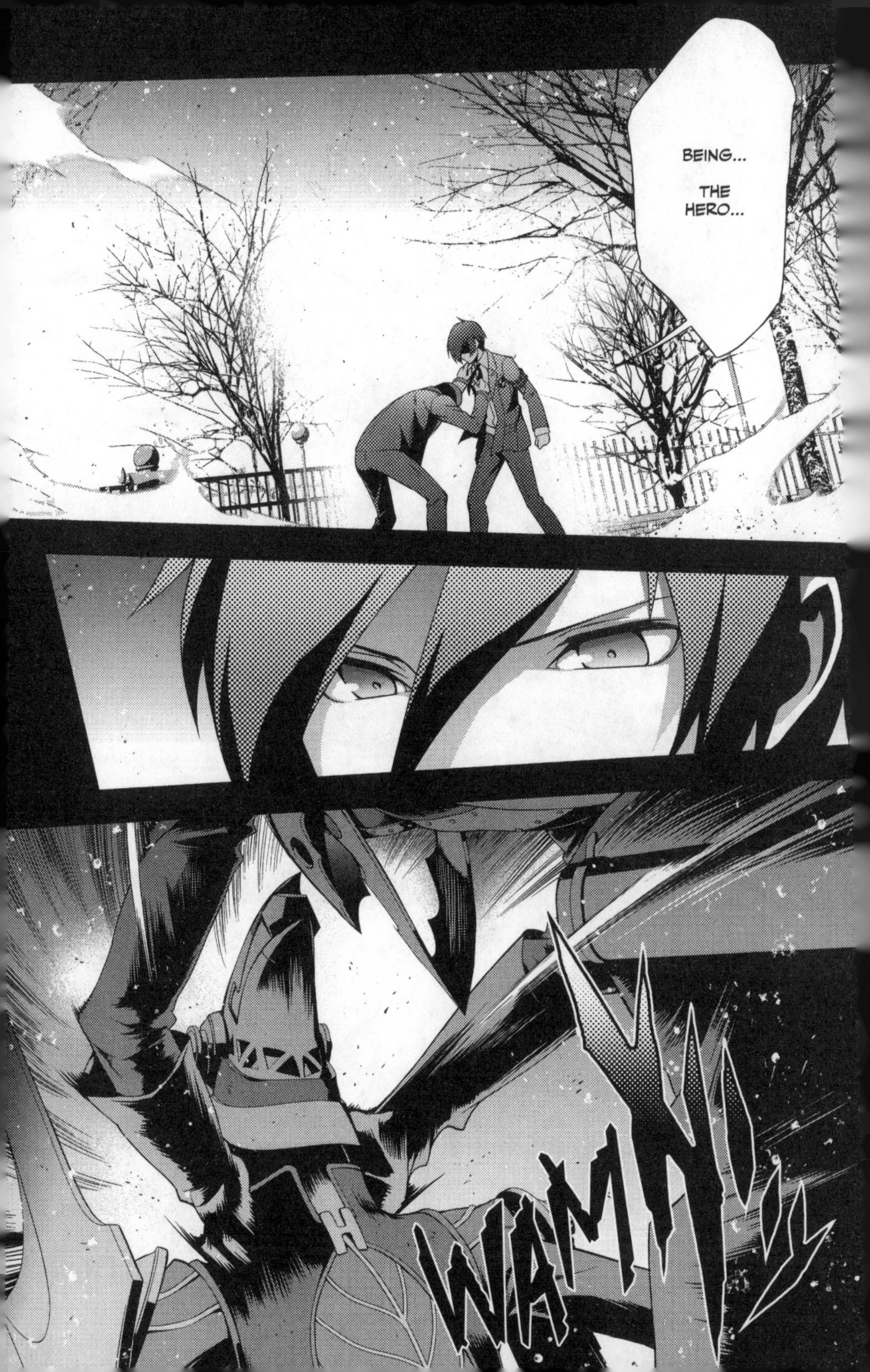
BEING... THE HERO...
WAM

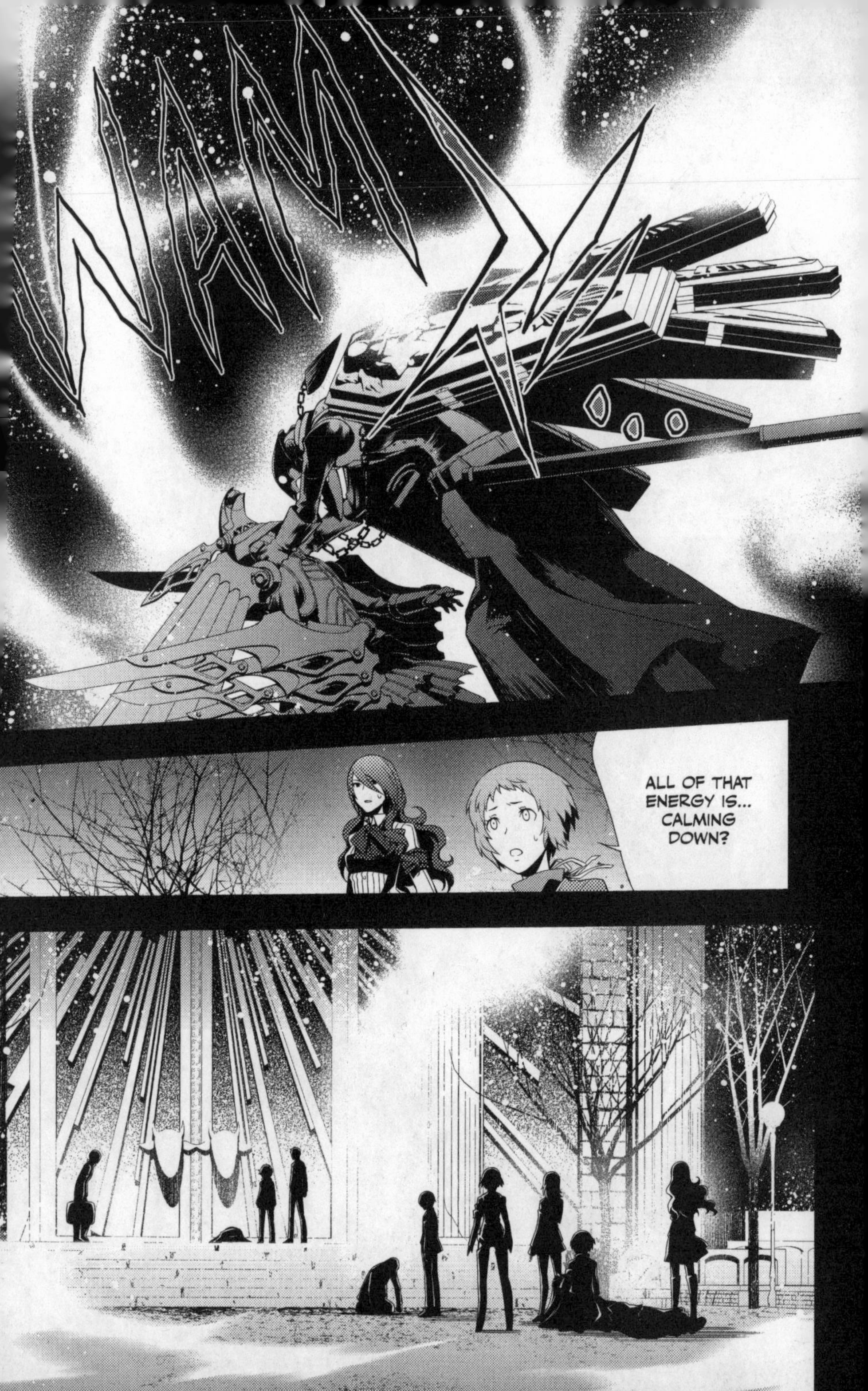
ALL OF THAT ENERGY IS... CALMING DOWN?

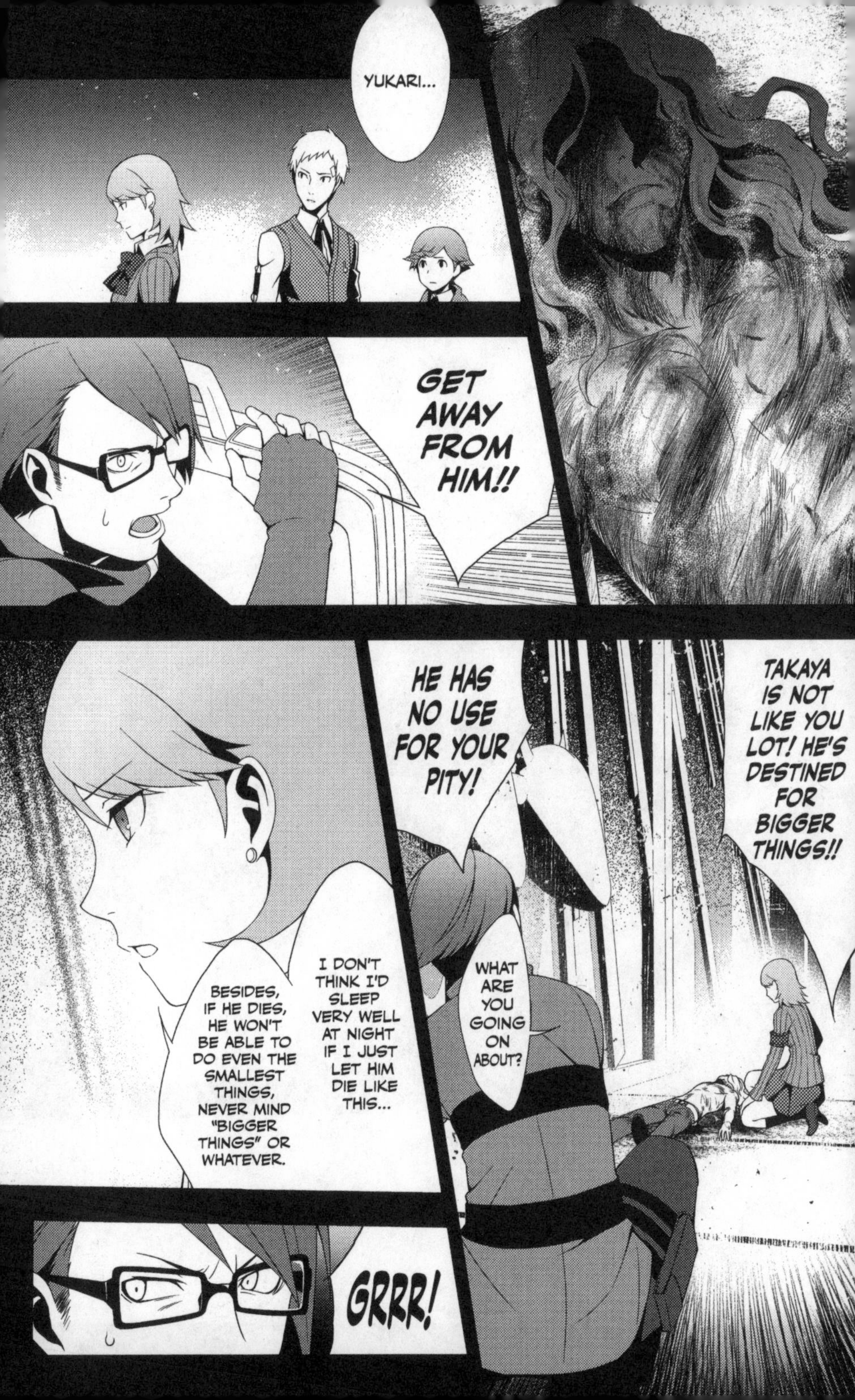
YUKARI...
GET AWAY FROM HIM!!
TAKAYA IS NOT LIKE YOU LOT! HE'S DESTINED FOR BIGGER THINGS!!
HE HAS NO USE FOR YOUR PITY!
WHAT ARE YOU GOING ON ABOUT?
I DON'T THINK I'D SLEEP VERY WELL AT NIGHT IF I JUST LET HIM DIE LIKE THIS...
BESIDES, IF HE DIES, HE WON'T BE ABLE TO DO EVEN THE SMALLEST THINGS, NEVER MIND "BIGGER THINGS" OR WHATEVER.
GRRR!

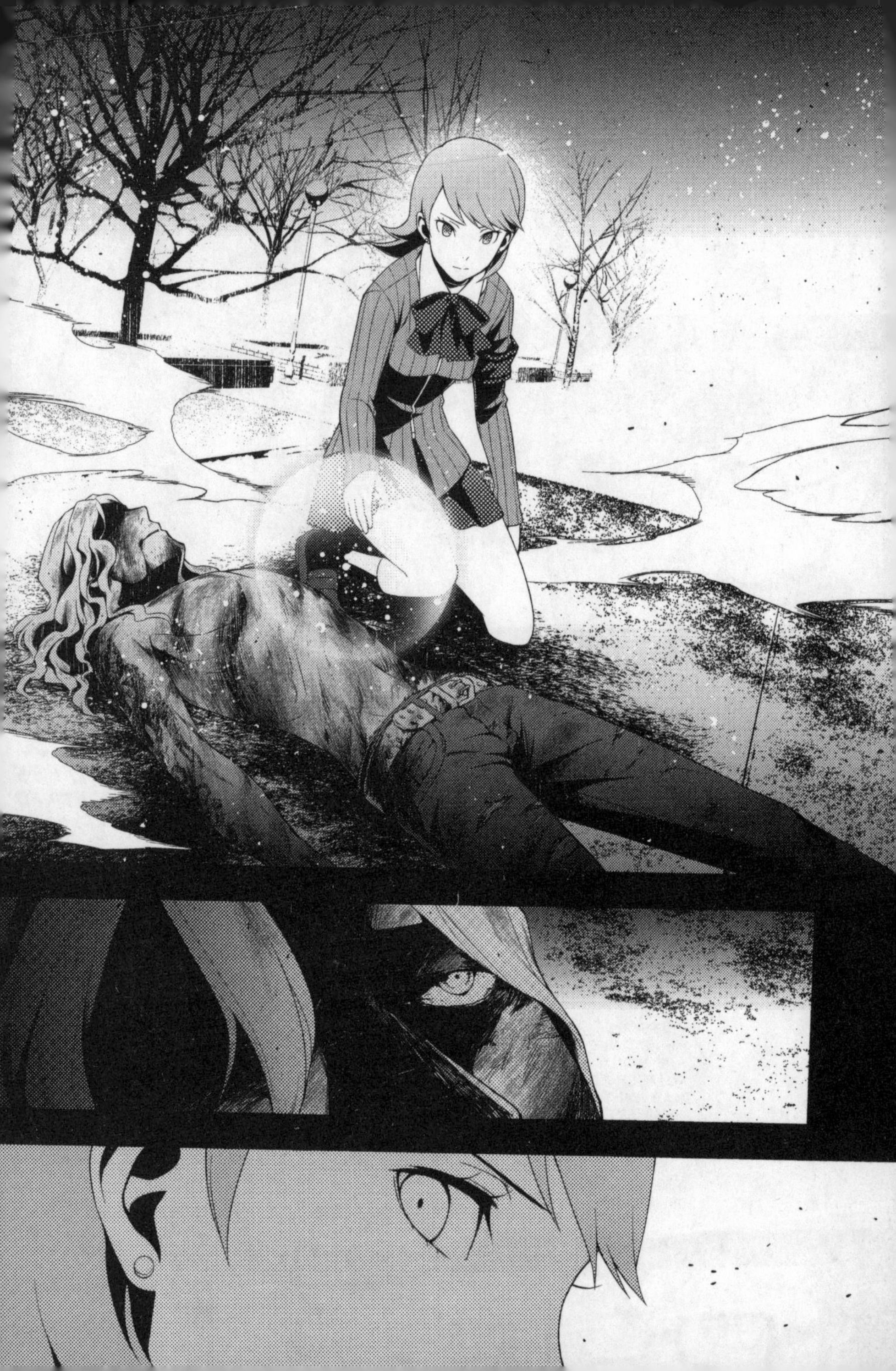

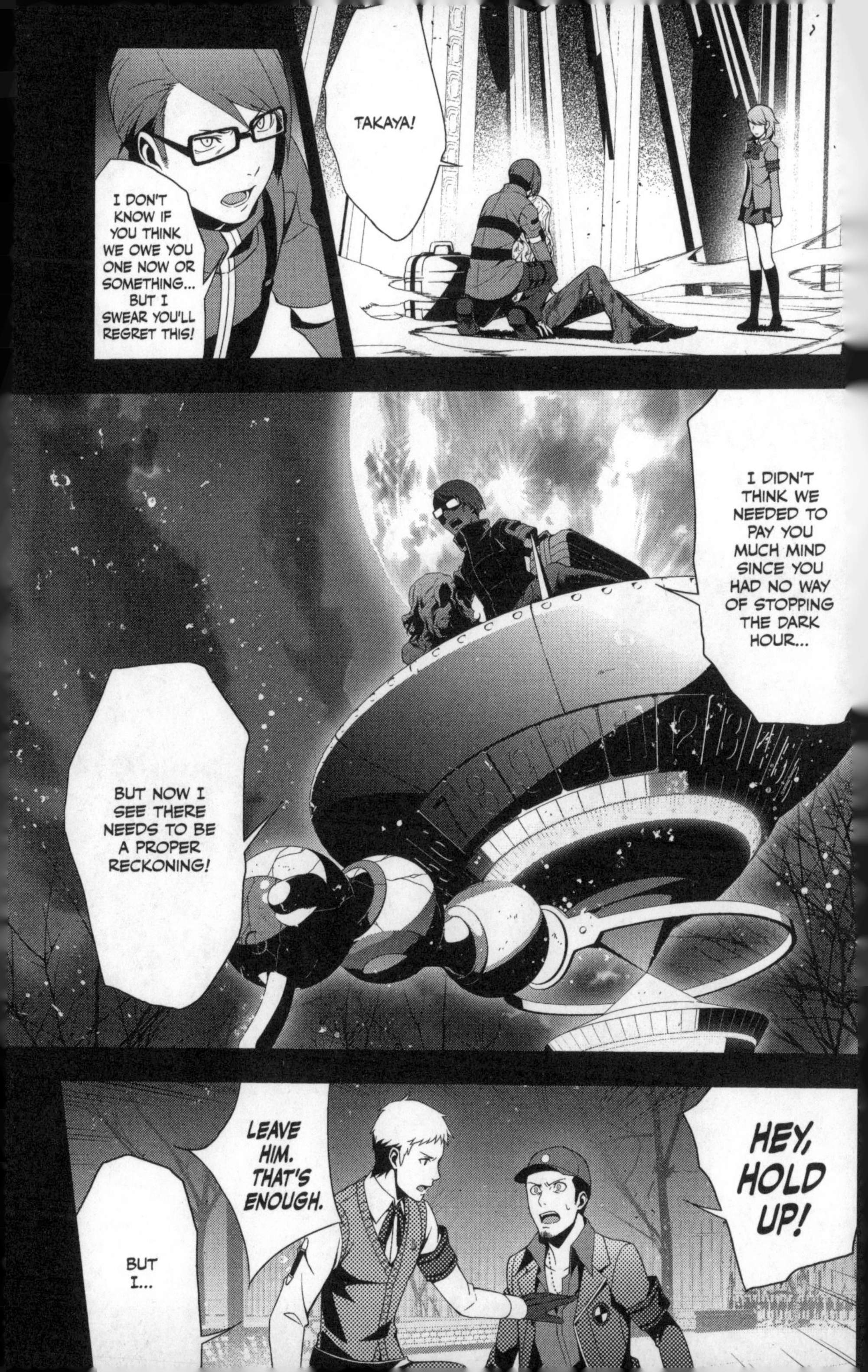
TAKAYA!
I DON'T KNOW IF YOU THINK WE OWE YOU ONE NOW OR SOMETHING... BUT I SWEAR YOU'LL REGRET THIS!
I DIDN'T THINK WE NEEDED TO PAY YOU MUCH MIND SINCE YOU HAD NO WAY OF STOPPING THE DARK HOUR...
BUT NOW I SEE THERE NEEDS TO BE A PROPER RECKONING!
HEY, HOLD UP!
LEAVE HIM. THAT'S ENOUGH.
BUT I...

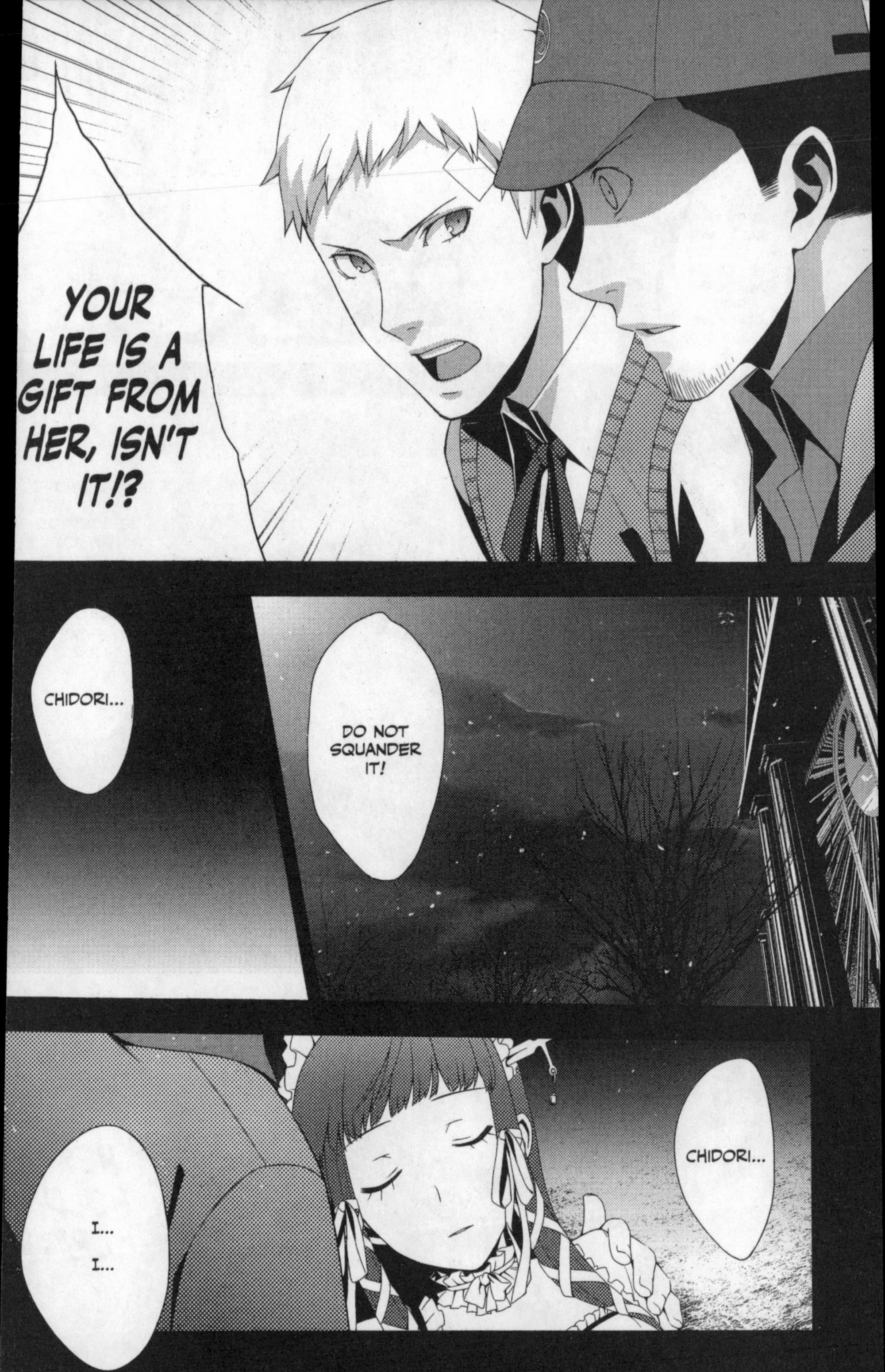
YOUR LIFE IS A GIFT FROM HER, ISN'T IT!?
DO NOT SQUANDER IT!
CHIDORI...
CHIDORI...
I... I...

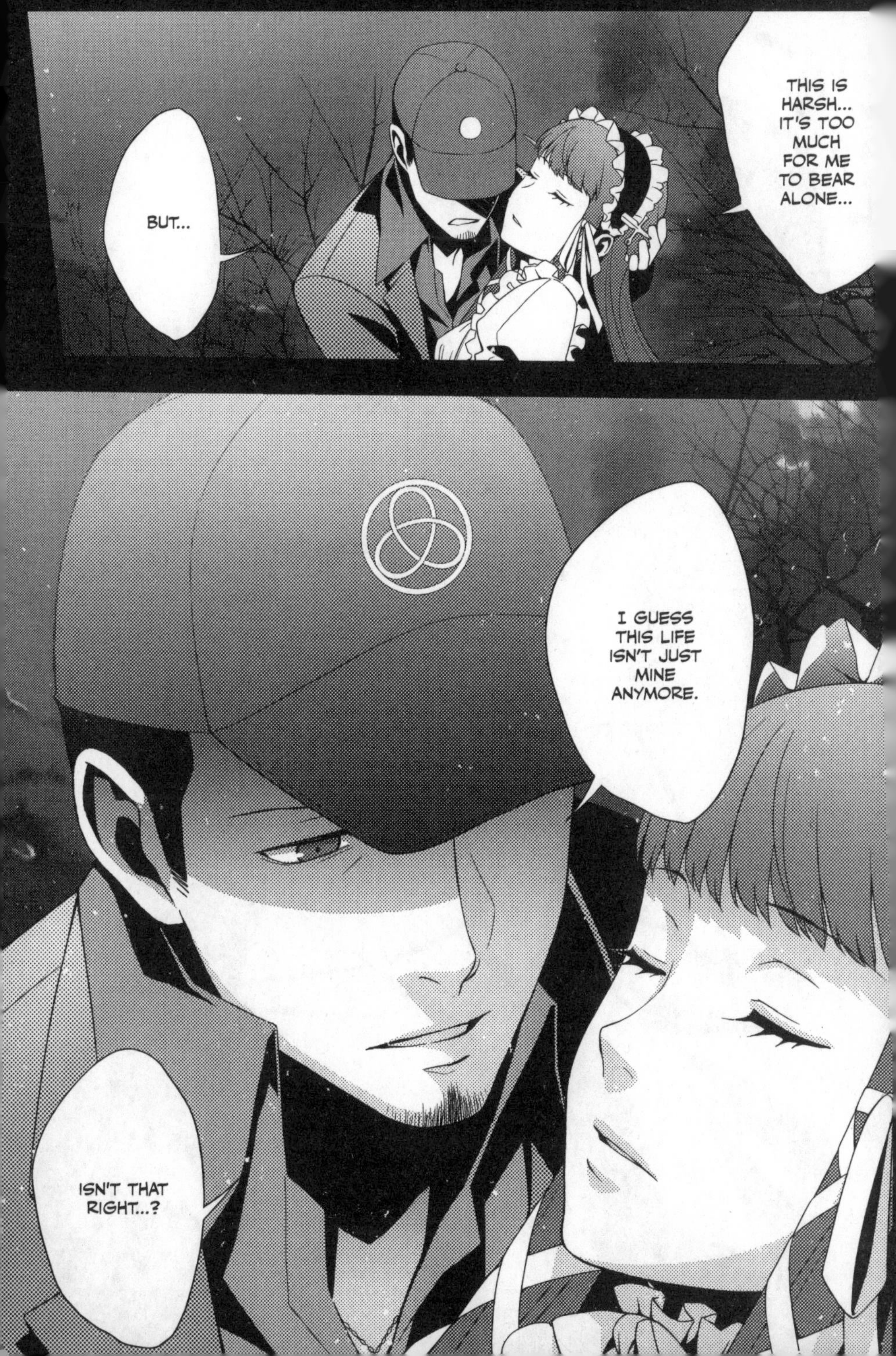
THIS IS HARSH... IT'S TOO MUCH FOR ME TO BEAR ALONE...
BUT...
I GUESS THIS LIFE ISN'T JUST MINE ANYMORE.
ISN'T THAT RIGHT...?

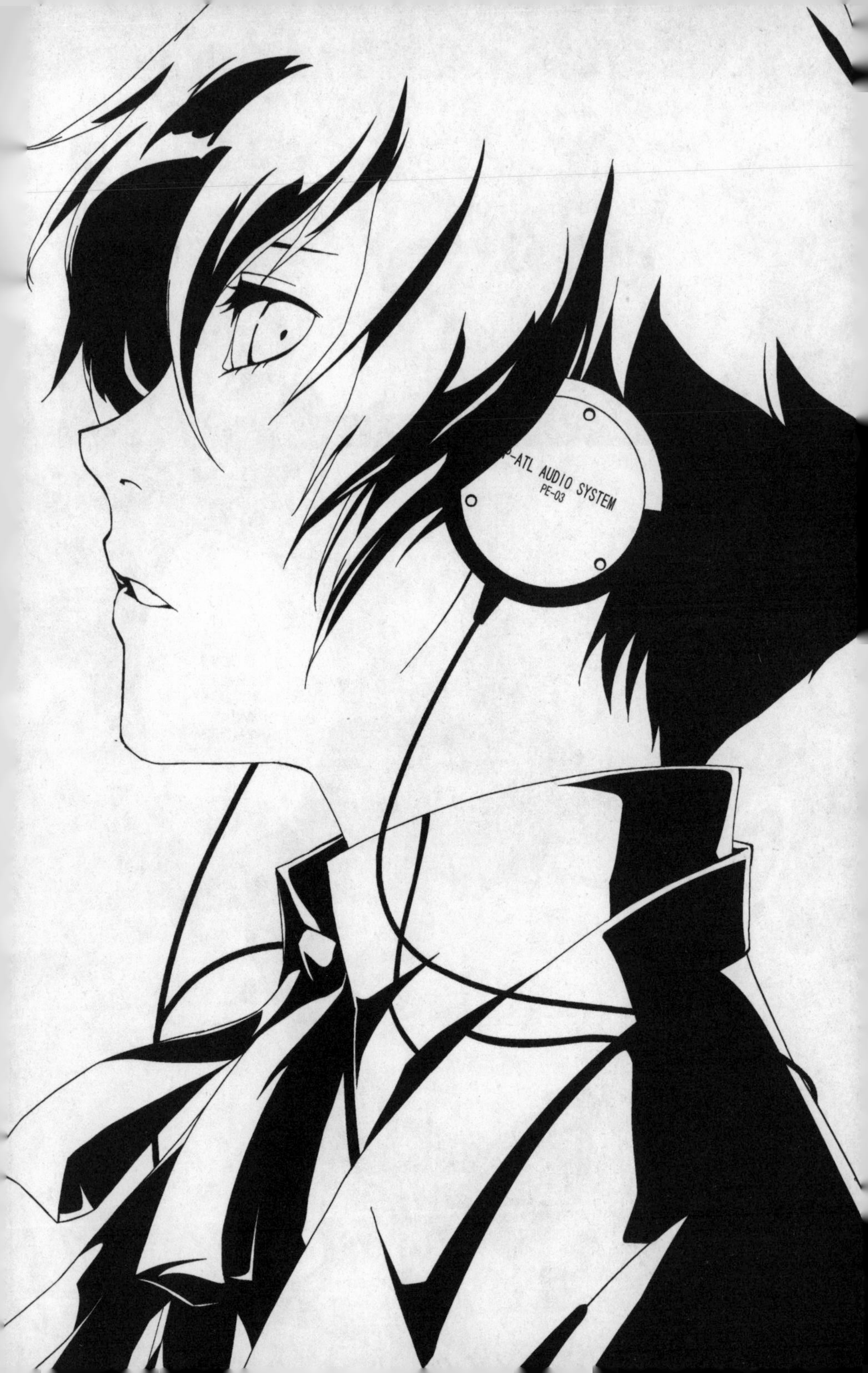
-ATL AUDIO SYSTEM
PE-03

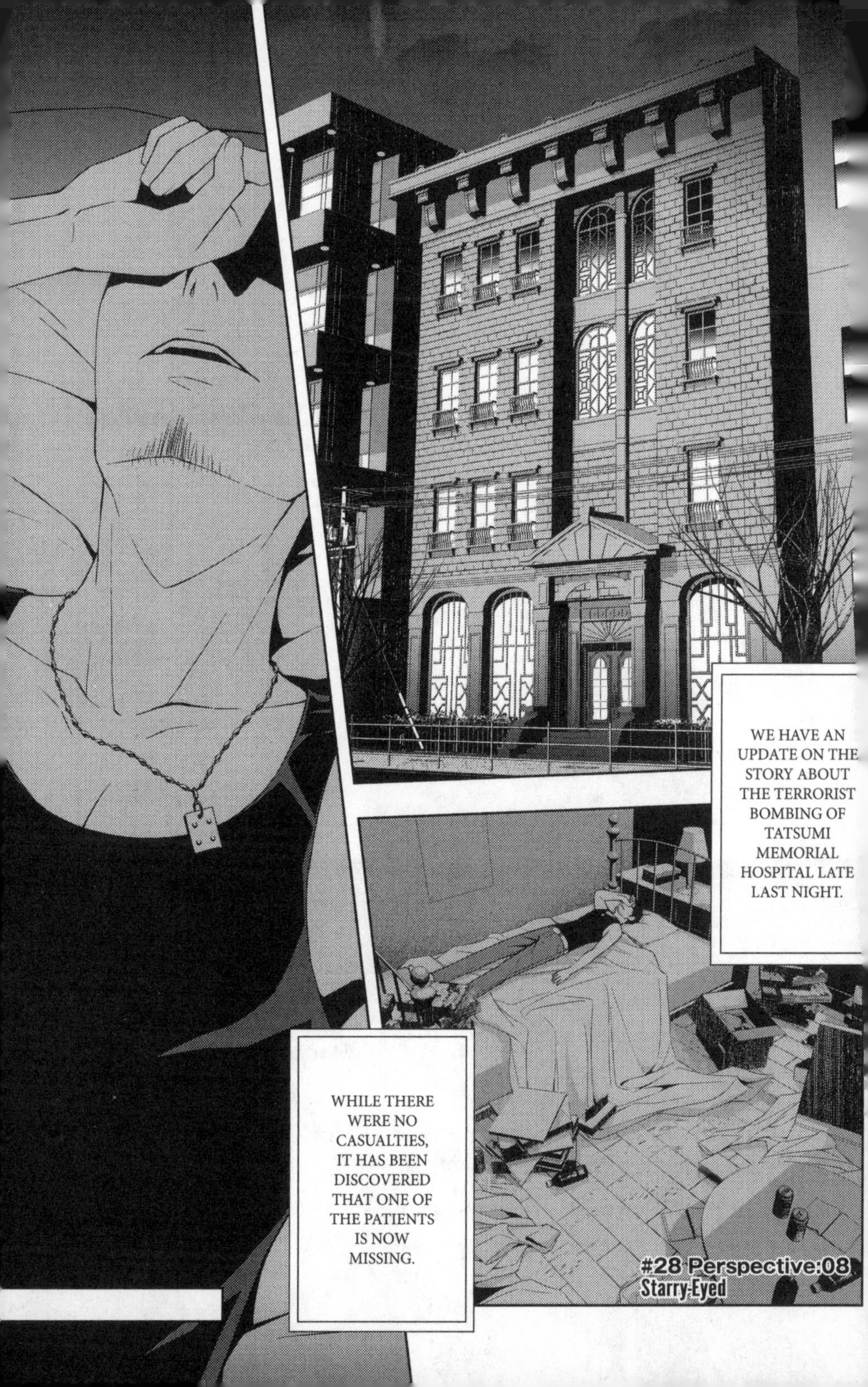
WE HAVE AN UPDATE ON THE STORY ABOUT THE TERRORIST BOMBING OF TATSUMI MEMORIAL HOSPITAL LATE LAST NIGHT.
WHILE THERE WERE NO CASUALTIES, IT HAS BEEN DISCOVERED THAT ONE OF THE PATIENTS IS NOW MISSING.
#28 Perspective:08
Starry-Eyed

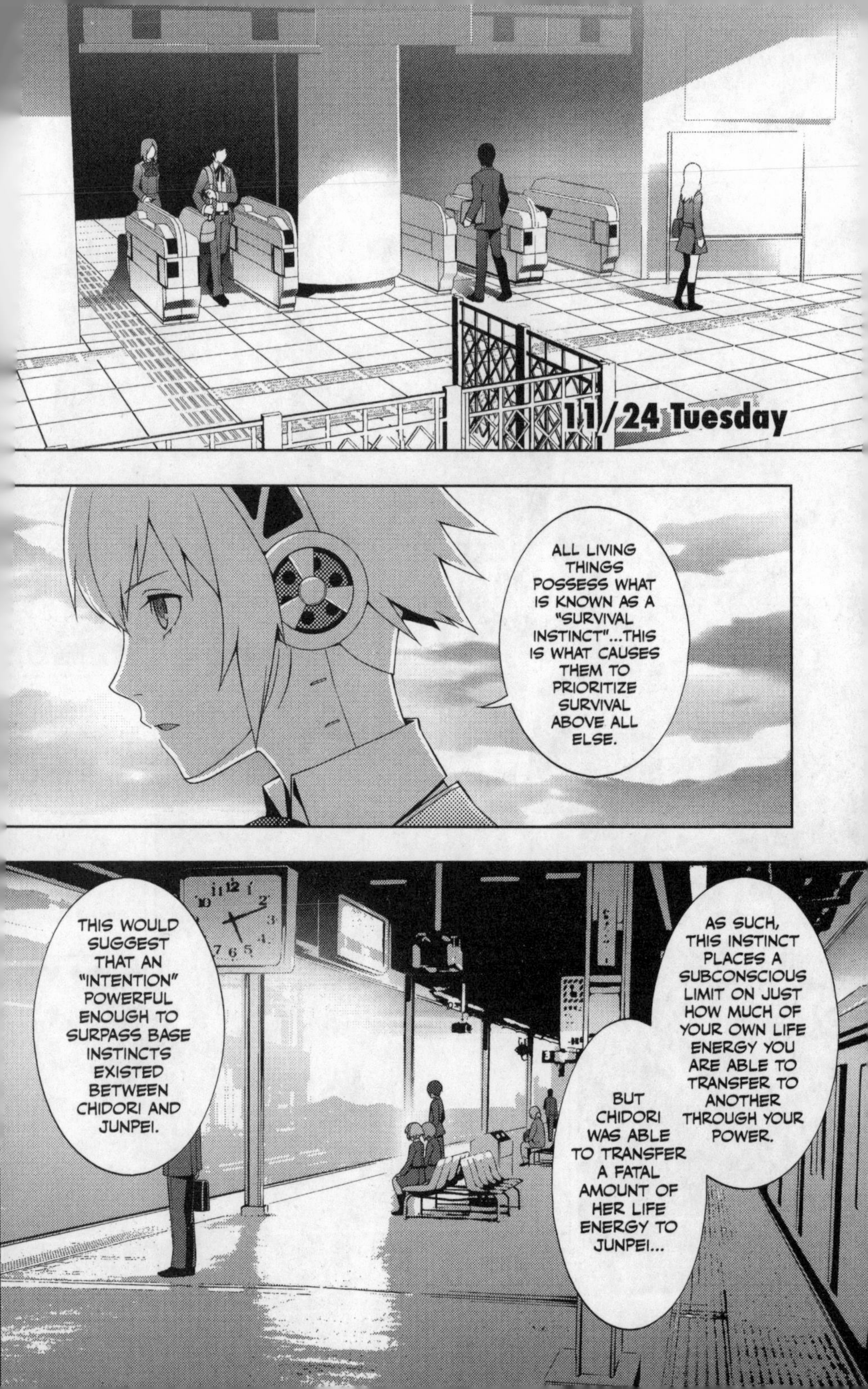
11/24 Tuesday
ALL LIVING THINGS POSSESS WHAT IS KNOWN AS A "SURVIVAL INSTINCT"...THIS IS WHAT CAUSES THEM TO PRIORITIZE SURVIVAL ABOVE ALL ELSE.
AS SUCH, THIS INSTINCT PLACES A SUBCONSCIOUS LIMIT ON JUST HOW MUCH OF YOUR OWN LIFE ENERGY YOU ARE ABLE TO TRANSFER TO ANOTHER THROUGH YOUR POWER.
BUT CHIDORI WAS ABLE TO TRANSFER A FATAL AMOUNT OF HER LIFE ENERGY TO JUNPEI...
THIS WOULD SUGGEST THAT AN "INTENTION" POWERFUL ENOUGH TO SURPASS BASE INSTINCTS EXISTED BETWEEN CHIDORI AND JUNPEI.

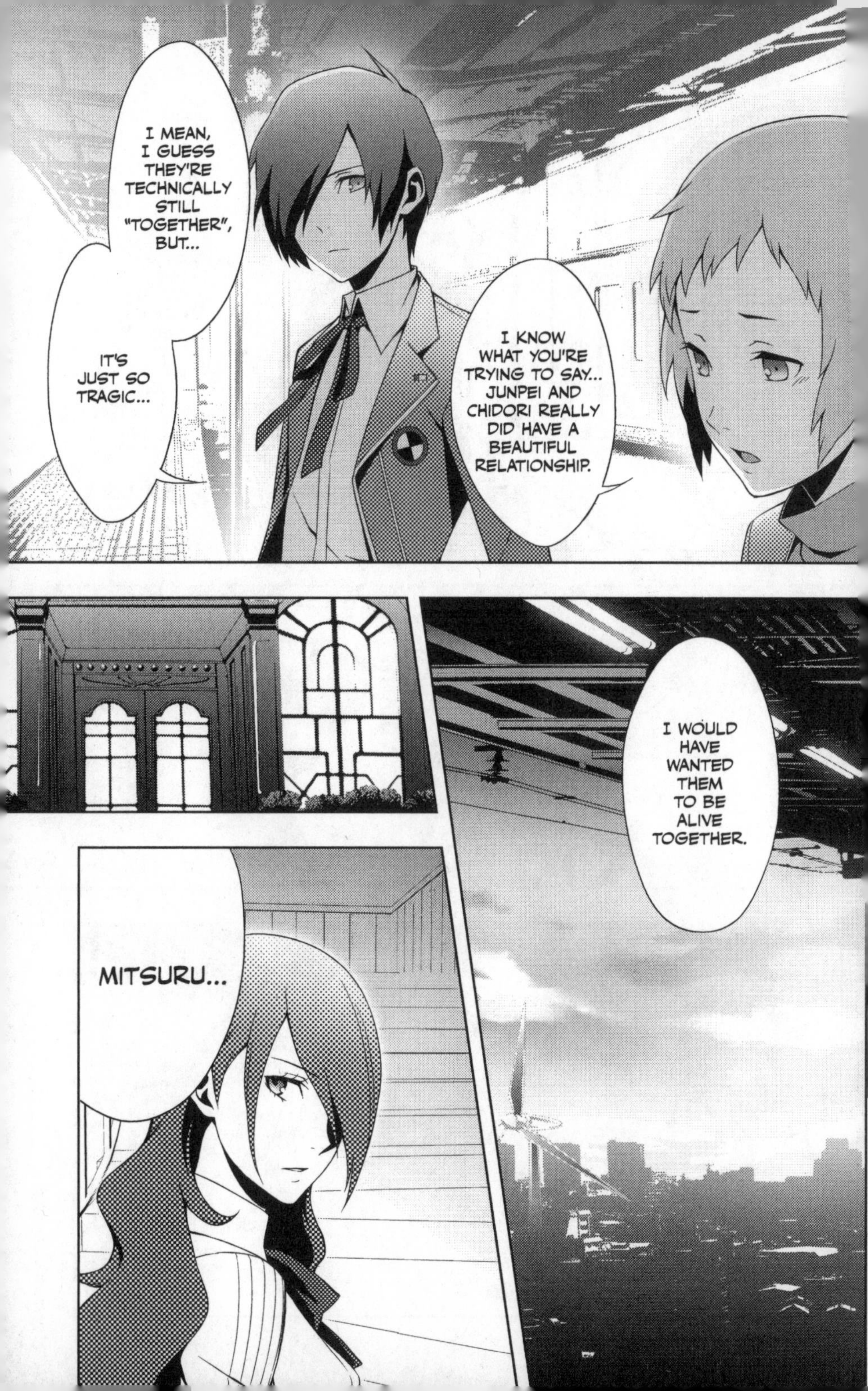
I KNOW WHAT YOU'RE TRYING TO SAY... JUNPEI AND CHIDORI REALLY DID HAVE A BEAUTIFUL RELATIONSHIP.
I MEAN, I GUESS THEY'RE TECHNICALLY STILL "TOGETHER", BUT...
IT'S JUST SO TRAGIC...
I WOULD HAVE WANTED THEM TO BE ALIVE TOGETHER.
MITSURU...

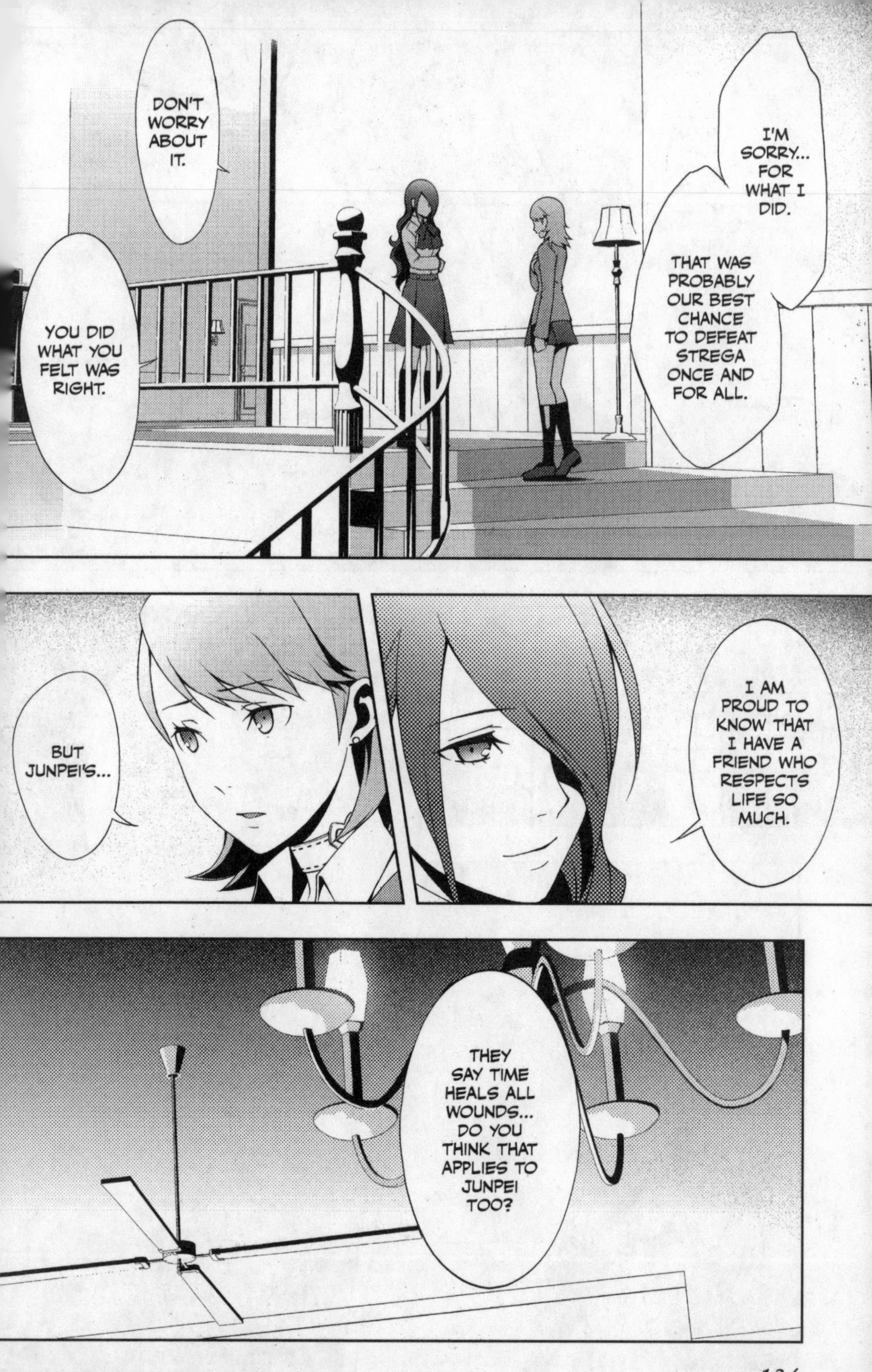
I'M SORRY... FOR WHAT I DID.
THAT WAS PROBABLY OUR BEST CHANCE TO DEFEAT STREGA ONCE AND FOR ALL.
DON'T WORRY ABOUT IT.
YOU DID WHAT YOU FELT WAS RIGHT.
I AM PROUD TO KNOW THAT I HAVE A FRIEND WHO RESPECTS LIFE SO MUCH.
BUT JUNPEI'S...
THEY SAY TIME HEALS ALL WOUNDS... DO YOU THINK THAT APPLIES TO JUNPEI TOO?

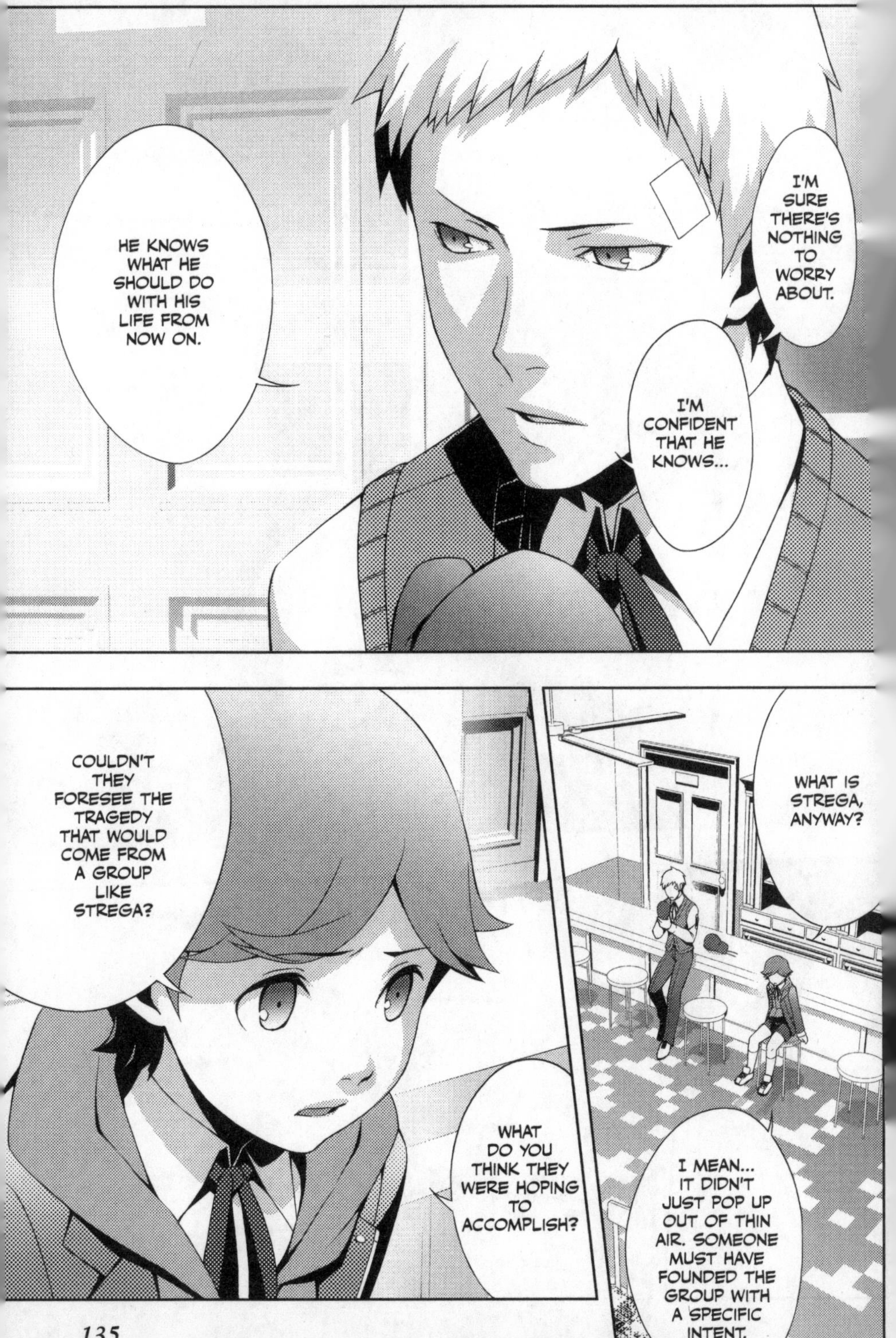
I'M SURE THERE'S NOTHING TO WORRY ABOUT.
I'M CONFIDENT THAT HE KNOWS...
HE KNOWS WHAT HE SHOULD DO WITH HIS LIFE FROM NOW ON.
WHAT IS STREGA, ANYWAY?
I MEAN... IT DIDN'T JUST POP UP OUT OF THIN AIR. SOMEONE MUST HAVE FOUNDED THE GROUP WITH A SPECIFIC INTENT.
WHAT DO YOU THINK THEY WERE HOPING TO ACCOMPLISH?
COULDN'T THEY FORESEE THE TRAGEDY THAT WOULD COME FROM A GROUP LIKE STREGA?

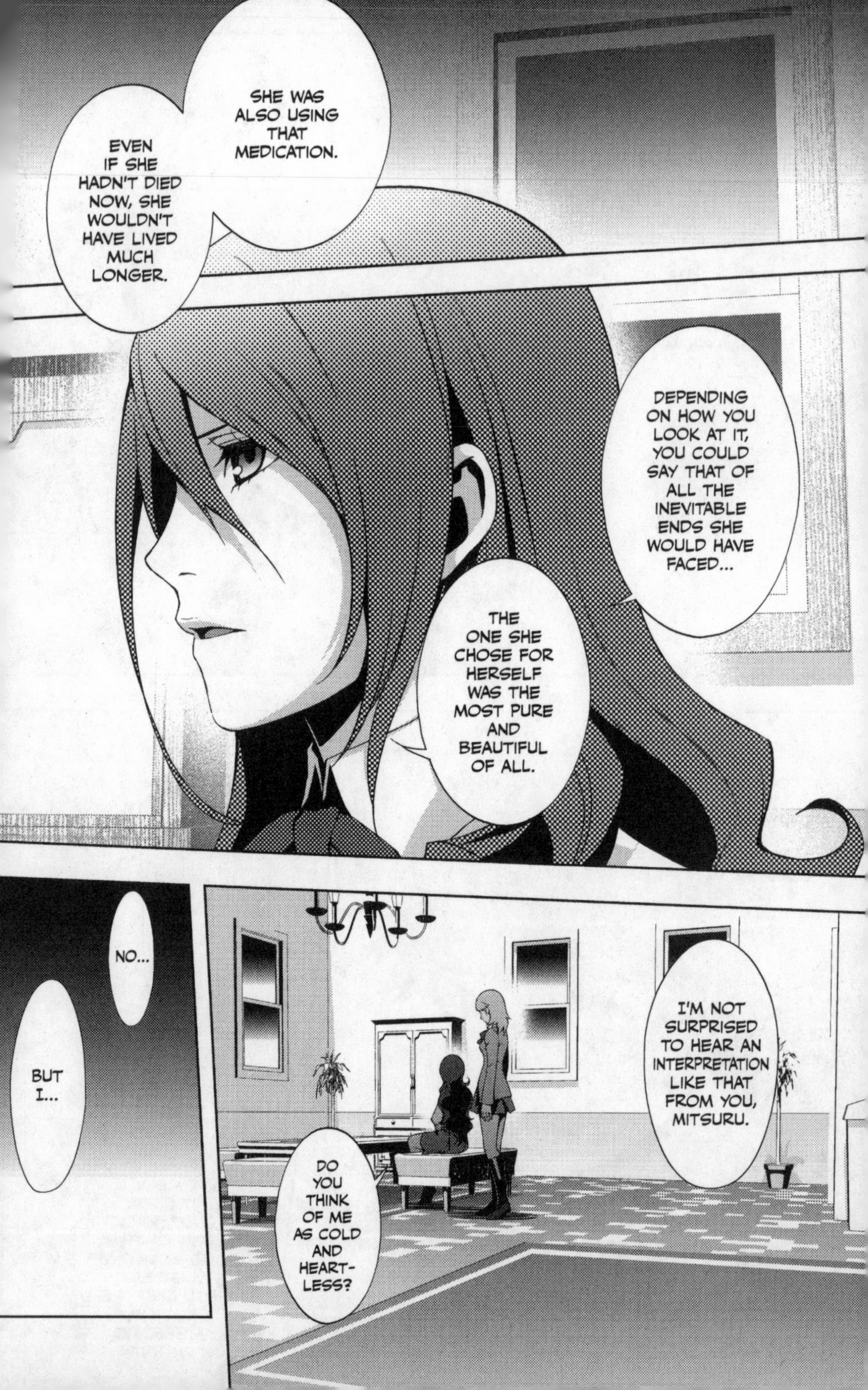
SHE WAS ALSO USING THAT MEDICATION.
EVEN IF SHE HADN'T DIED NOW, SHE WOULDN'T HAVE LIVED MUCH LONGER.
DEPENDING ON HOW YOU LOOK AT IT, YOU COULD SAY THAT OF ALL THE INEVITABLE ENDS SHE WOULD HAVE FACED...
THE ONE SHE CHOSE FOR HERSELF WAS THE MOST PURE AND BEAUTIFUL OF ALL.
I'M NOT SURPRISED TO HEAR AN INTERPRETATION LIKE THAT FROM YOU, MITSURU.
DO YOU THINK OF ME AS COLD AND HEART-LESS?
NO...
BUT I...

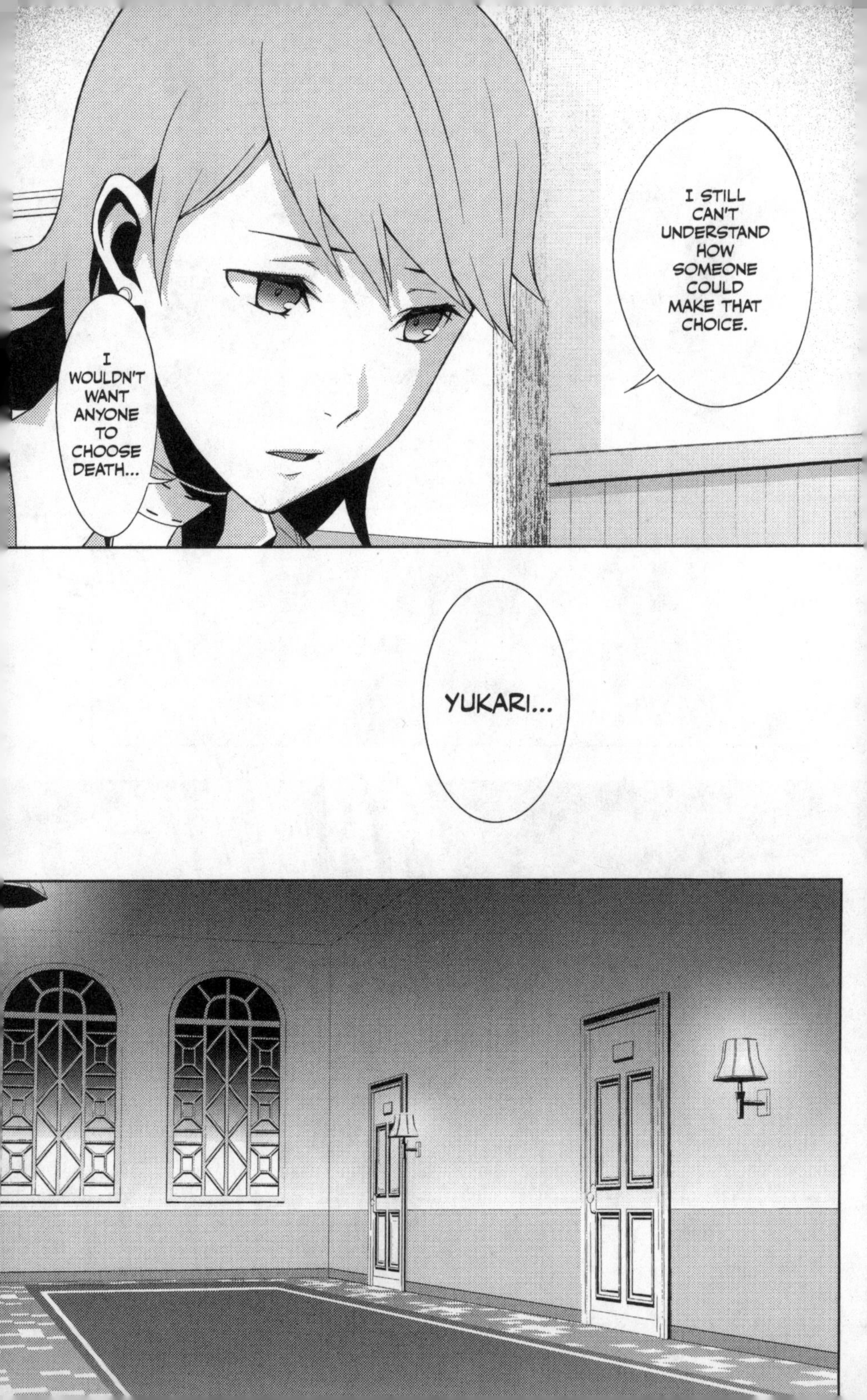
I STILL CAN'T UNDERSTAND HOW SOMEONE COULD MAKE THAT CHOICE.
I WOULDN'T WANT ANYONE TO CHOOSE DEATH...
YUKARI...

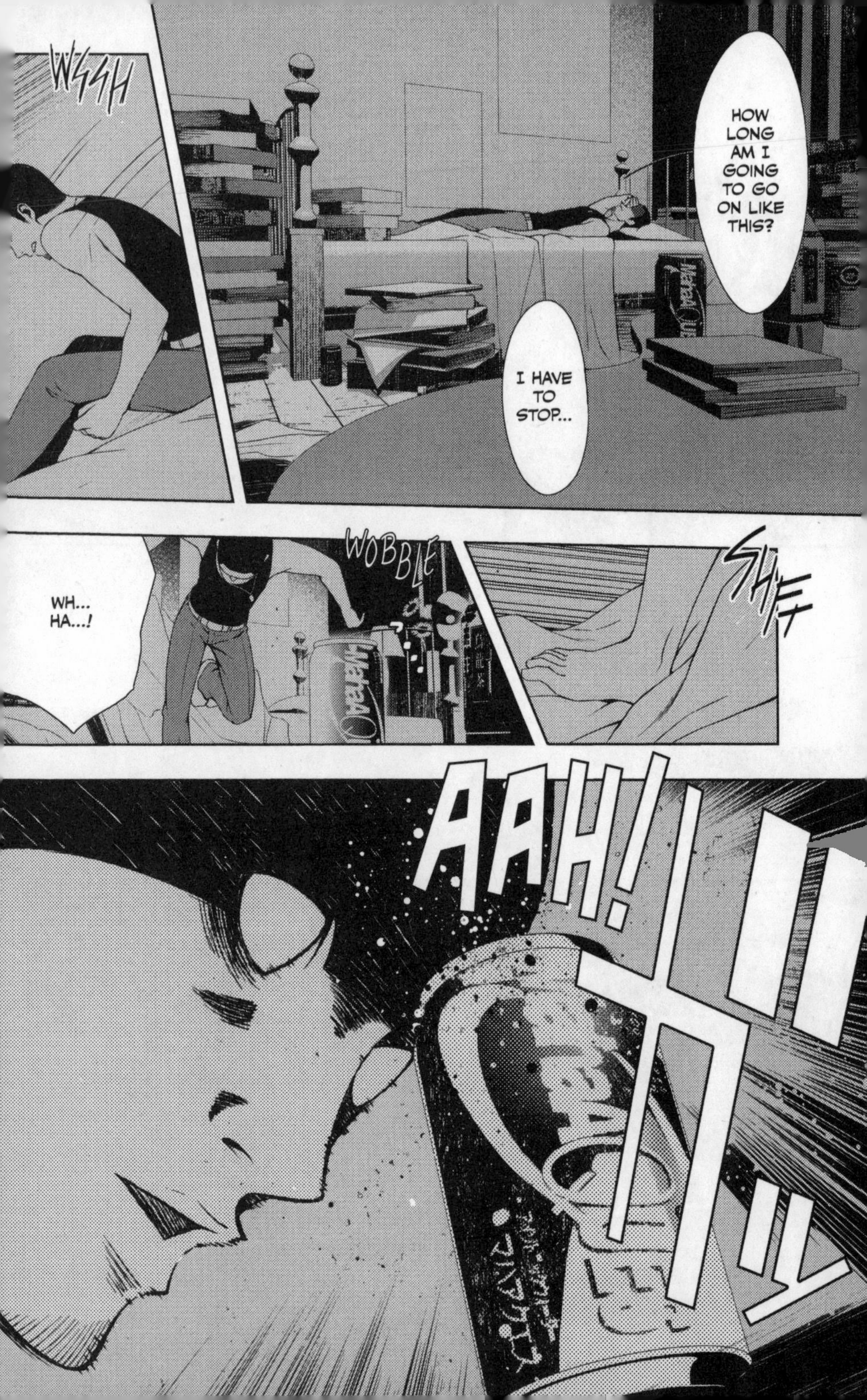
HOW LONG AM I GOING TO GO ON LIKE THIS?
I HAVE TO STOP...
WSSH
SHIFT
WOBBLE
WH... HA...!
AAH!!

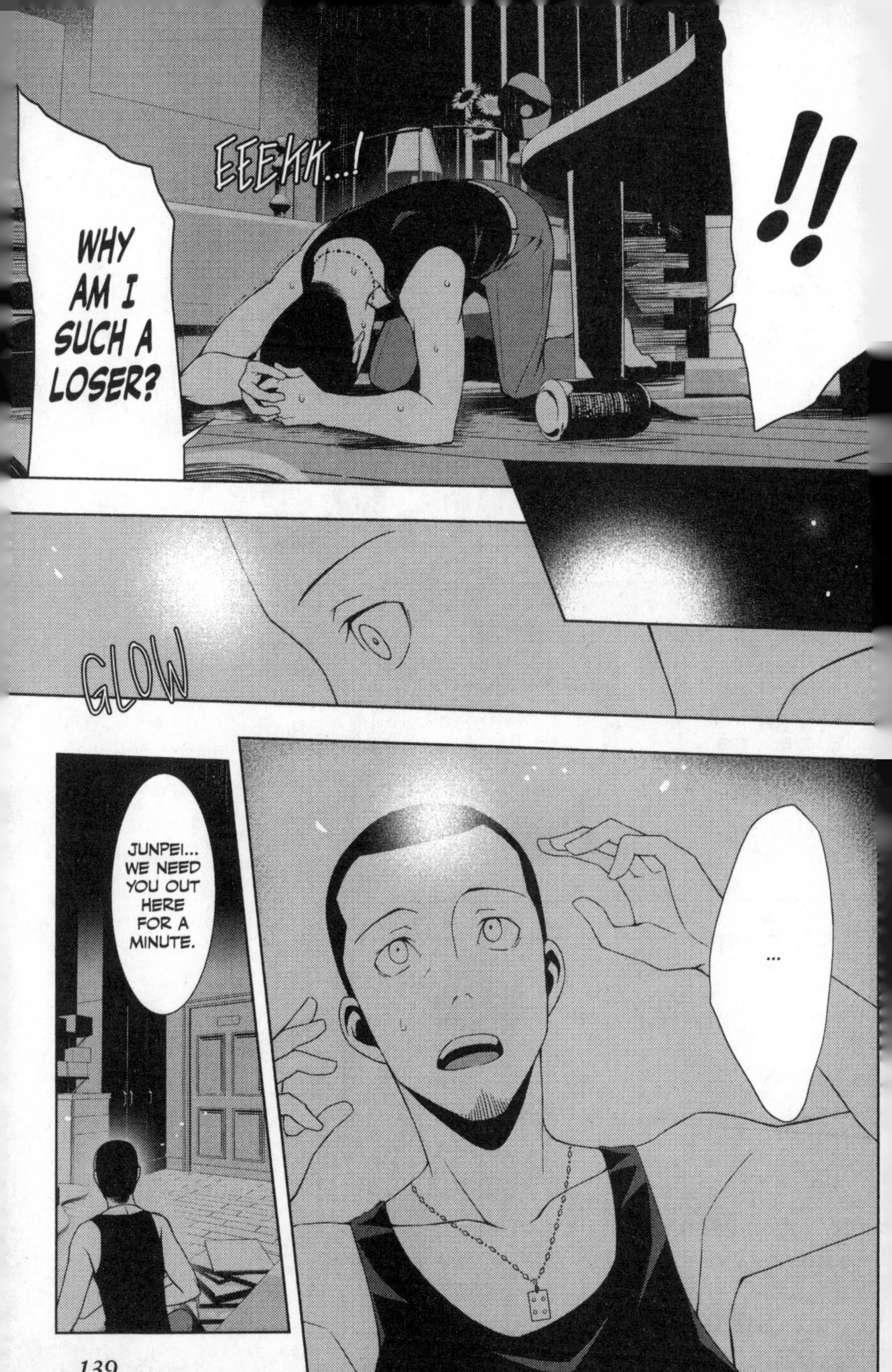
!!
EEEKK...!
WHY AM I SUCH A LOSER?
GLOW
...
JUNPEI... WE NEED YOU OUT HERE FOR A MINUTE.

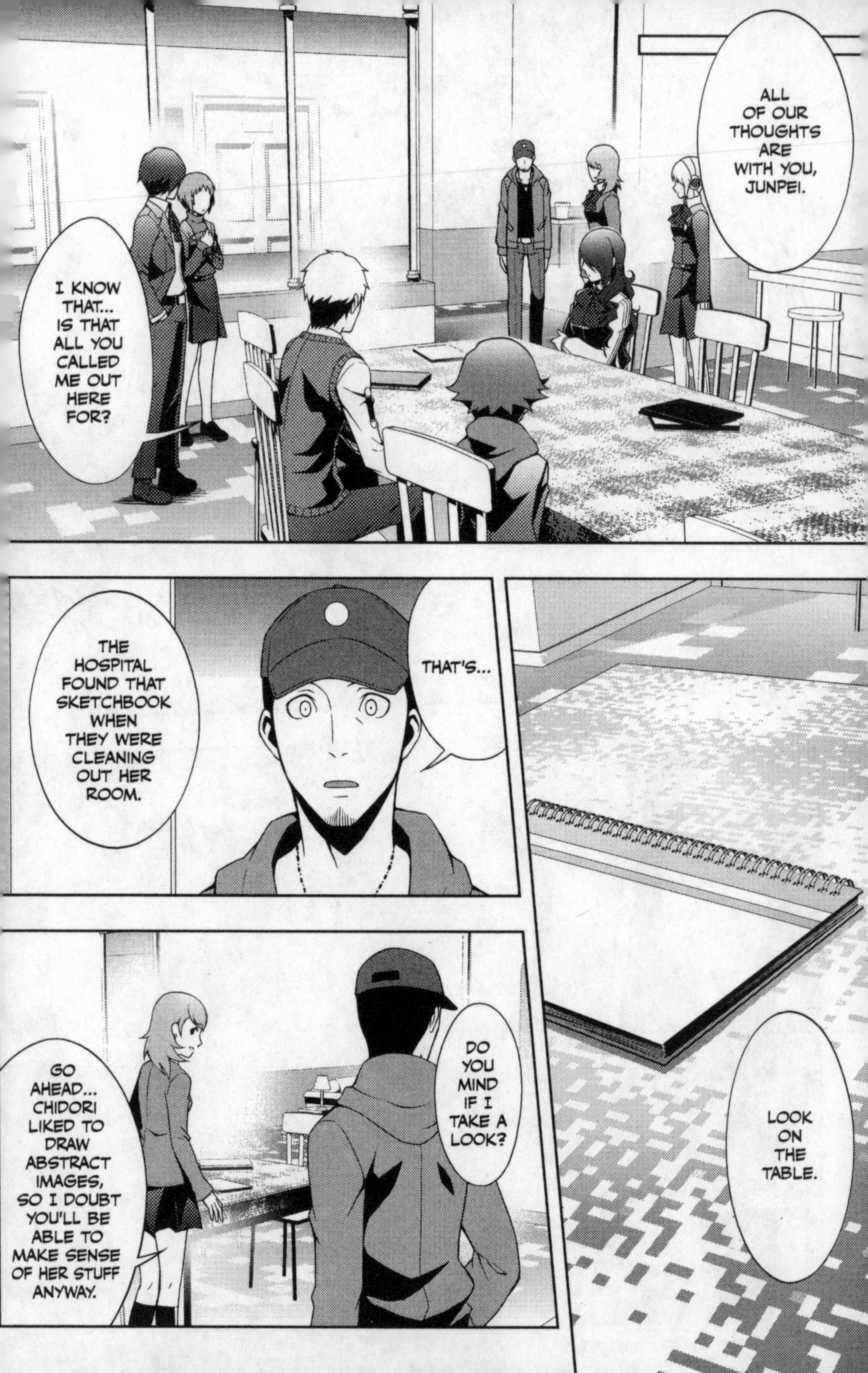
ALL OF OUR THOUGHTS ARE WITH YOU, JUNPEI.
I KNOW THAT... IS THAT ALL YOU CALLED ME OUT HERE FOR?
LOOK ON THE TABLE.
THAT'S...
THE HOSPITAL FOUND THAT SKETCHBOOK WHEN THEY WERE CLEANING OUT HER ROOM.
DO YOU MIND IF I TAKE A LOOK?
GO AHEAD... CHIDORI LIKED TO DRAW ABSTRACT IMAGES, SO I DOUBT YOU'LL BE ABLE TO MAKE SENSE OF HER STUFF ANYWAY.

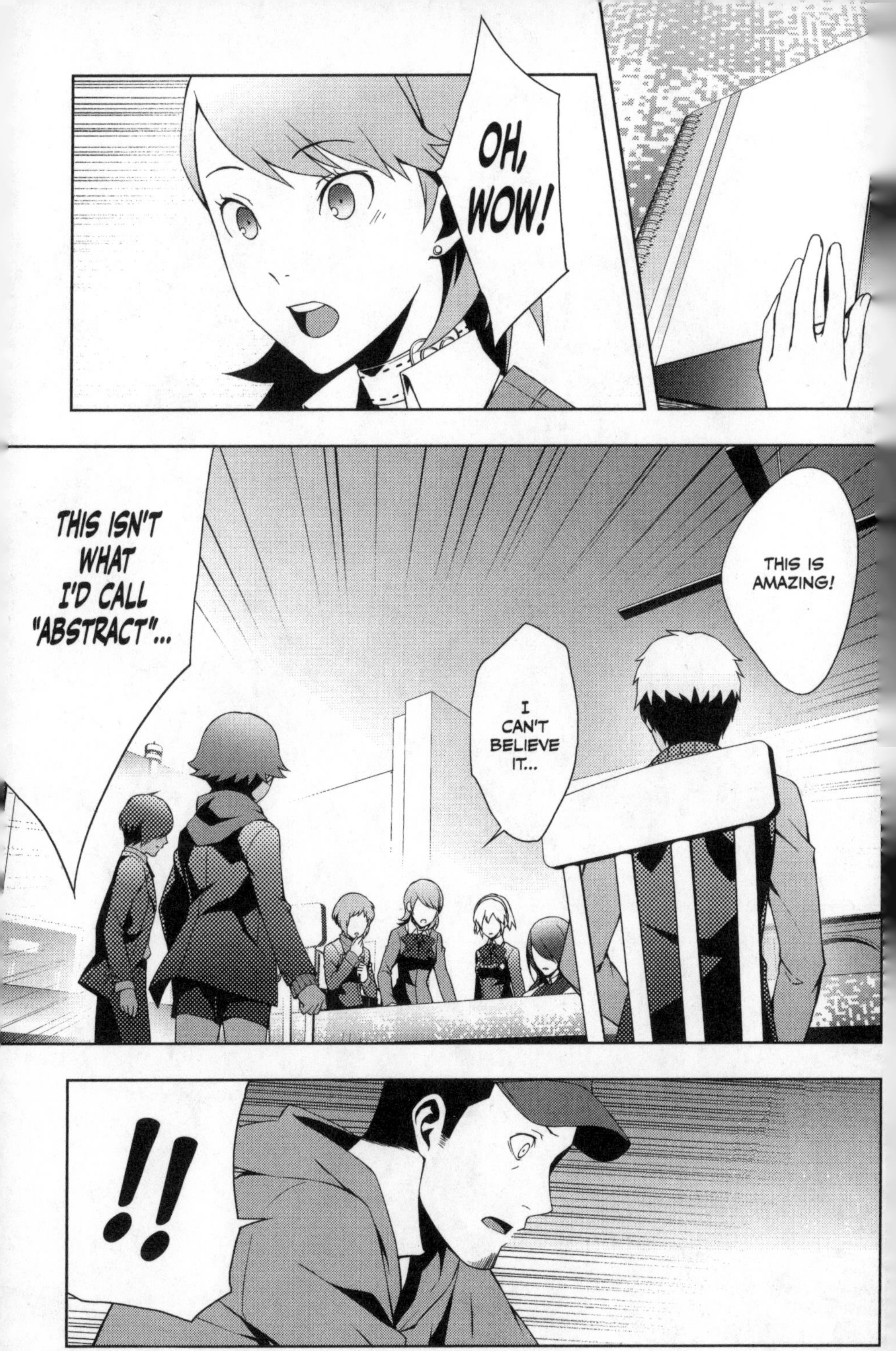
OH, WOW!
THIS IS AMAZING!
I CAN'T BELIEVE IT...
THIS ISN'T WHAT I'D CALL "ABSTRACT"...
!!

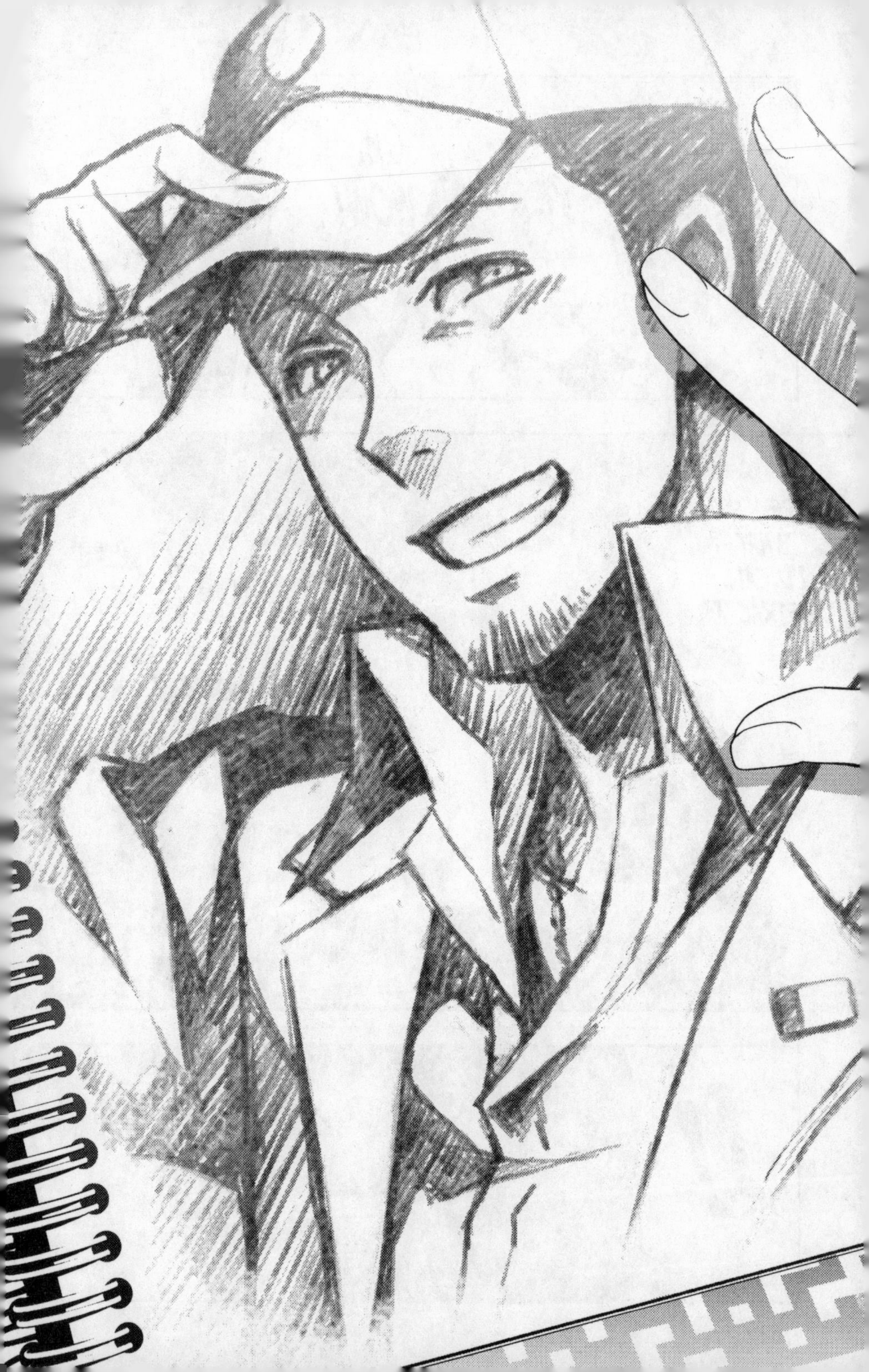

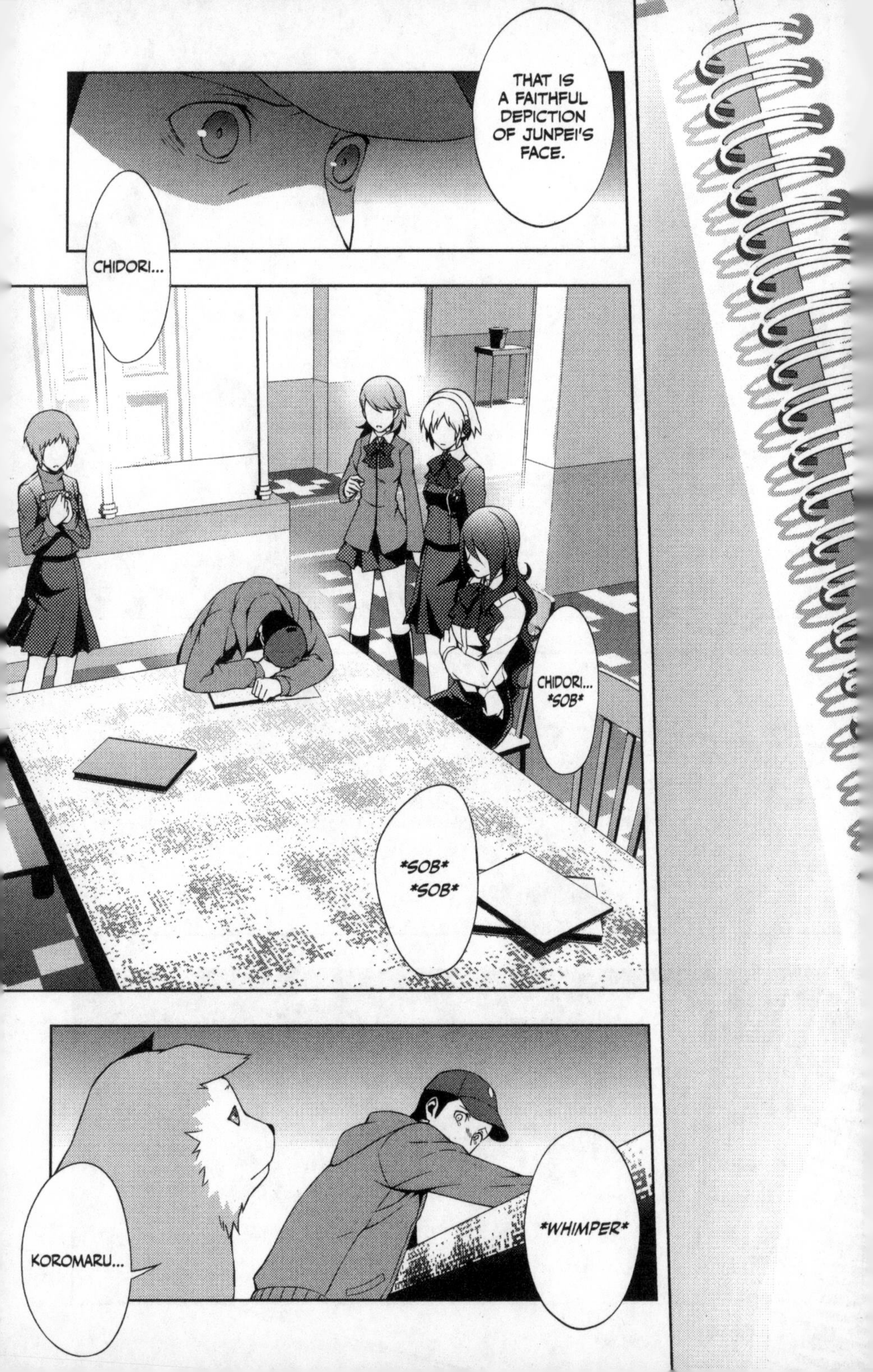
THAT IS A FAITHFUL DEPICTION OF JUNPEI'S FACE.
CHIDORI...
CHIDORI... *SOB*
SOB *SOB*
WHIMPER
KOROMARU...

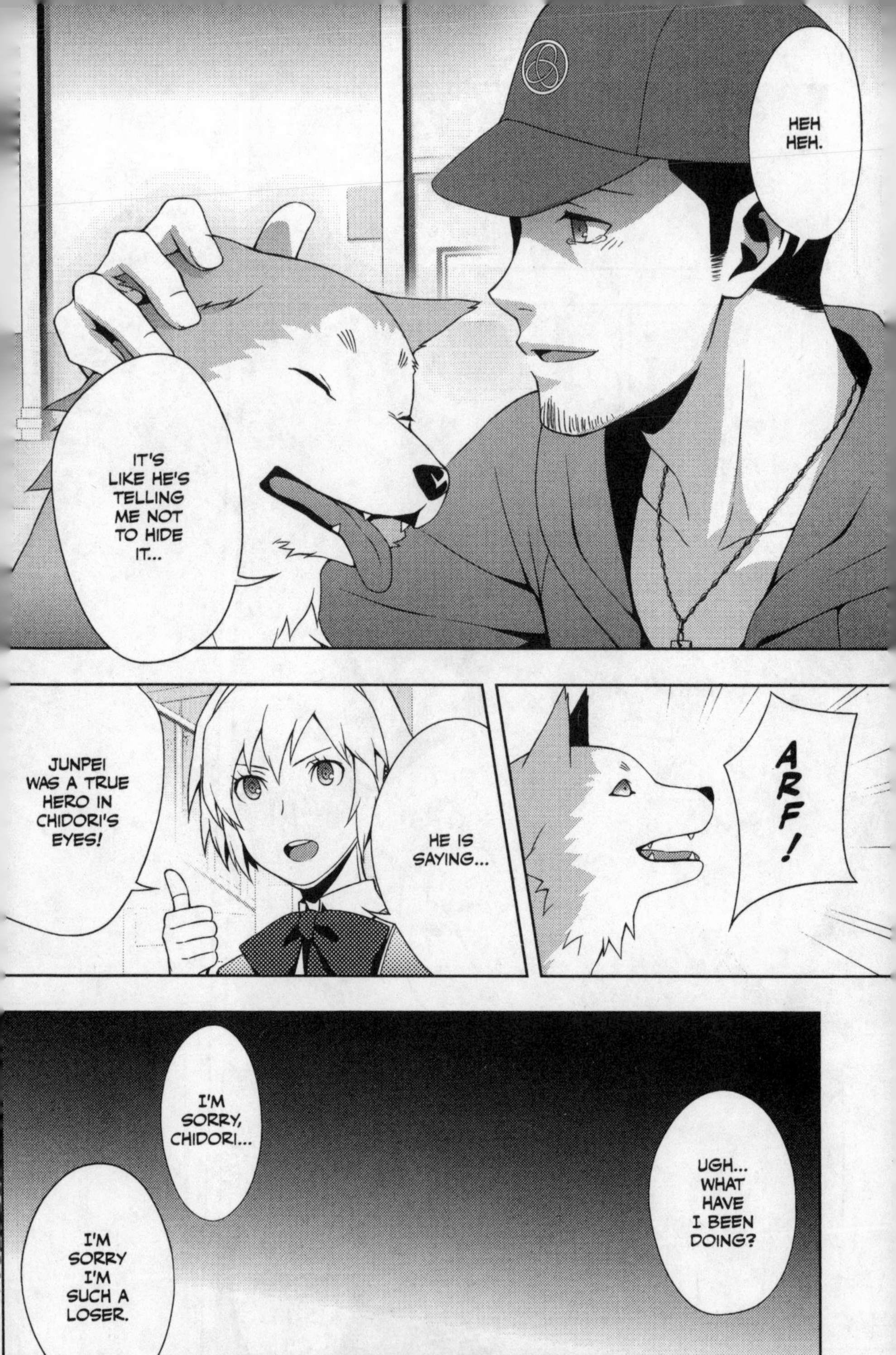
HEH HEH.
IT'S LIKE HE'S TELLING ME NOT TO HIDE IT...
ARF!
HE IS SAYING...
JUNPEI WAS A TRUE HERO IN CHIDORI'S EYES!
UGH... WHAT HAVE I BEEN DOING?
I'M SORRY, CHIDORI...
I'M SORRY I'M SUCH A LOSER.

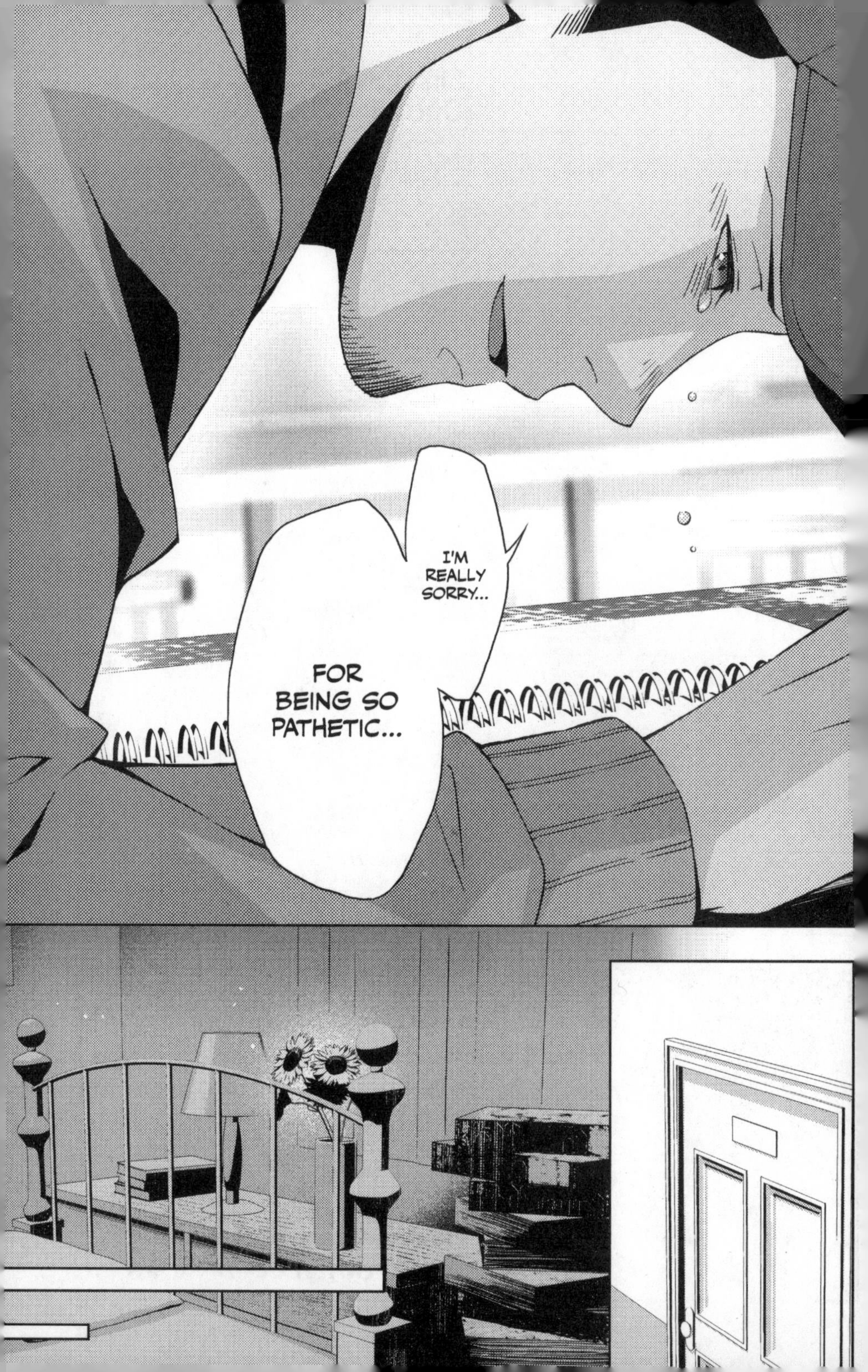
I'M REALLY SORRY...
FOR BEING SO PATHETIC...

PERSONA 3
Chapitre SIX
STAFF LIST

Original Work
アトラス
ATLUS

Original Art Director
副島成記 (Index)
Shigenori SOEJIMA

Original Scenario Writer
田中裕一郎 (Index)
Yuichiro TANAKA

Manga

曽我部修司 (FiFS)
Shuji SOGABE

worked by FiFS

Art Director
今泉昭彦
Teruhiko IMAIZUMI

Design

セキケイコ (SELFISH GENE)
Keiko SEKI

FiFS

Editing
飯島直樹
Naoki IIJIMA

Editing Assistance
岡本紗耶香
Sayaka OKAMOTO

藤倉さつき
Satsuki FUJIKURA

Translation
タノヴァン・フィリップ
TANOVAN Philippe

Special Thanks
森純一 (Index)
Junichi MORI

ペルソナ 3 オリジナルスタッフ
PERSONA3 ORIGINAL STAFF

FiFS on Twitter
https://twitter.com/FiFS_PR

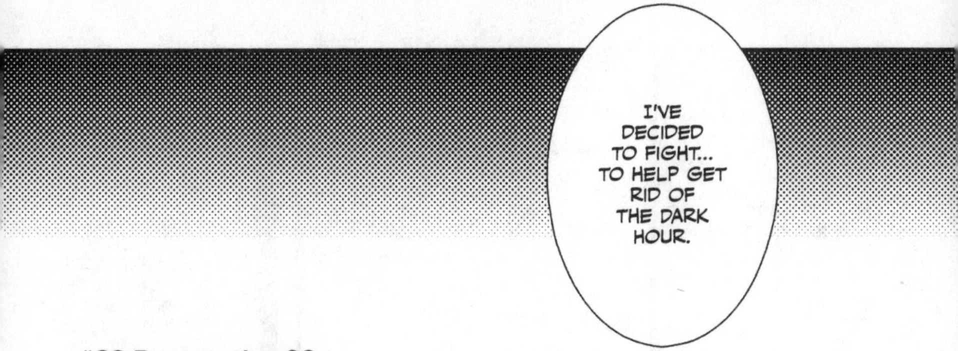
I'VE DECIDED TO FIGHT... TO HELP GET RID OF THE DARK HOUR.

#29 Perspective:09
Another Echo

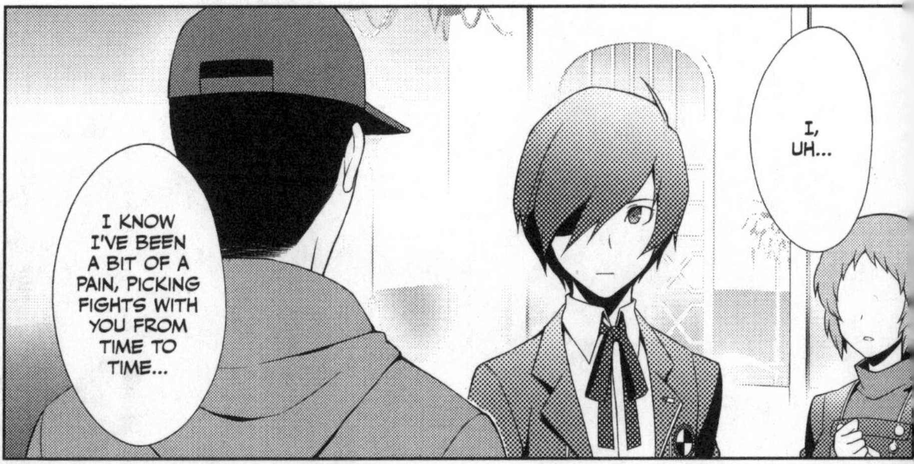
I, UH...
I KNOW I'VE BEEN A BIT OF A PAIN, PICKING FIGHTS WITH YOU FROM TIME TO TIME...

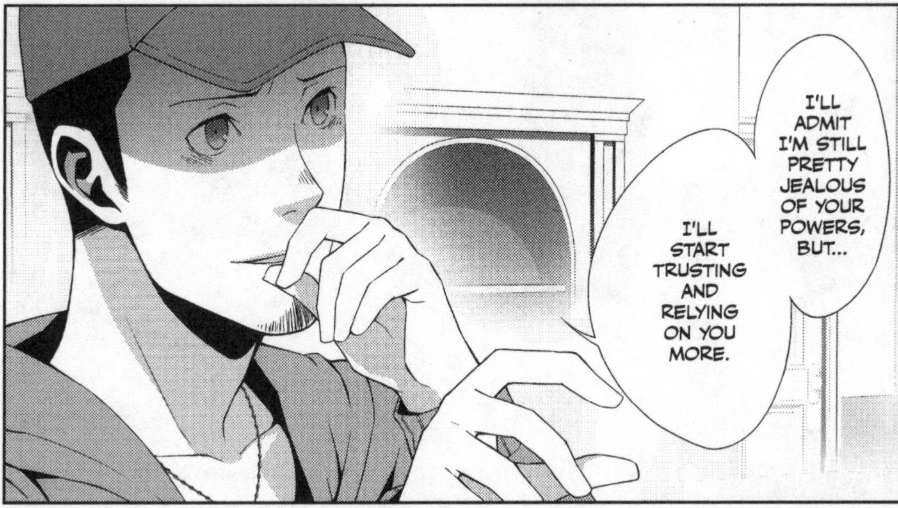
I'LL ADMIT I'M STILL PRETTY JEALOUS OF YOUR POWERS, BUT...
I'LL START TRUSTING AND RELYING ON YOU MORE.

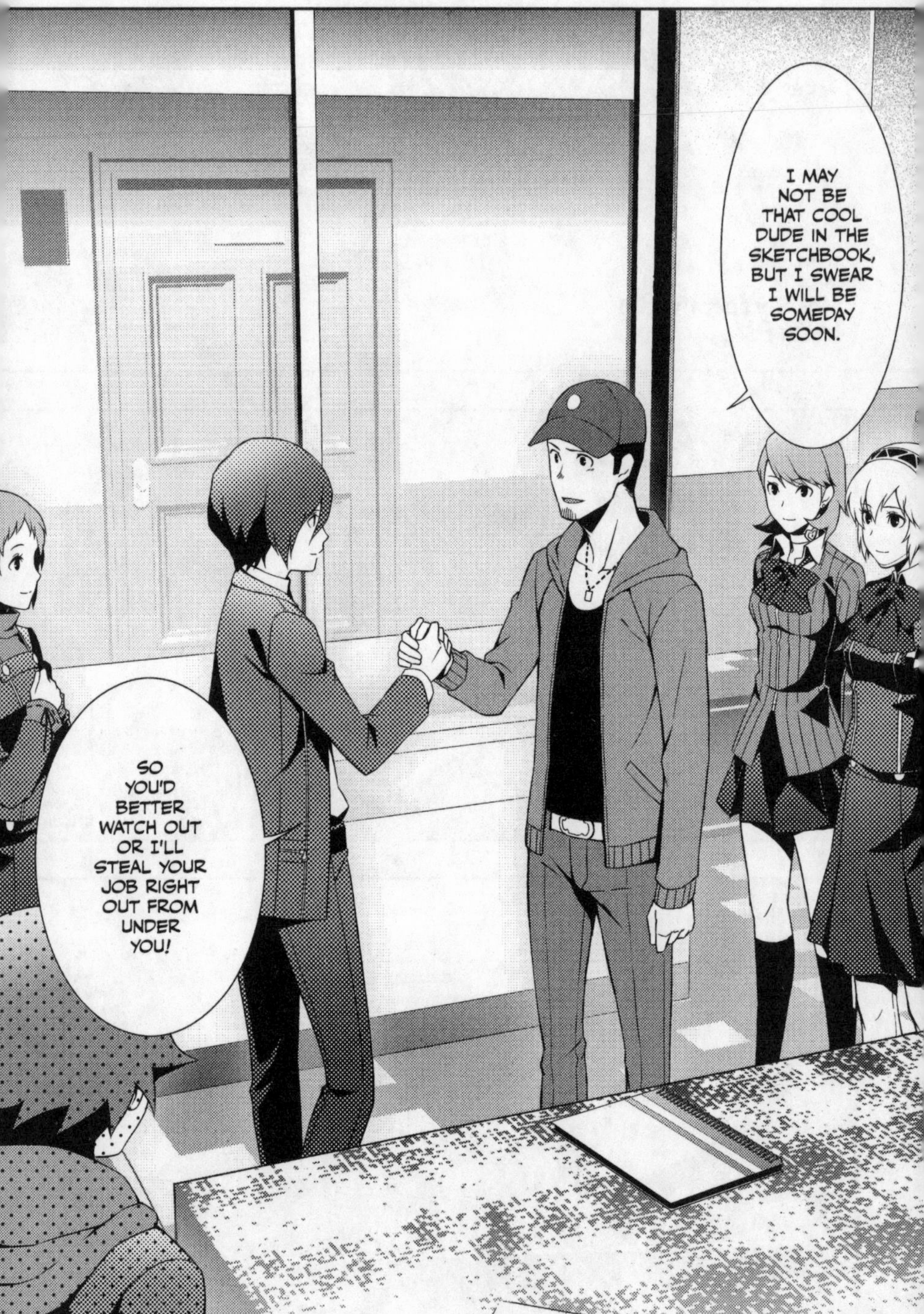
I MAY NOT BE THAT COOL DUDE IN THE SKETCHBOOK, BUT I SWEAR I WILL BE SOMEDAY SOON.
SO YOU'D BETTER WATCH OUT OR I'LL STEAL YOUR JOB RIGHT OUT FROM UNDER YOU!

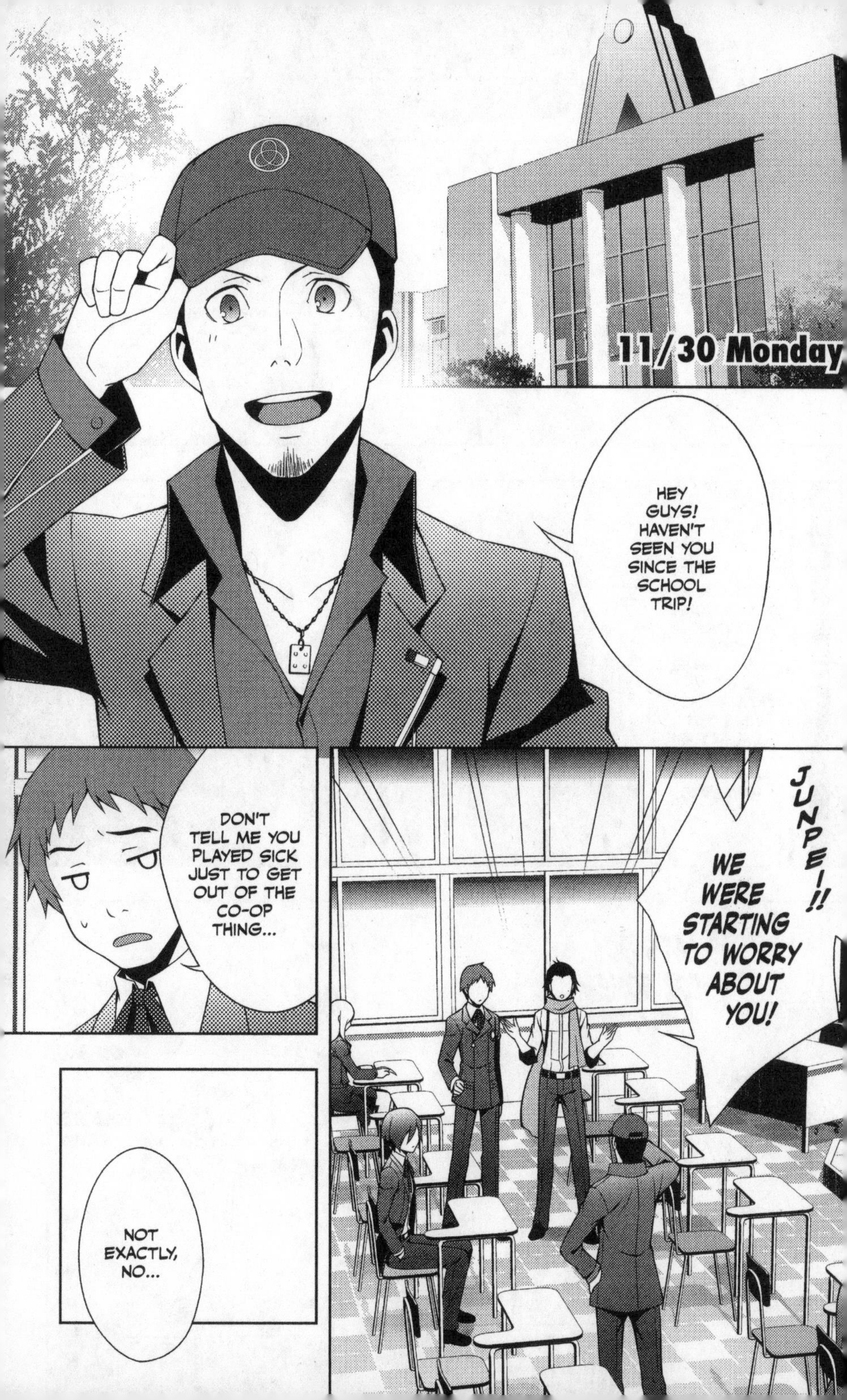
11/30 Monday
HEY GUYS! HAVEN'T SEEN YOU SINCE THE SCHOOL TRIP!
JUNPEI!! WE WERE STARTING TO WORRY ABOUT YOU!
DON'T TELL ME YOU PLAYED SICK JUST TO GET OUT OF THE CO-OP THING...
NOT EXACTLY, NO...

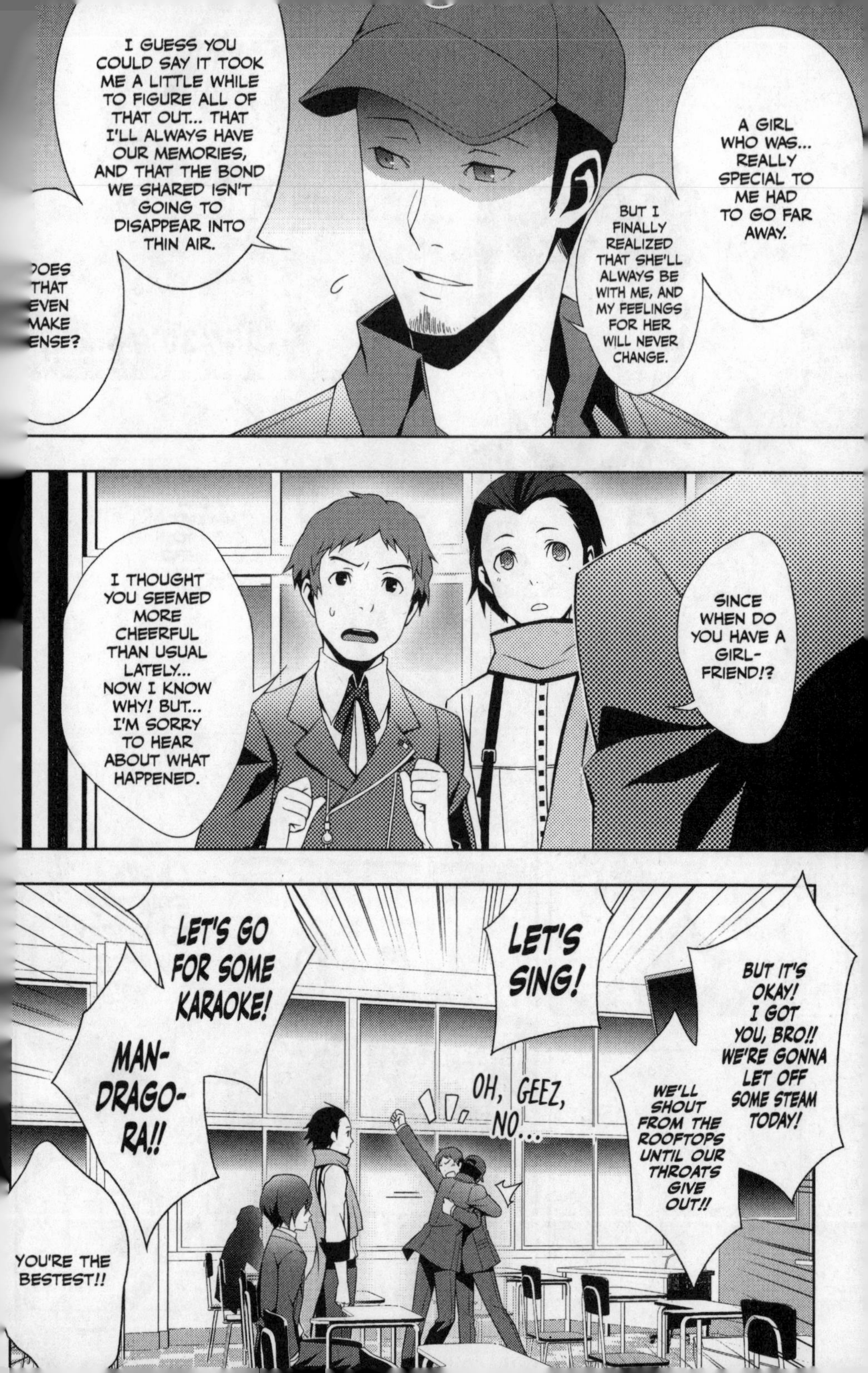

A GIRL WHO WAS... REALLY SPECIAL TO ME HAD TO GO FAR AWAY.
BUT I FINALLY REALIZED THAT SHE'LL ALWAYS BE WITH ME, AND MY FEELINGS FOR HER WILL NEVER CHANGE.
I GUESS YOU COULD SAY IT TOOK ME A LITTLE WHILE TO FIGURE ALL OF THAT OUT... THAT I'LL ALWAYS HAVE OUR MEMORIES, AND THAT THE BOND WE SHARED ISN'T GOING TO DISAPPEAR INTO THIN AIR.
DOES THAT EVEN MAKE ENSE?
SINCE WHEN DO YOU HAVE A GIRL-FRIEND!?
I THOUGHT YOU SEEMED MORE CHEERFUL THAN USUAL LATELY... NOW I KNOW WHY! BUT... I'M SORRY TO HEAR ABOUT WHAT HAPPENED.
BUT IT'S OKAY! I GOT YOU, BRO!! WE'RE GONNA LET OFF SOME STEAM TODAY!
WE'LL SHOUT FROM THE ROOFTOPS UNTIL OUR THROATS GIVE OUT!!
LET'S SING!
OH, GEEZ, NO...
LET'S GO FOR SOME KARAOKE!
MAN-DRAGO-RA!!
YOU'RE THE BESTEST!!

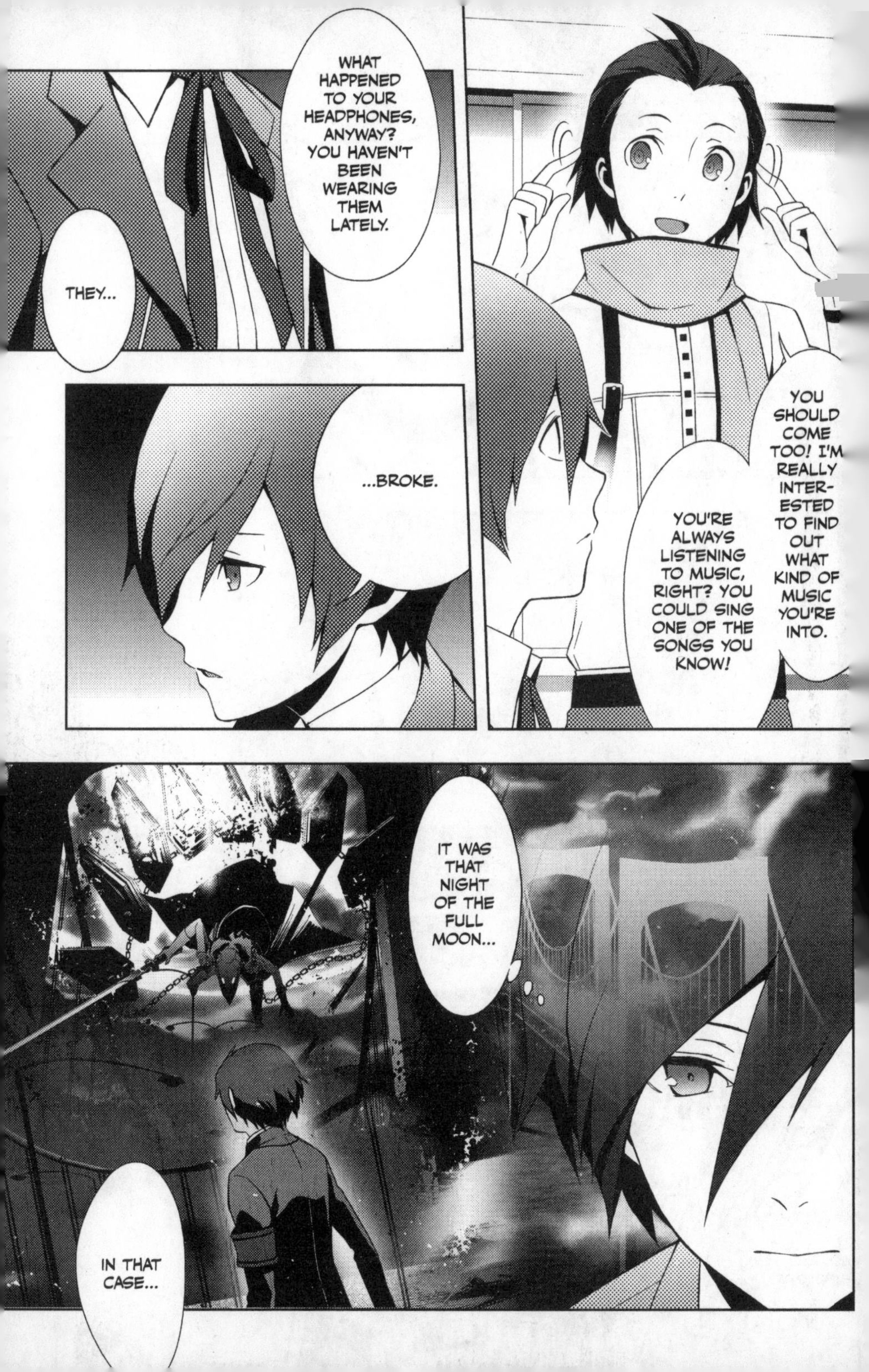
YOU SHOULD COME TOO! I'M REALLY INTER-ESTED TO FIND OUT WHAT KIND OF MUSIC YOU'RE INTO.
YOU'RE ALWAYS LISTENING TO MUSIC, RIGHT? YOU COULD SING ONE OF THE SONGS YOU KNOW!
WHAT HAPPENED TO YOUR HEADPHONES, ANYWAY? YOU HAVEN'T BEEN WEARING THEM LATELY.
THEY...
...BROKE.
IT WAS THAT NIGHT OF THE FULL MOON...
IN THAT CASE...

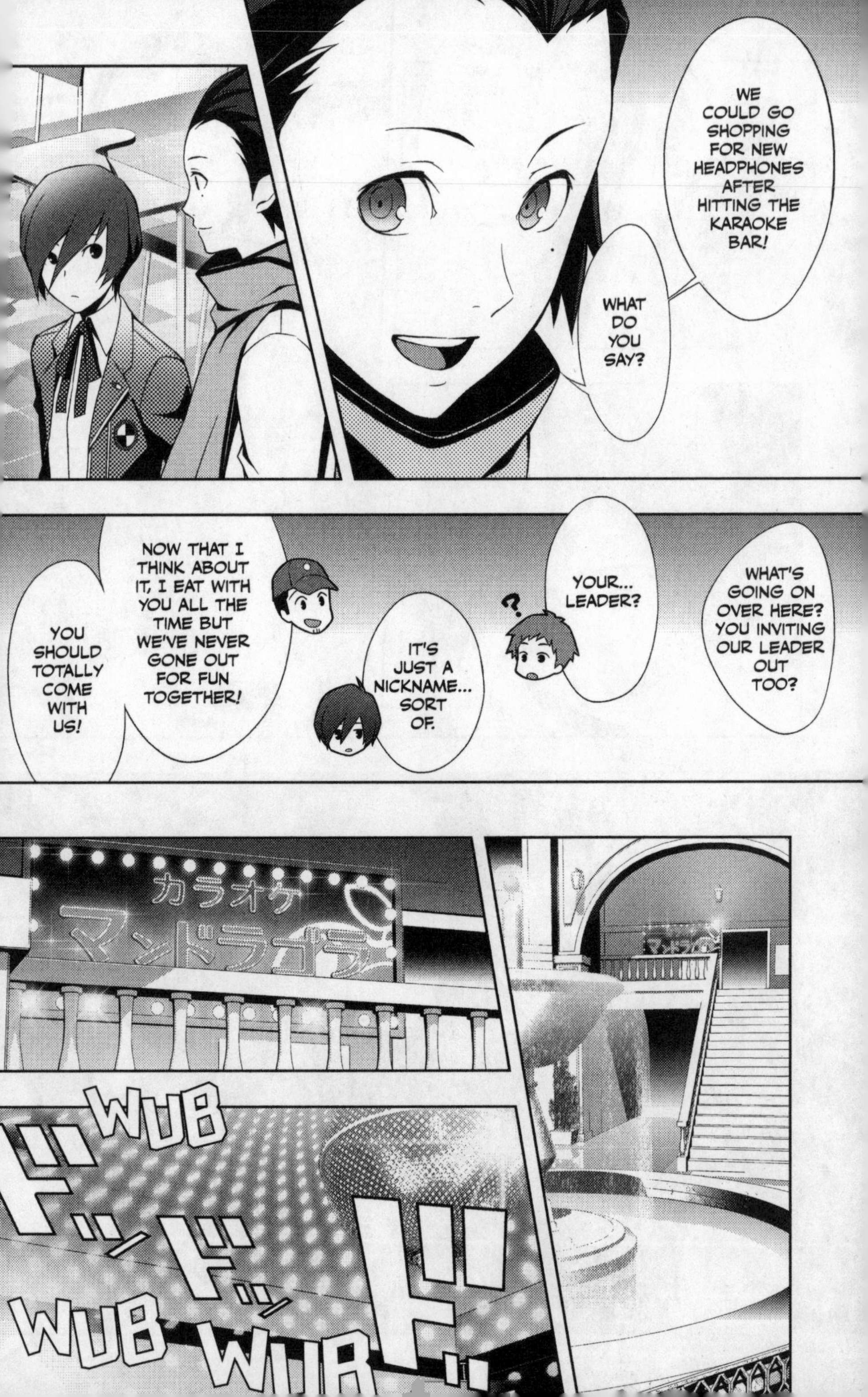
WE COULD GO SHOPPING FOR NEW HEADPHONES AFTER HITTING THE KARAOKE BAR!
WHAT DO YOU SAY?
WHAT'S GOING ON OVER HERE? YOU INVITING OUR LEADER OUT TOO?
YOUR... LEADER?
IT'S JUST A NICKNAME... SORT OF.
NOW THAT I THINK ABOUT IT, I EAT WITH YOU ALL THE TIME BUT WE'VE NEVER GONE OUT FOR FUN TOGETHER!
YOU SHOULD TOTALLY COME WITH US!
カラオケ
マンドラゴラ
WUB
WUB
ドッ
ドッ
ドッ

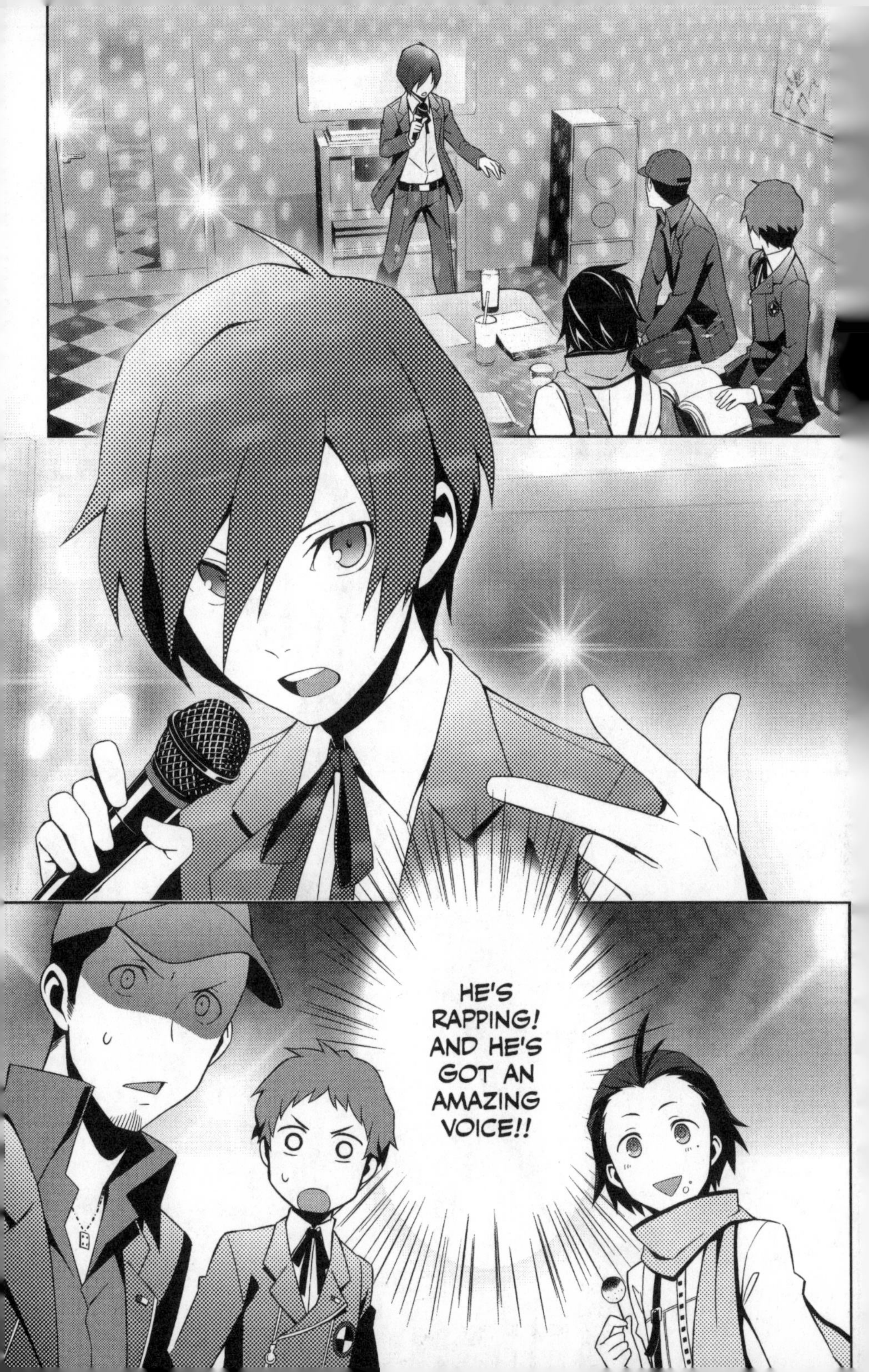
HE'S RAPPING! AND HE'S GOT AN AMAZING VOICE!!

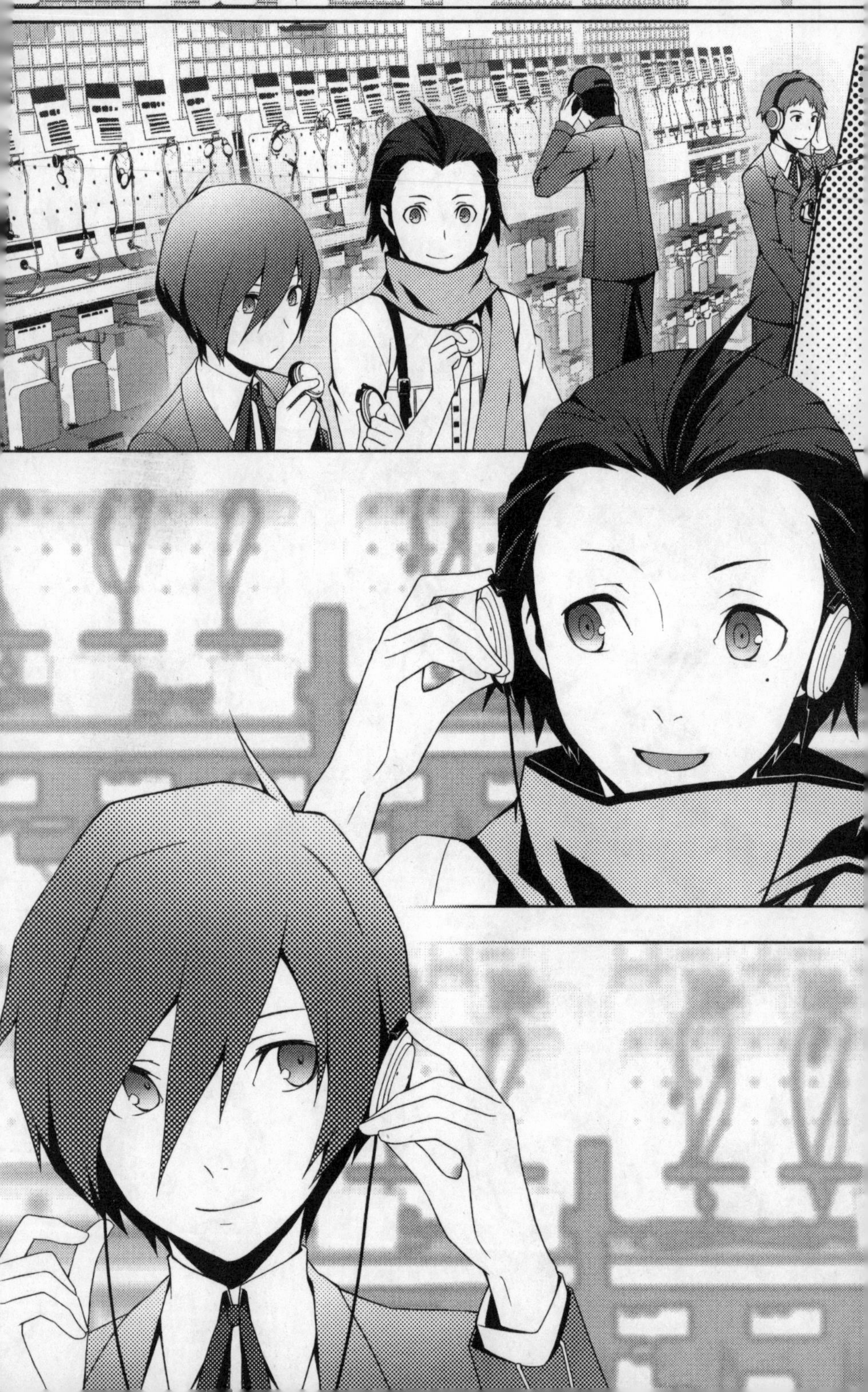

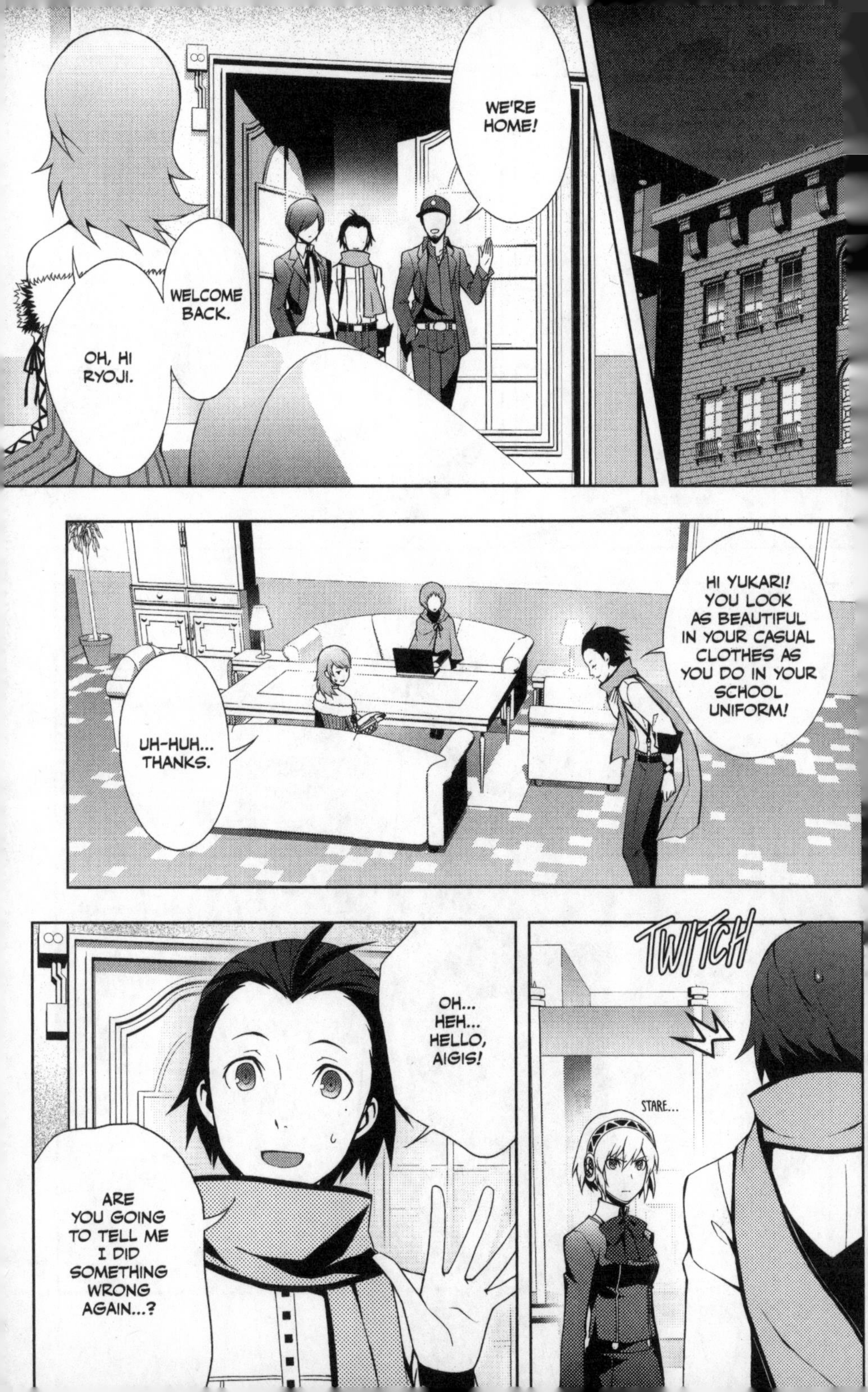
WE'RE HOME!
WELCOME BACK.
OH, HI RYOJI.
HI YUKARI! YOU LOOK AS BEAUTIFUL IN YOUR CASUAL CLOTHES AS YOU DO IN YOUR SCHOOL UNIFORM!
UH-HUH... THANKS.
TWITCH
STARE...
OH... HEH... HELLO, AIGIS!
ARE YOU GOING TO TELL ME I DID SOMETHING WRONG AGAIN...?

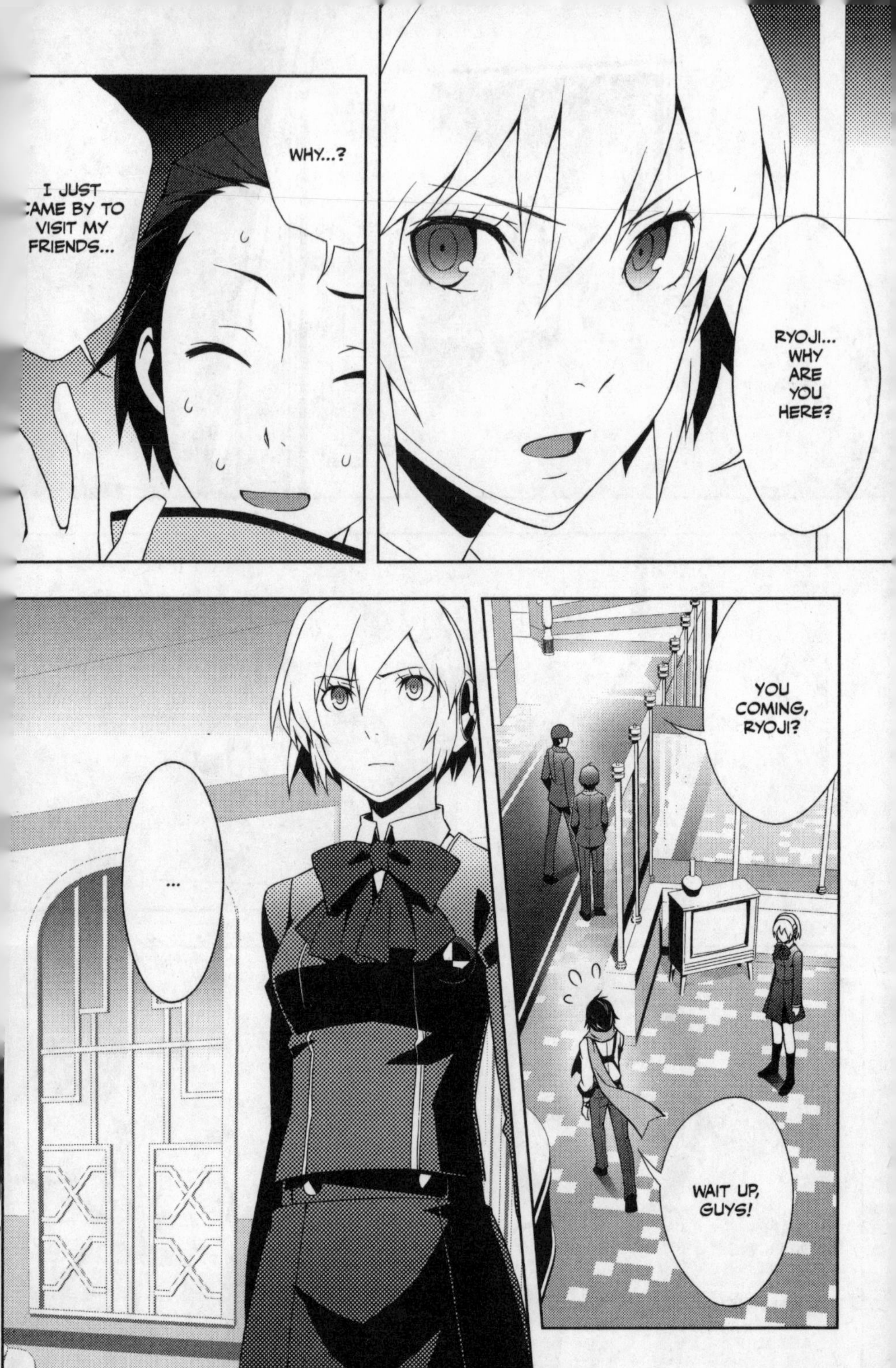
RYOJI... WHY ARE YOU HERE?
WHY...?
I JUST CAME BY TO VISIT MY FRIENDS...
YOU COMING, RYOJI?
WAIT UP, GUYS!
...

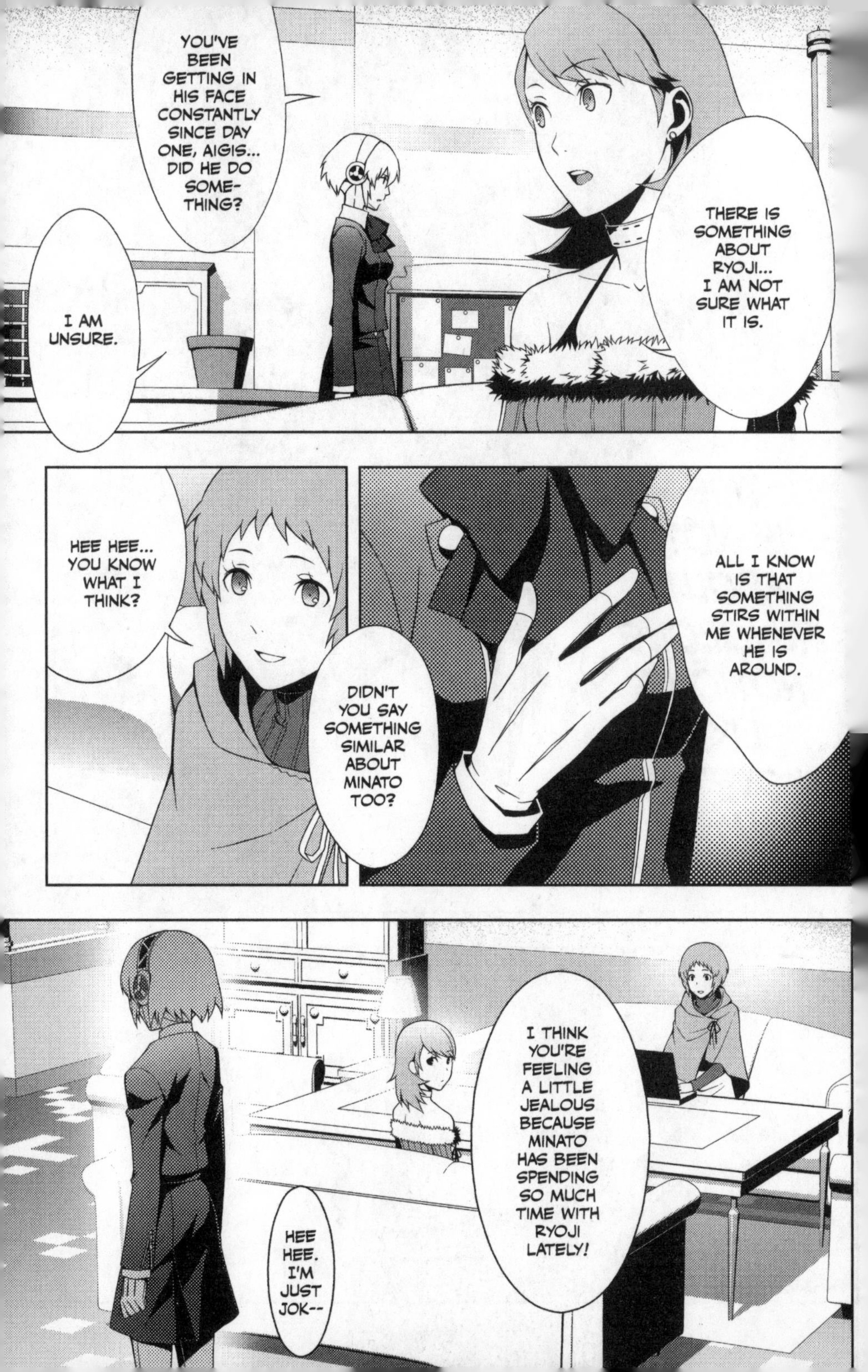
YOU'VE BEEN GETTING IN HIS FACE CONSTANTLY SINCE DAY ONE, AIGIS... DID HE DO SOME-THING?
I AM UNSURE.
THERE IS SOMETHING ABOUT RYOJI... I AM NOT SURE WHAT IT IS.
ALL I KNOW IS THAT SOMETHING STIRS WITHIN ME WHENEVER HE IS AROUND.
DIDN'T YOU SAY SOMETHING SIMILAR ABOUT MINATO TOO?
HEE HEE... YOU KNOW WHAT I THINK?
I THINK YOU'RE FEELING A LITTLE JEALOUS BECAUSE MINATO HAS BEEN SPENDING SO MUCH TIME WITH RYOJI LATELY!
HEE HEE. I'M JUST JOK--

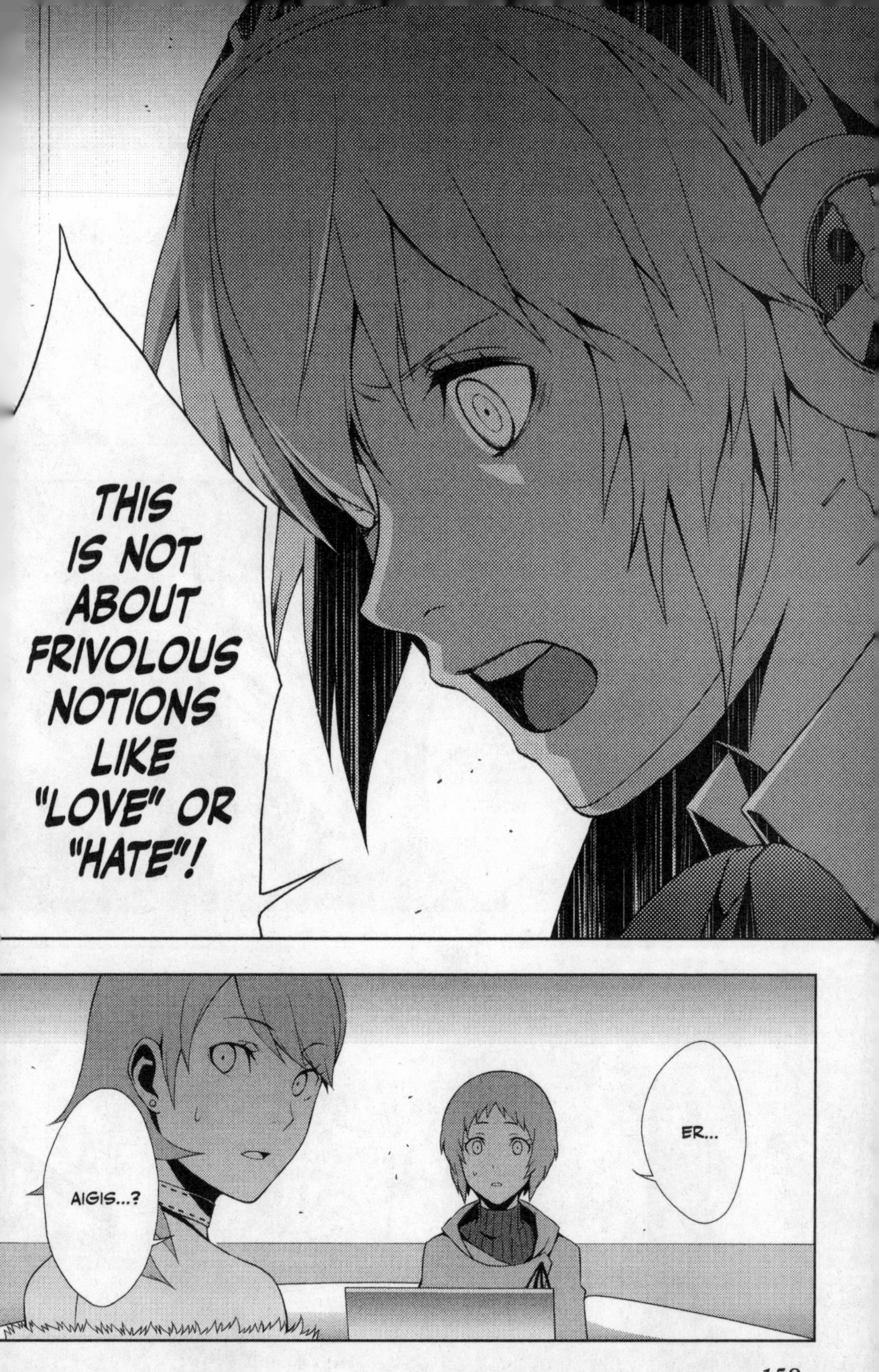
THIS IS NOT ABOUT FRIVOLOUS NOTIONS LIKE "LOVE" OR "HATE"!
ER...
AIGIS...?

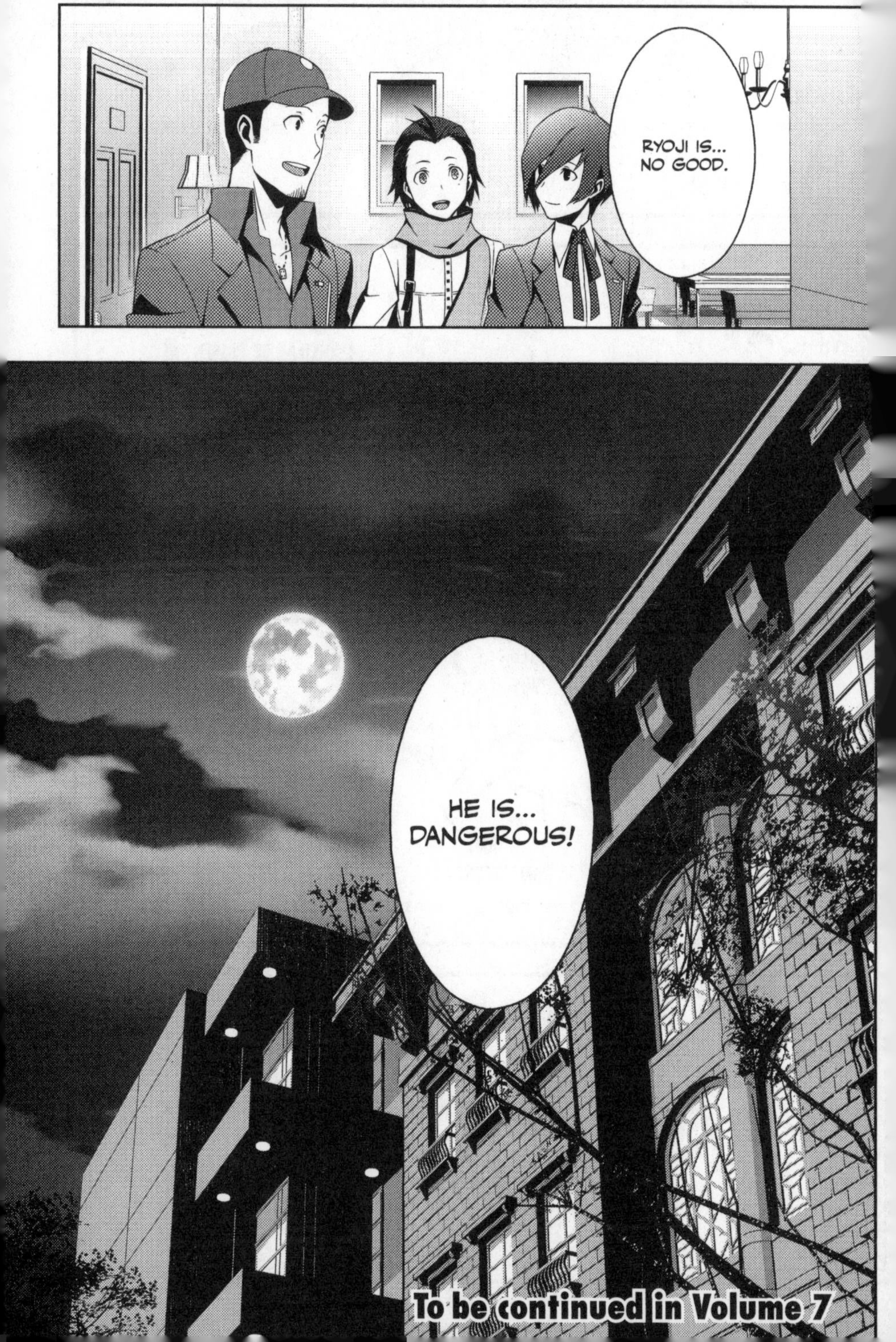
RYOJI IS... NO GOOD.
HE IS... DANGEROUS!
To be continued in Volume 7

Sogabenow 12-2

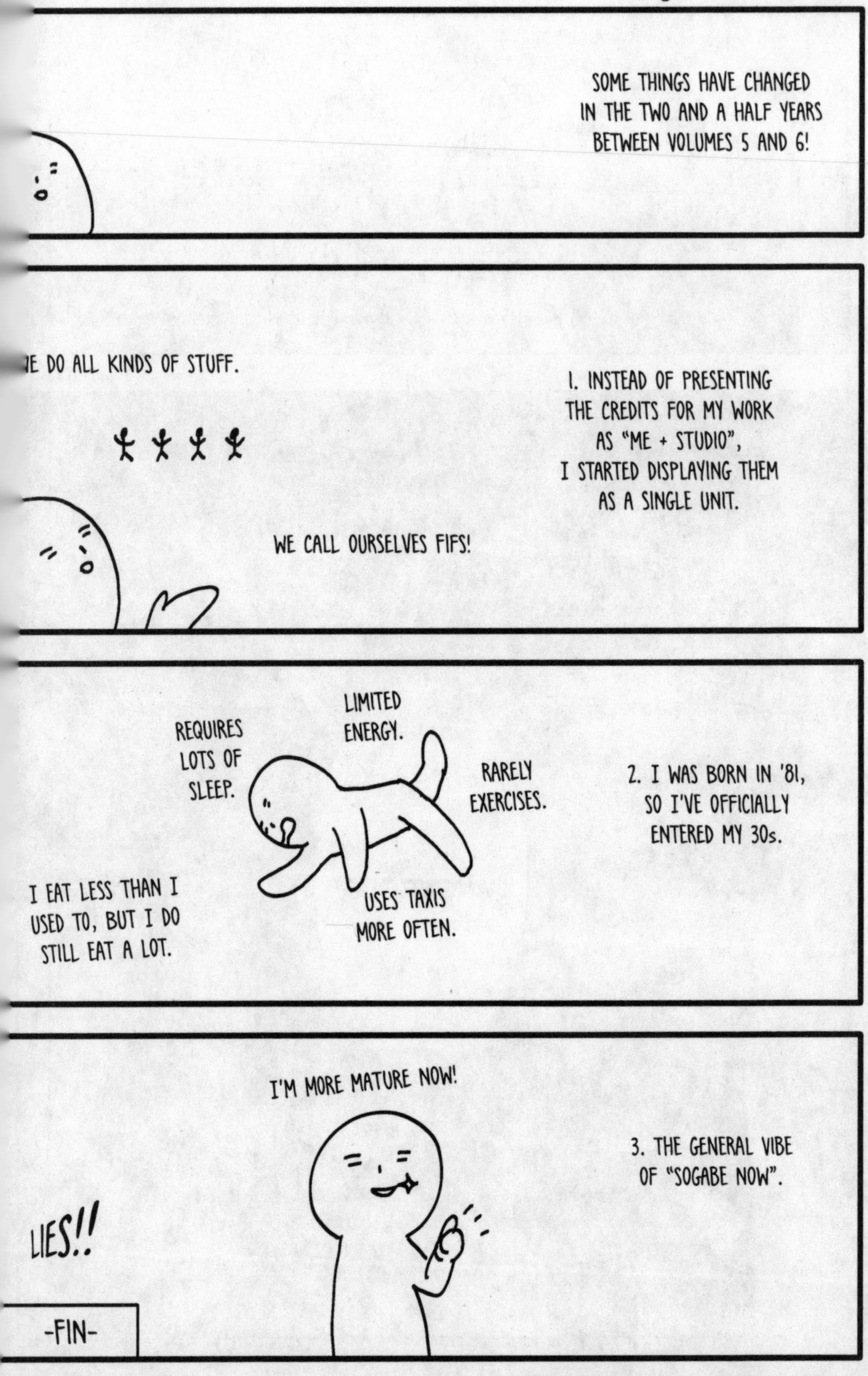
SOME THINGS HAVE CHANGED IN THE TWO AND A HALF YEARS BETWEEN VOLUMES 5 AND 6!
1. INSTEAD OF PRESENTING THE CREDITS FOR MY WORK AS "ME + STUDIO", I STARTED DISPLAYING THEM AS A SINGLE UNIT.
E DO ALL KINDS OF STUFF.
WE CALL OURSELVES FIFS!
2. I WAS BORN IN '81, SO I'VE OFFICIALLY ENTERED MY 30s.
RARELY EXERCISES.
LIMITED ENERGY.
REQUIRES LOTS OF SLEEP.
USES TAXIS MORE OFTEN.
I EAT LESS THAN I USED TO, BUT I DO STILL EAT A LOT.
3. THE GENERAL VIBE OF "SOGABE NOW".
I'M MORE MATURE NOW!
LIES!!
-FIN-

The following message was originally included in the Japanese edition of
PERSONA 3 VOLUME 6 to explain the series' return after a 2.5-year hiatus.

REGARDING THE RELEASE OF PERSONA 3 VOLUME 6

The "Persona 3" manga series was originally published in "Dengeki Maoh", and the overwhelming support it got from fans like you made it possible for me to start the "Persona 4" manga in Maoh's quarterly magazine, "Dengeki Black Maoh".

After six months of running both manga series in parallel, it was decided that the two magazines would trade series so that the more current and relevant "Persona 4" series would be published monthly instead of quarterly.

Then came the unexpected merging of the two magazines!

Since the P4 manga was already running in Dengeki Maoh, the P3 manga had nowhere to go. So within a year of P3P's release, the P3 manga was sent packing to seek a new home.

We explored all kinds of possibilities, from other manga magazines to gaming magazines, the Internet, and even straight-to-tankoubon routes. It got to the point where I felt like I'd settle for any forum as long as it meant I could finish the series, but even then we had a hard time nailing down any solid leads and I couldn't bring myself to announce defeat.

I tackled lots of other projects in the meantime, but it was the periodic comments from fans on my blog and Twitter saying, "We still believe. We're waiting for the P3 series to resume!" that kept me going.

Just as the P4 manga caught up to the P3 manga in terms of content volume, I got some happy news!

With the anime "P4: The Animation" leading the way, the fighting game "P4 Arena" was released and quickly followed by the revamped port "P4 Golden"! These releases set the world ablaze in a Persona boom, making the Persona-exclusive magazine "Persona Magazine" a reality!

At last, someone had built the perfect stage for me to play out the rest of the P3 story. The invitation was formed less like, "Would you like to...?" and more like, "We know you want to!" So I was like, "Heck yeah! I've been waiting for this!!"

I am sorry that you had to wait two and a half years from the release of volume 5 before you could get your hands on volume 6.

All I can say is that I hope I can make good use of the experience I've gained in the meantime to make the P3 manga even better than it would have originally been. I hope you will stick with me through this exciting journey!

Shuji Sogabe

FiFS

Persona 3

Vol.6: Shuji SOGABE /ATLUS

ENGLISH EDITION
Translation: M. KIRIE HAYASHI
Lettering: MARSHALL DILLON

UDON STAFF
Chief of Operations: ERIK KO
Director of Publishing: MATT MOYLAN
Director of Operations: MARSHALL DILLON
VP of Business Development: CORY CASONI
Director of Marketing: MEG MAIDEN
Japanese Liaison: ANNA KAWASHIMA

ペルソナ３ 6
PERSONA 3 Volume 6

©ATLUS ©SEGA All rights reserved.
©Shuji Sogabe 2012

First published in 2012 by KADOKAWA CORPORATION, Tokyo.
English translation rights arranged with KADOKAWA CORPORATION, Tokyo

English language version published by UDON Entertainment Inc.
118 Tower Hill Road, C1, PO Box 20008
Richmond Hill, Ontario, L4K 0K0 CANADA

www.UDONentertainment.com

Third Printing: April 2024
ISBN: 978-1-927925-90-4

Printed in Canada